FROM POLITICAL WON'T
TO POLITICAL WILL

FROM POLITICAL WON'T TO POLITICAL WILL

Building Support for Participatory Governance

Edited by
Carmen Malena

Ipas Resource Center

From Political Won't to Political Will
Published in 2009 in the United States of America by Kumarian Press
22883 Quicksilver Drive, Sterling, VA 20166-2012 USA

Copyright © 2009 Kumarian Press

The text of this book is set in 10/12.5 Sabon

Proofread by Publication Services, Inc.
Index by Publication Services, Inc.
Production and design by Publication Services, Inc.

Printed in the United States of America
Text printed with vegetable oil-based ink.

∞ The paper used in this publication meets the minimum requirements of the American National Standard for Information Sciences-Permanence of Paper for printed Library Materials, ANSI Z39.48-1984

Library of Congress Cataloging-in-Publication Data

From political won't to political will : building support for participatory governance / edited by Carmen Malena.
    p. cm.
Includes bibliographical references and index.
ISBN 978-1-56549-311-7 (pbk. : alk. paper) — ISBN 978-1-56549-312-4 (cloth : alk. paper)
 1. Political participation—Cross-cultural studies. I. Malena, Carmen.
JF799.F76 2009
323'.042—dc22
                                                         2009019066

CONTENTS

Tables and Illustrations ix

Foreword xi

Preface xiii

Acronyms xv

Part 1—Introduction 1

Chapter 1   Building Political Will for Participatory
            Governance: An Introduction 3
            Carmen Malena

Chapter 2   Revisiting Participatory Governance: An Instrument
            for Empowerment or Co-optation? 31
            Henedina Abad

Chapter 3   Building Political Will for Participatory
            Governance: Overcoming the Obstacles 37
            John Clark

Part 2—Generating Political Will for Participatory
       Governance at the Local Level 49

Chapter 4   Lessons from the Work of the Aga Khan
            Foundation in Promoting Good Local
            Governance in Tajikistan, Kenya, and Tanzania 51
            *Richard Holloway, Shahribonu Shonasimova,
            Margaret Ngari, and Achim Chiaji*

v

Chapter 5   Neighborhood Democracy and Participation:
            Formal Representatives and Empowered
            Citizens Move From Competition to
            Mutual Interests 73
            Mary Jacksteit

Chapter 6   Building Political Will for Participatory Governance
            at the Local Level in the United Kingdom 93
            Tricia Zipfel

Chapter 7   Building Pressure from Below:
            Lessons from Uganda 113
            Harriet Namisi

Chapter 8   Beyond Lip Service: Using Social Contracts
            to Achieve Participatory and Accountable
            Governance in the Philippines 135
            Emmanuel C. Areño

Part 3—Nurturing Political Will for Participatory Budgeting 155

Chapter 9   Building Political Will for Participatory
            Budgeting in Rural Zimbabwe: The Case
            of Mutoko Rural District Council 157
            Takawira Mumvuma

Chapter 10 Building Political Will for Participatory
            Budgeting in Canada: The Case of the
            Guelph Neighbourhood Support Coalition 175
            Elizabeth Pinnington

Chapter 11 From Command to Consent in Bolivia:
            How and Why to Gain Political Will
            for Citizen Participation 189
            Ronald MacLean-Abaroa

**Part 4—Building Political Will for Participatory
Governance at the National Level** 209

Chapter 12 Building Political Will for Refining
Public Participation Policy in South Africa 211
Janine Hicks and Imraan Buccus

Chapter 13 Building Political Will for Enhanced
Citizen Access to Information: Lessons
from Latin America 227
Anabel Cruz

Chapter 14 Transparency International's Advocacy and
Legal Advice Centres: Experiences in
Fostering Citizen Participation and
Government Responsiveness 245
Angela Keller-Herzog

Part 5—Conclusion 265

Chapter 15 Participatory Governance: Where There Is
Lack of Will, Is There a Way? 267
Carmen Malena

Index 291

About CIVICUS 303

About the Contributors 305

TABLES

1.1. Examples of Participatory Governance
Practices at the Local and National Levels 4

8.1. Comparative Success of Social Contracts in Building
Political Will for Participatory Governance 150

9.1. Mutoko District Council Participatory Budgeting Cycle 162

ILLUSTRATIONS

1.1. Key Elements of Political Will 8

5.1. Community Roundtable Event Organized
by Collaboration D.C. 84

7.1. A Group of Citizens Attending One of the Community
Meetings in the Bukedea District 123

7.2. A Group of Youth in the Katakwi District Expressing
their Plight using Music, Dance, and Drama in the
Magoro Internally Displaced Person's Camps 125

8.1. Filipino Citizens Participating in the
Social Contract Process 139

8.2. Covenant Signing is Witnessed by Multisectoral
Representatives in Bingawan, Iloilo, 2004 146

14.1. ALAC Client Interviewing on Behalf of his
Daughter's Rights—Lenkaran, Azerbaijan 257

15.1. Key Reasons for Political Won't 269

FOREWORD

When this diverse group of practitioners, donors, and government representatives, whose collective work this publication embodies, met in
Glasgow, in 2008, the consequences of the yawning gaps between the
ideals of democracy and its practice were already glaringly obvious in the
looming food, energy, and climate crises. Since then, financial and economic meltdowns have uncovered, with stunning clarity, the scale and
severity of the lack of transparency, accountability, and public participation in decisions that determine the fates of billions of citizens across our
planet. Each day, we witness security forces combating growing waves of
protestors on the streets of our cities, communities resorting to violence in
a last ditch effort to get their voices heard, multitudes withdrawing from
democratic processes amidst growing skepticism of their effectiveness, and
citizens across nations questioning the legitimacy of the decisions their
governments make in their names. National security, the so-called war on
terror, historical grievances, real politik, logistical constraints, pragmatic
realism, and culture have all been cited as excuses for ignoring, bypassing,
or silencing citizens' voices in policymaking and governance in self-
proclaimed bastions of democracy and overtly repressive states alike.

The benefits of genuine democracy and authentic citizen participation
in governance are uncontested. Social stability, political accountability,
effective development, and equitable resource distribution are but a few
of the goals espoused, if only in words rather than action. Whether it is
dealing with the aftermath of a natural disaster, drafting a constitution,
formulating the annual budget, delivering public services, or holding free
and fair elections, it seems apparent that efficiency, justice, equity, and

effective democracy require informed, empowered, active participation from all citizens, especially those whose access to voice, assets, and power are limited.

Given the current context of global public outrage, amidst the concurrent spread of democratic forms of government, this publication could not be better timed. It seeks to uncover, through the direct experiences of practitioners in diverse contexts, the barriers to, and solutions toward, achieving political will for participatory governance. Aside from providing detailed analysis of real-life constraints, tangible instances of success, and practical pathways, tools, and mechanisms for achieving citizen participation, it will, we hope, also be a beacon of hope to the many who are still excluded from the institutions and practice of democracy, and inspire belief in the power of ordinary citizens everywhere to effect democratic change at a time when both hope and belief are severely stretched.

Ingrid Srinath,
Secretary General
CIVICUS: World Alliance for
Citizen Participation

PREFACE

A publication of this type is a true team effort. This book would not have been possible without the dedicated efforts of a large number of people who deserve to be mentioned here.

First and foremost, I would like to acknowledge the excellent work of the authors of the various chapters, each of whom generously took time out of their busy schedules to reflect on and write about their experiences as participatory governance practitioners. Their collective wisdom and insights give this book its substance, and their tremendous commitment and goodwill made the process of pulling the book together a genuine pleasure. Thank you!

Very special thanks to all the members of the CIVICUS Participatory Governance Programme team—Anu Pekkonen, Mahi Khallaf, and Guy Holloway—each of whom provided skillful, efficient, and unfailingly cheerful support, both toward the preparation of this book and the organization of the global conference that spawned it. Thanks as well to Eva Rehse and the staff and volunteers of the Scottish Council for Voluntary Organisations (SCVO), who provided invaluable assistance in organizing and conducting the conference.

Indispensable support was also provided by the CIVICUS senior management team—in particular, Ingrid Srinath, Katsuji Imata, Mandy Poole, and Liz Robson—all of whom continue to guide and support the work of the program on a daily basis.

We are also extremely grateful to the members of our CIVICUS Participatory Governance International Advisory Group, who provide invaluable ongoing intellectual, operational, and moral support to our program. Special thanks to Alnoor Ebrahim and Sarah Lister for reviewing and providing thoughtful and practical comments on the introductory and concluding chapters of the book.

Priscilla Ryan did an exceptional job of copyediting and formatting the various chapters of the book, and our colleagues at Kumarian Press, in particular Jim Lance and Erica Flock, expertly transformed our manuscript into a final publication with equal amounts of professionalism and good humor.

The *Building Political Will for Participatory Governance* conference, held in Glasgow, Scotland, in June 2008, would not have taken place, and this book would not have been published without the generous support of our donors. On behalf of CIVICUS, I would like to acknowledge and thank Irish Aid, the main supporter of the event and this publication, and the UK Department for International Development (DfID) that provided grants for many southern participants to travel to Glasgow. Thanks also to other donors who provide core support to our program and to CIVICUS as a whole—the Canadian International Development Agency (CIDA), Oxfam Novib, the Swedish International Development Agency (SIDA), the Charles Stewart Mott, Foundation, the Tides Foundation, Oxfam Great Britain, the Rockefeller Brothers Foundation, the International Development and Research Center (IDRC), the Conrad Hilton Foundation, Oxfam US, the Commonwealth Foundation, and Ibis.

Thanks also to all the participants, from around the world, who attended and contributed to the conference. The rich discussions and honest sharing of experiences that occurred at that event inspired and nourished this book. We hope that each one of you sees some of your questions, ideas, and concerns reflected in these pages.

Our greatest hope is that the experiences and reflections shared in this book will in turn serve to inform and inspire participatory governance practitioners working in different countries, and sometimes difficult circumstances, around the world. We welcome your feedback to this book and we invite you to join our growing global *community of practice,* by contacting us at *governance@civicus.org.*

Carmen Malena,
Stoneham, Quebec, Canada
April 2009

ACRONYMS

AGESIC	Agency for e-Government, Information, and Knowledge
AKF	Aga Khan Foundation
AKF/MSDSP	Aga Khan Foundation's Mountain Societies Development Support Programme
ALACs	Advocacy and Legal Advice Centres
ANC	Advisory Neighbourhood Commission
CBCC	Community Benefits Coordinating Committee
CBOs	community based organizations
CBTF	Community Benefits Task Force
CCM	Chama Cha Mapinduzi
CDO	Community Development Officer
CHAMP	clean, honest, accountable, meaningful, and peaceful
CIDA	Canadian International Development Agency
CPF	Commonwealth People's Forum
CPI	Corruption Perceptions Index
CPP	Centre for Public Participation
CRSP	Coastal Rural Support Programme
CRSP(K)	Coastal Rural Support Programme—Kenya
CSOs	civil society organisations

CUF	Civic United Front
DAO	District Administrative Officer
DC	District Commissioner
DCC	District Community Coordinator
DCLG	Department for Communities and Local Government
DENIVA	Development Network of Indigenous Voluntary Associations
DfID	Department for International Development
DILG	Department of Interior and Local Government
DPLG	Department of Provincial and Local Government
FSE	Fondo Social de Emergencia
GAIP	Grupo de Archivos y Acceso a la Información Pública
GBAO	Gorno-Badakhshan Autonomous Oblast
GGLN	Good Governance Learning Network
GTZ	Gesellschaft für Technische Zusammenarbeit
HIPCs	Heavily Indebted Poor Countries
HSRC	Human Sciences Research Council
ICODE	Iloilo Caucus of Development NGOs
IDPs	internally displaced persons
IDRC	International Development and Research Center
IRAs	internal revenue allocations
KADIVDO	Kamwenge District Voluntary Development Organisation
KANIVA	Kakuuto Network of Indigenous Voluntary Associations
KAUFO	Katakwi Urafiki Foundation
KZN	KwaZulu-Natal

LDCs	Local Development Councils
LND	Law of the National Dialogue
LG	local government
LGAs	Local Government Authorities
LGC	Local Government Code
LOGOCAT	Local Good Governance Capacity Assessment Tool
LPP	Law of Popular Participation
LPU	Local Public Administration
LSP	Local Strategic Partnership
MAS	Movimenta al Socialismo
MoU	Memoranda of Understanding
MP	Member of Parliament
MSDSP	Mountain Societies Development Support Programme
NDP	National Development Plan
NGO	non-governmental organisation
NGORC	Non-Governmental Organisation Resource Centre
NPM	New Public Management
NSC	Neighbourhood Support Coalition
OAIP	Offices for Access to Public Information
OAS	Organization of American States
OTBs	Organizacions Territoriales de Base
PADED	Participatory Development in Agriculture Program
PEAP	Poverty Eradication Action Plan
PFB	Pressure from Below
PO	Planning Officer
PP	Popular Participation

PPP	private-public partnership
PRDP	Peace, Recovery, and Development Plan for Northern Uganda
RFEs	Rapid Funding Envelopes
SCVO	Scottish Council for Voluntary Organisations
SIDA	Swedish International Development Cooperation Agency
SWNA	Southwest Neighbourhood Assembly
TAFAF	Tanzania Social Action Funds
TGLP	Tajikistan Governance and Livelihood Programme
TI	Transparency International
TIS	Transparency International's Secretariat
TMOs	Tenant Management Organisations
UKNZ	University of KwaZulu-Natal
USAID	United States Agency for International Development
VDCs	Village Development Committees
VOs	village organizations
WOs	women's organizations
ZANU-PF	Zimbabwe African National Union-Patriotic Front

PART 1

INTRODUCTION

CHAPTER 1

BUILDING POLITICAL WILL FOR PARTICIPATORY GOVERNANCE: AN INTRODUCTION

Carmen Malena

Introduction

There is growing consensus that poor governance is a, if not *the*, principal obstacle to the achievement of poverty reduction and other critical human development goals (UNDP 1997; World Bank 1992, 1994). Every day, around the globe lack of good governance results in intolerable human suffering, wasted resources, lost development opportunities, and social injustice.

There is also growing consensus that *good*—for example, transparent, accountable, effective, and equitable—governance cannot be achieved by governments alone. Good governance requires strong, effective government *and* the active involvement of citizens and civil society organizations (CSOs) (UNDP 1997; Hyden, Court, and Mease 2004; Tandon and Mohanty 2002). Around the world, citizens and CSOs have responded to this challenge by affirming citizen rights and supporting initiatives that empower citizens to participate in and influence governance processes, beyond simply voting once every few years. Many dedicated government actors, at both local and national levels, have also proactively created space and mechanisms for citizens to participate more meaningfully in processes of public decision making that affect their lives. Participatory governance has thus become widely recognized as a crucial element of development. (See Table 1.1.)

Despite the impressive successes and significant impacts of this ever-expanding universe of participatory governance experiences, lack of political will for participatory governance remains a stumbling block. Although

Table 1.1. Examples of Participatory Governance Practices at the Local and National Levels

Governance Functions	National Level	Local Level
Public agenda-setting, policymaking, and planning	Evidence-based policy advocacy and dialogue (Nicaragua, Uruguay); preparation of draft bill by civil society coalition (Uruguay); public participation in legislative committees (South Africa); advocacy for legal and administrative reforms (Transparency International).	Participatory development planning (Bolivia, Kenya, Philippines, Tajikistan, Tanzania); people's manifestos (Uganda); multi-stakeholder and citizen/community roundtables (United States); public hearings (Zimbabwe).
Public budgets	National dialogue on resource allocation (Bolivia); independent budget analysis.	Participatory budgeting (Canada, Bolivia, United Kingdom, Zimbabwe).
Public expenditures	Nationally mandated vigilance committees (Bolivia); participatory public expenditure tracking (Uganda).	Overview and scrutiny committees (United Kingdom); joint budget action committees (Zimbabwe).
Public services	Citizen evaluation of public services (public opinion polls, citizen report cards); anti-corruption hotlines and walk-in centers (Transparency International).	Community-driven projects and programs (Canada, Uganda); community management organizations (United Kingdom); community monitoring and feedback on services (Uganda); community assessment of local government performance (Philippines, South Africa).
Public oversight	Right to information legislation (Honduras); independent transparency councils (Chile); Advocacy and Legal Advice Centers (Transparency International).	Social contracts (Philippines, Zimbabwe); municipal social accountability ordinances (Philippines).

participatory governance practices offer important concrete benefits for citizens and state actors alike, initiatives that aim to improve public access to information, strengthen citizen voice, and enhance citizen participation in governance processes are frequently faced with *political won't*.

Why is political will for participatory governance lacking and what can be done about it? Which strategies and actions have proved most effective in nurturing political will and genuine support for participatory governance and why? What can we, as citizens, civil society actors, elected representatives, and government officials, do to build broad-based support for citizen empowerment and participatory governance? These are some of the key questions explored in this volume, drawing on an inspiring collection of firsthand experiences relayed by leading practitioners from around the world.

What is so Important about Participatory Governance?

Despite the recent wave of democratization around the world, traditional systems of representative democracy seem to be in crisis (Gaventa 2002; Paul 2002). Citizens, in both the North and the South, lack confidence in political leaders and express growing disillusionment with their governments—citing problems of lack of transparency, responsiveness, and accountability, especially vis-à-vis disadvantaged social groups (Commonwealth Foundation 1999; Narayan et al. 2000). Human and citizen rights are neither fully acknowledged nor respected. As a result, ordinary citizens—especially women, poor people, and other marginalized groups—are largely excluded from governance processes and the making of decisions that directly affect their lives. Around the world, citizens suffer from a lack of adequate information, lack of awareness and acknowledgement of human and citizen rights, and inadequate opportunities for meaningful dialogue and negotiation with public actors.

The impacts of unresponsive and unaccountable government are most harshly felt by disadvantaged citizens of the global South, where corruption and governance failures are a principal cause of poverty and human suffering and a stubborn barrier to the realization of urgent priorities, such as the Millennium Development Goals. *Democracy deficits* at the local, national, and international levels result in the wanton waste of precious development resources. They seriously compromise the quality and effectiveness of public policymaking and the provision of public services to meet basic human needs. They also deny citizens their inherent right to participate in decisions that directly affect their lives and to hold government officials accountable for the public resources with which they are entrusted.

A spectrum of creative participatory governance practices have emerged in response to this crisis. Over the past decade, a growing global community of both civil society and state actors have dedicated themselves to developing and experimenting with a multitude of *participatory governance* practices aimed at: enhancing citizen access to essential public information; strengthening citizen voice, especially that of disadvantaged and marginalized groups; promoting active citizen participation in key governance processes, such as agenda-setting, policymaking, the allocation of public funds, and the delivery of public services; and empowering citizens to hold the state accountable and negotiate real change. A range of exciting participatory governance approaches—including participatory policymaking, community-driven development planning, participatory budgeting, independent budget analysis, participatory expenditure tracking, citizen monitoring of public services, and citizen/CSO involvement in formal public oversight bodies—have been tried, tested, and proved to have an impact (World Bank 2004; Krafchik 2003; Malena, Forster, and Singh 2004; Paul 2002; Songco 2001).

As participatory governance practices expand and evolve, there is growing evidence of the important and concrete benefits they can bring, in terms of: (i) *improved governance*, particularly greater government transparency, responsiveness, and accountability; (ii) *enhanced development*, as a result of better-informed policies, more responsive programs, and more efficient and equitable service delivery; and (iii) *citizen empowerment*, particularly, enhanced citizen information, voice, and influence. Experience has also shown that participatory governance practices bring important *concrete benefits to state actors*, including enhanced legitimacy, popularity, stability, and resources.

Why Focus on Political Will?

Experience shows that one of the key challenges participatory governance practitioners face is lack of political will. For example, a recent needs assessment survey of more than 250 practitioners from around the world, undertaken by the CIVICUS Participatory Governance Programme, identified *lack of political will* as a principal obstacle in promoting participatory governance—outranking other obstacles, such as lack of knowledge and skills, limited citizen capacity, a disabling political/policy environment, and lack of access to public information (CIVICUS 2007, 4).

While some groundbreaking participatory governance practices have been initiated by governments themselves—for example, the now world-famous practice of participatory budgeting introduced by local government authorities in Brazil—there is often initial resistance from political actors and government officials who are unfamiliar with such approaches, unconvinced about the benefits of participation, threatened by the prospect of *power-sharing*, distrustful of civil society actors, or intolerant of what they see as illegitimate meddling in the affairs of government. For example, almost every case study examined in this book reports initial skepticism or resistance on the part of government actors. Yet, without government *buy-in* and support, participatory governance initiatives are unlikely to have significant or sustainable impact.

Lack of political will is frequently cited as a serious problem, but is poorly understood and under-analyzed. While the field of participatory governance has attracted a tremendous amount of interest in the past several years and much has been written about new theories, methods, and case studies of active citizenship and participatory governance, this essential theme of *how to build genuine political will for participatory governance* remains under-explored, scantily documented, and, as a result, inadequately addressed. Anecdotal evidence suggests that it *is* possible to change political attitudes and build genuine political will for citizen participation.

This volume seeks to fill a gap, by analyzing a range of participatory governance experiences, with a view to exploring and understanding reasons for political won't. Most importantly, it seeks to identify and analyze strategies that have proved effective in strengthening relationships between government and CSOs/citizens and building genuine political will for participatory governance (Figure 1.1).

The Concept and Practice of Participatory Governance?

What is Participatory Governance?

Participatory governance is a broad and complex concept that means different things to different people and can be defined and interpreted in different ways. For the purposes of this book, participatory governance is understood as *empowering citizens to influence and share control in processes of public decision making that affect their lives* (CIVICUS 2006, 2).

Participatory governance is based on the premise that citizens have both the *right* and the *responsibility* to contribute to processes of public decision making. Frequently, however, citizens lack the opportunity and ability to do so. Therefore, *citizen empowerment* and the promotion of *active citizenship,* through rights awareness-raising, citizen education, mobilization, legal reforms, or the introduction of mechanisms and platforms for citizen participation, lie at the heart of participatory governance.

The term *participation* and *participatory* are used to describe an extremely wide range of actions and behaviors. The *level* of participation can be assessed both according to breadth, how inclusive it is, and according to depth, how intensive it is. Many practitioners acknowledge a ladder

Figure 1.1. Key Elements of Political Will

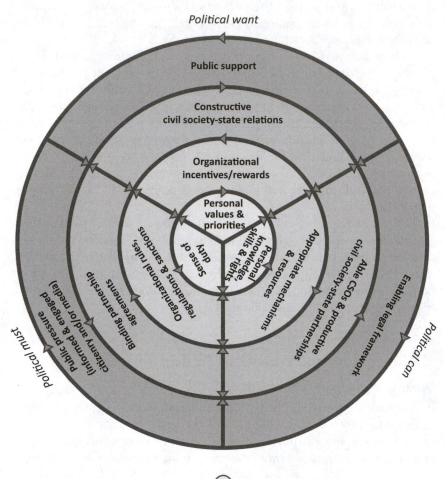

of participation that starts out with information-sharing and evolves, through consultation and deliberation, to extensive collaboration, empowerment and joint decision making, and in some cases, even to self-government. The appropriate, or possible, breadth and depth of participation depends on specific context and circumstance. In many cases, participatory governance practices evolve and deepen over time, for example, beginning with improved information-sharing between citizens and the state and, as trust and relations are strengthened, gradually developing into more meaningful and intensive forms of participation. In terms of breadth, the goal of participatory governance is not to have every citizen participate in every decision, but rather to ensure an equitable representation of different interests and societal groups, especially of disadvantaged or marginalized groups, in those decisions and processes that most directly affect peoples' lives. The working definition adopted here suggests that some level of *influence* and *shared control*—for example, something beyond just *information-sharing* or *consultation*—is required for an initiative to be considered an example of participatory governance.

Related concepts

Participatory governance is closely linked to other key concepts and agendas. A number of development institutions, such as the World Bank and the UK Department for International Development (DfID), use the term *demand for good governance* to refer to citizen involvement in governance processes. The term *social accountability* is also broadly used to refer to participatory governance practices, with an emphasis on how citizens and CSOs can use these practices to exact accountability from public officials (Malena, Forster, and Singh 2004). As mentioned above, participatory governance is closely connected to the concepts of *active citizenship* and *civic engagement* and the broader agendas of *citizen empowerment* and enhanced *civil society–state relations*.

Participatory Governance in Practice

Participatory governance is about: (i) affirming a set of *principles* around the respective rights and responsibilities of citizens and state actors, and (ii) putting those rights and responsibilities into *practice*. A wide range of strategies and mechanisms can be used to enhance citizen participation in diverse aspects of governance. Experience shows there are important opportunities for citizen participation at different stages throughout the cycle of public agenda-setting, policymaking, planning, budgeting, expenditures, service delivery, and oversight.

The potential for participatory governance is perhaps greatest at the local level, where citizens can directly engage with local authorities on issues of direct relevance to their daily lives, such as community development, the management of shared resources, and the provision of essential services. Much exploration and experimentation of participatory governance practices has occurred at this level. However, given that power, resources, and crucial decision making are often concentrated at the central level, efforts to expand and deepen citizen participation in national level governance processes are also extremely important.

Table 1.1 provides a summary overview of some of the various participatory governance practices discussed in this book. While far from comprehensive, these examples represent a useful and illustrative cross section of participatory governance approaches and methodologies at the local and national levels.

Public agenda-setting, policymaking, and planning

Citizen participation in agenda-setting and policymaking sometimes takes the form of public consultation or deliberative processes, where citizens/CSOs are invited to contribute information and ideas to decision makers, for example, through public hearings or legislative committee work. More frequently, citizens and CSOs themselves take a lead in raising public and government awareness of priority concerns, reviewing or critiquing proposed policies, or advocating for new policies or programs. At the local level, participatory development planning, through the use of community dialogue, multi-stakeholder roundtables, and joint civil society and local government planning committees, are increasingly common means of enhancing the relevance and effectiveness of local development initiatives.

Public budgets

Citizen involvement in preparing and analyzing public budgets is another important category of participatory governance. Participatory budget formulation is most common at the local level, as illustrated in cases from Canada, the United Kingdom, and Zimbabwe. The case of Bolivia, however, offers an innovative example of how participatory budgeting principles were also applied to the allocation of poverty reduction funds at the national level. More common examples of budget-related participatory governance practices at the national level include efforts to raise public awareness about budget-related issues, undertake independent analyses of the impact of budget allocations, and expose discrepancies between stated government policy priorities and resource allocations.

Public expenditures

An important aspect of participatory governance is for citizens to be able to hold government accountable for how it handles public funds. For example, in an increasing number of countries local governments now publicly disseminate information about accounts and expenditures and invite citizens to serve on joint budget action or overview committees. Public expenditure tracking surveys and independent or government-mandated vigilance committees are examples of participatory governance practices that have been applied at the national level, with the aim of monitoring the flow of public resources. These approaches often involve analyzing information received from finance ministries' disbursement records, accounts submitted by line agencies, and information obtained from end users, using tools like social audits to track expenditures from allocation to destination, identify leakages and/or bottlenecks in the system, and demand accountability.

Public services

Another important category of participatory governance practice aims at enhancing the relevance, accessibility, and quality of public goods and services. At the local level, these typically involve citizen participation in the development, management, monitoring, or evaluation of priority services. A variety of methods—such as community monitoring, participatory performance assessment, and public feedback sessions—can be used to help citizens monitor, evaluate, and improve public services and government performance. At the national level, methods such as public opinion polls or citizens' report cards are used to solicit citizen feedback, exact accountability, and lobby for change. Anticorruption hotlines and complaint centers, especially when combined with an advocacy function, allow citizens to flag problems with public services and performance, and to seek redress and reform.

Public oversight

A final category of participatory governance practice aims to improve public oversight or enhance the effectiveness of conventional oversight mechanisms. Examples include the creation of local and national citizen oversight committees, the inclusion of citizen/civil society representatives on public boards and regulatory bodies, and civil society efforts to solicit, aggregate, and act upon citizen complaints, for example, in the context of legal advice centers. Demanding access to information and requiring public officials to regularly report to and account to citizens, according to social contracts or municipal ordinances, are other important participatory governance practices aimed at enhancing public oversight.

Key Stakeholders in Participatory Governance

Participatory governance practices involve a wide range of actors and stakeholders, each with different rights and responsibilities. We often refer broadly to *state* or *government* stakeholders on the one hand and *civil society* stakeholders on the other, but it is important to unpack these terms and to acknowledge that each of these spheres is inhabited by a highly heterogeneous mix of actors and interests. Key government actors include mayors and local councilors, members of parliament, chief executives, other bureaucrats, public service providers, as well as *independent* government institutions, such as the judiciary, the ombudsman, and anti-corruption agencies. Key civil society actors include ordinary citizens, community-based membership organizations, community leaders and activists, independent media, advocacy organizations, non-governmental organizations (NGOs), social movements, professional associations, trade unions, academics, think tanks, and other CSOs. Actors that are sometimes perceived as inhabiting the *border* between government and civil society are traditional authorities and political parties. Participatory governance involves strengthening linkages and relationships between these different actors, challenging traditional *us* and *them* categories, and identifying and collaborating with allies from across all sectors.

Participatory governance initiatives are frequently launched and owned by either civil society or government actors with varying levels of success in *reaching out to* or *getting buy-in from* the other side. Success, however, has been greatest where multiple stakeholders, from both civil society and government, have succeeded in developing joint initiatives or establishing participatory governance mechanisms based on a process of negotiation and mutual agreement. Participatory governance initiatives often involve other parties such as international NGOs or donors or private sector actors, such as local businesses, companies involved in public–private partnerships, or investors. While this book is largely focused on the dynamics between citizens/CSOs and government actors, it is important to acknowledge the potential roles and impacts of this broader universe of stakeholders.

Benefits of Participatory Governance

As discussed above, numerous important advantages are associated with participatory governance. Some principal benefits to citizens and society at large include *improved governance*, *enhanced development*, and *citizen empowerment*. In addition, and of particular significance to the theme of building political will, participatory governance also brings significant *direct benefits to government actors*.

Improved governance

Participatory governance can help make governance processes more transparent, responsive, and accountable. Participatory governance can help public officials better understand citizen priorities and needs and help to identify and address problems that are neglected by mainstream politics. In particular, it can help articulate and draw attention to the interests of underprivileged and marginalized social groups. Participatory governance practices allow citizens to contribute to the achievement of common public goals, to better understand governance processes, and to extract accountability from public officials, bureaucrats, and service providers. Its purpose is not to replace, but rather to improve and complement existing democratic institutions.

Enhanced development

As shown in the case studies in this book, participatory governance can result in improved public policies, better public services, and, as a result, enhanced development outcomes. Participatory governance can improve the quality and quantity of information fed into public decision making by producing information that comes from an important but neglected perspective, or that is more accurate and more representative, and by generating better awareness of citizens needs, particularly of poorer, underprivileged groups. This, in turn, can lead to improved implementation through more effectively targeted programs and the need for fewer subsequent adjustments. Citizen monitoring can ensure the rational use of resources and provide a safeguard against leakages, while citizen evaluation can provide feedback on problems or shortcomings in service delivery and, ideally, propose collective solutions. In Kenya, Tajikistan, and Tanzania, for example, local level participatory governance initiatives supported by the Aga Khan Foundation have led to concrete improvements in priority sectors, such as education, health, water, and sanitation (Chapter 4). Participatory budgeting initiatives have resulted in improved roads and market infrastructure in Zimbabwe (Chapter 9), and decreased crime rates in Uganda and Canada (Chapters 7 and 10), while, in the Philippines, local government units, using social contracts, have realized millions of pesos in savings (Chapter 8).

Citizen empowerment

Although there is no single definition of empowerment, at its broadest it can be understood as the expansion of freedom of choice and action (World Bank 2002). Participation has an empowering effect on those who are involved, building their confidence to approach government and helping them find new ways to voice their preferences and take action toward fulfilling their needs. Participatory governance processes can act as a catalyst for innovation and creativity in civil society, to initiate and support programs and reforms. They can also encourage citizens to become more involved in the political arena, interacting with politicians, supporting campaigns, or even running as candidates themselves.

Direct benefits to government actors

Because this volume is concerned with building political will, identifying and highlighting ways in which participatory governance works to the advantage of and serves the self-interests of state actors is critical. Experience shows that there are many such benefits, including increased *legitimacy, effectiveness, popularity, resources,* and *political stability* for government actors.

Governments around the world suffer from a lack of *legitimacy*, with citizens citing corruption, weak accountability, and government unresponsiveness as reasons for their growing disillusionment. Chapter 3, for example, discusses some of the challenges and weaknesses of representative democracy. On the other hand, citizens' trust in government grows when they feel they have a say and an eye on government's activities, and when government listens and responds to their concerns. Therefore, participatory governance mechanisms play an important role in enhancing government credibility and legitimacy.

As described above, participatory governance can also lead to more relevant public policies and tangible improvements in programs and services, thus making public officials and service providers appear more *able* and *effective* in the eyes of citizens and users. Outcomes, such as improved health services, better roads and schools, expanded access to water and sanitation services, and improved security, not only respond to citizens' needs, but also enhance their esteem and respect for government actors.

Enhanced legitimacy and improved effectiveness can, in turn, lead to *greater popularity and public support for the government*. In Bolivia, for example, in the early years of municipal democracy, mayors were routinely voted out of office after the first year of being elected, but, after the implementation of the Popular Participation initiative, seven of the ten mayors of the main municipalities were reelected, signaling their increased popularity and enhanced ability to sustain public support.

Participatory governance practices can also lead to increased government resources, both from international donors, who increasingly request or require enhanced mechanisms of accountability, and from tax-paying citizens. The introduction of participatory budgeting in the rural district of Mutoko in Zimbabwe, for example, led to "a sharp decrease in residents' default rate on fees and charges owed to the local authority" (Chapter 9) and the use of social contracts in the municipality of Batad in the Philippines, resulted in a 250% increase in tax collection, in just one year (Chapter 8). Areño adds that participatory governance initiatives have helped local government units attract significant donor funds, and "by enhancing public trust and performance, they have led to increases in revenues and investment opportunities that surpass all initial expectations" (Chapter 8).

Finally, participatory governance approaches can contribute to *political stability and peace*. The risk of instability is increased when citizens lack trust in government, when government is perceived as corrupt or unresponsive, or when it fails to deliver essential services. Actions, such as public protests, street demonstrations, strikes, and riots, result when channels for more constructive dialogue and negotiation are lacking. As experienced in Zimbabwe (Chapter 9), participatory governance mechanisms create opportunities for informed and constructive dialogue and negotiation between citizens and government, thus breaking patterns of unproductive confrontation and conflict.

Potential risks of participatory governance

Participatory governance practices bring important benefits, but are also susceptible to some significant risks. In building political will for participatory governance, it is important to be cognizant of the potential risks, as well as strategies for mitigating them.

EXPOSING UNDERLYING CONFLICTS

Although participatory governance approaches can help to avoid confrontation and conflict between citizens and the state, in some circumstances, they can also serve to bring suppressed anger and disputes to the surface. By challenging existing systems of top-down decision making and creating opportunities for multistakeholder dialogue and negotiation, there is always potential for *pent-up frustrations* or *adversarial attitudes* to emerge. In particularly sensitive or politically charged contexts, the use of professional mediators, facilitators, or conflict management specialists may be required.

LIP SERVICE

If political will is lacking, there is a risk that public sector actors will only pay *lip service* to participatory governance approaches. If participatory processes are not meaningful and no concrete results are achieved, citizens and state actors alike can soon become demoralized and lose interest. This is precisely why building genuine political will for participatory governance is so important.

ELITE CAPTURE

As with almost any development intervention, participatory governance processes run the risk of being dominated by more powerful or influential stakeholders. Constant and specific efforts are required to guard against *elite capture* and to ensure the meaningful inclusion and participation of less organized and/or less powerful groups, such as poor people, women, youth, minorities, and special needs groups. Such efforts are described in several of the case studies and discussed in Chapter 15.

EXCLUSION OF CRITICS

Another risk is that participatory governance initiatives may involve only a limited universe of actors and *exclude more critical or radical viewpoints*. Even if it is not intentional, processes of dialogue and negotiation sometimes end up involving groups of *usual suspects* or moderate, *well-behaved* actors. Participatory governance practitioners must make explicit efforts to ensure the involvement of the broad universe of diverse viewpoints on the issue, or sector at hand, and promote meaningful interaction among diverse stakeholders.

CO-OPTATION OF CIVIL SOCIETY ACTORS

With enhanced inclusion of citizens and CSOs in processes of public dialogue and negotiation comes the risk of real or perceived co-optation. Civil society actors who become too closely associated with government processes can suffer weakened links with their constituencies and/or a loss of legitimacy. If their own power or interests are enhanced by their involvement in institutionalized mechanisms of dialogue or negotiation, they may be tempted to allow themselves to be co-opted, in order to sustain their newfound status or influence. In order to mitigate this risk, care must be taken in aiming for an optimal and appropriate level of *institutionalization* of participatory governance mechanisms, such as procedural or institutional mechanisms; safeguards against co-optation should be introduced; and state–civil society dialogue and negotiation should be made as open and transparent as possible.

POTENTIAL REPRISALS AGAINST CITIZENS

In some country contexts, individuals or organizations who dare to speak out or question current governance practices may do so at considerable personal risk. Participatory governance practitioners must take their primary responsibility to protect the security of individual citizens—in particular, those who are least powerful and most vulnerable—very seriously. Where basic rights and freedoms of information, association, and expression are not guaranteed, preliminary efforts should focus on building political will for developing these.

The Concept of Political Will

What is Political Will?

If there were a competition for the most frequently cited reason for unsuccessful development endeavors, lack of political will would probably win the prize. Indeed, lack of political will has been blamed for neglect and failure in such diverse arenas as anticorruption reforms (Brinkerhoff 2000), prevention of deadly conflicts (Jentleson 2000), environmental protection (Ng 2000), debt relief (Atkinson 2000), economic reforms (Hope 2000), health care reform (Moore 2000), and education reform (Marrin 2000).

Although lack of political will is repeatedly cited as a major obstacle to development goals, it is surprisingly under-analyzed and little understood. Woocher (2001, 181), for example, states that, "remarkably little systematic analysis of the concept and of its determinants seems to have been conducted." Hammenger (1998, 12) calls political will "the slipperiest concept in the policy lexicon," while Evans (2000) concludes that the difficulty with most discussions of political will is that we spend more time lamenting its absence than analyzing what it means.

Although this book is practical rather than theoretical in nature, it nevertheless seems necessary to devote at least some attention to unpacking and understanding the notion of political will, particularly from an operational perspective. What is really meant by political will in practical terms? How can we tell whether or not political will is present? What are some of its key elements and influencing factors?

Political will is simply and commonly defined as the "demonstrated credible intent of political actors" (UNDP 2008, 230; Stapenhurst et al. 2006, 41). A slightly more detailed and operationally-oriented definition of political will is "the commitment of political leaders and bureaucrats to undertake actions to achieve a set of objectives and to sustain the costs of those actions over time" (Brinkerhoff 2000, 242).

Despite this relatively straightforward definition, Brinkerhoff reminds us that political will is an extremely complex phenomenon, with many dimensions that cannot be easily defined or analyzed. Similarly, Woocher (2001) points out that political will reflects a large and multifaceted set of underlying factors; and Evans (2000) warns that thinking about political will as a single, simple factor underestimates the sheer complexity of what is involved.

Indicators of Political Will

On what basis can it be claimed that political will does or does not exist? Indicators of genuine political will would ideally include efforts on the part of the state to initiate or actively support participatory governance practices, actively seek to understand underlying problems and issues related to lack of participatory governance, introduce legal and regulatory reform to facilitate participatory governance, create platforms and mechanisms for participatory governance, allocate adequate resources for the purposes of participatory governance, mobilize stakeholders in support of participatory governance, and enforce sanctions for noncompliance with participatory governance principles.

On the other hand, indicators of lack of political will, as witnessed in many of the cases examined in this book, include failing to initiate participatory governance practices, refusing to accept or support participatory governance initiatives proposed by citizens or CSOs, labeling participatory governance practitioners as *opponents*, refusing to make information available and/or meet with citizens and CSOs, or not responding to calls for legal reforms or the introduction of participatory governance mechanisms. Ideally, political will would involve active support for participatory governance, but, in many country contexts, simply tolerating or not banning or punishing participatory governance practitioners would represent a significant improvement.

Although state actors sometimes openly reject or resist participatory governance initiatives, a much more common scenario is for government actors to publicly *claim* to support principles of transparency, accountability, citizen empowerment, and participation, but to fail to put these principles into practice. In such cases, lack of political will may be manifested by not following through on public declarations or promises, failing to allocate adequate resources to participatory governance initiatives, failing to implement policies or rules with regard to participatory governance, failing to enforce sanctions for noncompliance, or delaying or failing to give priority to participatory governance reforms or initiatives.

Principal Elements of Political Will

The purpose of this volume, however, is not just to assess whether political will for participatory governance is present, and shrugging our shoulders in resignation if that is not the case. The core premise of this volume is that the presence or absence of political will is not an external factor we must passively accept, but rather something we must actively seek to create and nurture. In order to generate and nurture political will, it is important to seek to understand (i) the principal elements of political will, and (ii) key influencing factors.

Taking the definition of political will as *the commitment of political leaders and bureaucrats to undertake action* as a starting point, it is important to reflect on the process whereby such *commitment to act* emerges and develops. My experience as a participatory governance practitioner and researcher has led me to identify three mutually reinforcing elements of political will: *political want*, *political can*, and *political must*. In order for power-holders to become committed to act, they need to *want* to undertake a given action, feel confident they *can* undertake that action, and feel they *must* undertake the action.

As pointed out in the literature (Brinkerhoff 2000; Allison and Zelikow 1999; Kpundeh 1998) and illustrated by the cases presented in this book, the real world of political will and political action is complex and unpredictable. Such a multitude of different visible and invisible factors come into play at different individual, organizational, relational, and societal levels. There is no guarantee that pushing these three buttons of political *want, can,* and *must* will necessarily result in political will. It is also quite possible that political will can emerge in the absence of one or more (or even all!) of these elements. Nevertheless, it is hypothesized that by looking at elements of *political want, political can,* and *political must*, we can begin to identify some important strategies for nurturing political will.

Political want

An important and rather obvious aspect of political will, but one which has probably received the least attention in both practice and theory, is *political want*. An ideal scenario for achieving participatory governance is not one in which political leaders and bureaucrats accept citizen participation in governance because they are *forced* to, but rather one in which they genuinely understand and support the principles and practices of participatory governance and *want* it to happen, because they are aware of the benefits.

Those who are cynical about the nature of political behavior, especially those who function in contexts of entrenched corruption and patronage, where political office is primarily viewed as a means of self-enrichment rather than public service, understandably have limited faith that political power-holders will ever willingly give more influence and control to citizens. Instead they tend to focus on tactics that force power-holders to listen and respond to citizens. However, experience, including a number of the examples described in this book, suggests that many political leaders and bureaucrats do have a genuine respect for participatory governance, and many others who are initially skeptical can eventually be genuinely *won over* to participatory governance when provided with sound evidence, and incentives.

Experience suggests that there are two categories of *champions* of participatory governance, the *natural* and the *converted*. Political leaders and bureaucrats who instinctively support the participatory governance agenda tend to do so as a result of personal beliefs and values that have instilled within them a participatory *mind-set*, a genuine commitment to democratic and inclusive ideals, and confidence in the ability and wisdom of *the people*.

Converted champions, although they may not be naturally predisposed (and, in some cases, may be initially stridently opposed!) to participatory governance, usually come to support it, as a result of seeing its concrete benefits, to themselves, to those they govern, or both. Bureaucrats, in particular sector specialists, sometimes subconsciously regard ordinary citizens as lacking technical knowledge and therefore unable to bring worthwhile ideas to the table. As several case studies show, government officials are often pleasantly surprised at the insights of ordinary people and discover perspectives they had not previously thought of. It is such revelations that can convince technocrats that participatory governance is not just political correctness, but can really add value. This *conversion* can take place over many years, as a result of iterative experience and learning, or may take the form of an instantaneous revelation, for example, based on firsthand experience in or exposure to a successful participatory governance initiative.

Political or *personal self-interest* is an important source of *political want*. Politicians, or bureaucrats, may come to *want* participatory governance for less than virtuous reasons, for example, because it allows them to attract donor funds, *expose* a political opponent, or direct public attention to one issue area while diverting it from another. In any case, the realization that participatory governance can potentially serve the political and personal interests of both governors and the governed is often an important turning point on the road to political want and political will for participatory governance.

Political can

While being *willing* and being *able* are obviously not the same thing, there is clearly a strong link between the two. Experience suggests that *political can* is an important element of political will. Political leaders and bureaucrats, who are confident in their own capacity and the capacity of others to successfully implement participatory governance, are much more likely to manifest political will. Conversely, lack of abilities, skills, mechanisms, resources, and support are likely to result in a lack of political will to support or undertake participatory governance practices.

Therefore, developing participatory governance skills and establishing mechanisms and conditions that enhance the ability of state actors to undertake participatory governance are also key elements of nurturing political will. In order to acquire a sense of *political can*, state actors need confidence, not only in their own capabilities, but also in the will and capabilities of other key stakeholders, particularly, citizens and CSOs. Building such confidence may require helping state actors discover and appreciate the existing capabilities of citizens and/or CSOs, as well as strengthening the capacity and agency of these actors, where it is lacking.

The ability of *all* stakeholders to implement participatory governance is also dependent upon factors such as an enabling legislative and regulatory framework, creating appropriate mechanisms and platforms, and the provision of adequate resources and support. Therefore, all of these factors play a potentially important role in creating a sense of *political can* and *political will*.

Political must

In addition to *political want* and *political can*, a final key element of political will is what might be called *political must*. Politics is an arena of stiff and constant competition for limited attention, time, and resources. Even if a political leader or bureaucrat genuinely *wants* to undertake an action and has the capacity to do so, the chance of action actually occurring is much greater if this *want* and *can* are accompanied by some compelling force or pressure that demands action and renders inaction politically costly.

Such pressure can be generated by a situation of political, economic, or social crisis, when business as usual is no longer an option and power-holders are forced to consider alternative approaches, or, in the context of a political regime, change that espouses fresh ideas or new directions. Pressure can come from *above*, in the form of instructions from political leadership, or, very importantly for CSO practitioners, can be created from *below*, through citizen mobilization, in the form of public demonstrations, rallies, petitions, and strikes, or media campaigns, advocacy, and lobbying tactics. A sense of *political must* can also be created through constitutional, legal, or regulatory reforms—for example, by adopting laws requiring state actors to publicly share information, or consult with or account to citizens, and by sanctioning those who fail to abide by these laws.

Key Factors Influencing Political Will

Political want, political can, and *political must* have been identified as key elements of political will. As mentioned above, each of these elements is influenced by a wide range of underlying factors at the *individual, organizational, relational,* and *societal* levels. Although political will is normally understood as the commitment or credible intent of individual political actors, it is also potentially useful to consider how political will is manifested at the organizational, relational, and societal levels and to reflect on the dynamics among these different levels of political will.

Figure 1.1 outlines a framework for identifying and thinking about how variables at different levels can potentially influence key elements of political will. The multidimensional arrows are meant to reflect the fact that political will is a complex and multifaceted phenomenon, and that each different category of factors can influence one another. This framework is intended to help analyze the various case studies presented in this book. It could also potentially prove useful to participatory governance practitioners, who are faced with political won't and are struggling to identify strategies to nurture political will. In any given situation, it could be helpful to map both positive and negative factors in each compartment of the multidimensional circle of political will. This could help in identifying where there are potential strengths and/or important gaps.

Figure 1.1 proposes some examples of individual, organizational, relational, and societal level factors that can impact *political want, can,* and *must*. The implication is not that every single compartment of the political will circle needs to be addressed, but rather that by taking into account factors at each of these levels, and, in particular, assessing to what degree factors of *political want, can,* and *must* are simultaneously addressed, practitioners can potentially better understand the problems of political won't and tackle these in a more multidimensional and strategic manner.

Individual

Any conception of political will must be based on a theory about the way in which governments make decisions and take actions. *Rational actor* models of political behavior tend to emphasize decisions made by individual actors to meet certain goals. The actions or decisions of individual political actors, be they at the top levels of political leadership or the front lines of public service delivery, are undeniably extremely important in shaping citizen–state relations and achieving political change. An important part of nurturing participatory governance, therefore, is nurturing the political will of key individual actors (Evans 2000).

At the most basic level, the willingness of an individual political actor to support participatory governance or not is linked to that person's personal beliefs and values, in other words a result of his/her character, background, upbringing, education, instincts, experiences, relationships, and the myriad factors that shape his or her perspective and understanding of the world, as well as attitudes and goals. For example, individual political actors may hold elitist or populist beliefs. They may be arrogant or humble by nature, and autocratic or democratic. They may believe the masses to be wise or ignorant. They may also be corrupt or honest, and concerned with self-enrichment or public service.

All of these beliefs, values, and traits play a role in determining political will, in determining to what extent individual actors are *intrinsically motivated* (Treadway et al. 2005, 230). Direct advocacy with an individual can also serve to shift his or her perceptions or priorities, thus influencing political will and behavior (Woocher 2001). Factors at the organizational, relational, and societal levels also have an important impact on the political will of individuals.

Organizational

Organizational behavior theory emphasizes the importance of looking beyond the individual to understand how organizational factors, such as organizational mandates, culture, established practices, and procedures, influence political will and political actions. Organizations are thought to act according to the *logic of appropriateness* (March and Simon 1993), guided by compliance with formal and informal norms and preestablished patterns of behavior, rather than rational consideration of consequences. Although it is conceptually difficult to think about organizations having a *will* or *lack of will*, it is clear that there can be important manifestations of political will for participatory governance at the organizational level, such as an organizational mandate that prioritizes participatory governance; an organizational culture that values and rewards accountability, responsiveness, and public service; established practices and procedures for participatory governance; or incentives for promoting participatory governance and sanctions for failing to do so.

It is clear that these organizational-level factors can have an important influence on the political will—or political want, can, and must—of individuals therein. Such links between individual and organizational political will have important operational implications, for example, in terms of taking into account organizational-level factors when seeking to generate political will on the part of individual power-holders and understanding the challenges and needs of participatory governance "champions" functioning within a broader organizational context.

Relational

Until now, attention has been focused on the political will of state power-holders since *buy-in* from this group of actors is both crucially important and frequently lacking. Participatory governance by nature, however, requires political will on the part of a range of state and non-state actors to interact with one another and work together. In some circumstances, a lack of political will among citizens or CSOs may be as problematic as lack of will on the part of government officials. Political will for participatory governance on the part of citizens, civil society actors, and other stakeholders is essential to the achievement of participatory governance and plays an important role in nurturing political will on the part of state actors.

Political systems theory sees government actions as resulting from a process of political bargaining dependent upon established relationships and the respective power, perceptions, and preferences of different players (Woocher 2001). Therefore, the manifestation of political will for participatory governance on the part of individual citizens and CSOs, as well as the nature of civil society–state relationships and the impact of these on political *want, can,* and *must* are extremely important factors. It can be particularly difficult to nurture political will in situations where citizens are disempowered or disengaged, CSOs are weak or disorganized, or where civil society–state relations are characterized by mutual distrust or hostility.

Societal

Political will for participatory governance on the part of individuals and organizations, within the state and civil society spheres, is influenced by a wide range of societal-level factors. Political, legal, socioeconomic, and cultural characteristics all play a role in enabling or constraining political will. Political traditions and norms have a particularly strong impact on promoting or blocking political will for participatory governance. Where there is a legacy of authoritarianism or dictatorship, and where notions of democracy and active citizenship are still being consolidated, building political will for participatory governance requires patience and perseverance.

In so-called *hybrid* or *neopatrimonial* states, real decision-making power frequently lies outside formal government institutions, in the hands of *big men* and their cronies, who seek to serve their own vested interests rather than the well-being of ordinary citizens or national betterment (Cammack 2007). In circumstances such as these, building political will for participatory governance is difficult, because public officials benefiting from corruption are likely to resist calls for transparent citizen participation and oversight and others may be powerless to act. Situations where corruption and political patronage are endemic pose particular challenges for building political will for participatory governance, but, as illustrated by several chapters (Chapters 8, 11, and 14) of this book, can also offer important opportunities and motivations for action.

Legal factors, such as an enabling or disabling constitutional and legislative framework and policies, regulations, and mechanisms that facilitate or discourage citizen participation also have a strong impact on building political will. A variety of socioeconomic factors are also influential. High rates of poverty and illiteracy, low levels of trust and social capital, gender inequities, and sociocultural barriers to women's participation in public life can also have a negative impact on political will. Therefore, societal-level factors must be taken into account in analyzing lack of *political want, can, and must* and in reflecting on strategies for building political will. It is important to remember that "changing the context in which the game is played can influence individual players' behavior" (Woocher 2001, 195).

Overview of the Volume

This volume is based on the learnings and insights of a diverse group of leading practitioners, each of whom draws on extensive firsthand experience working to nurture political will for participatory governance. As mentioned above, the case studies represent a broad range of participatory governance practices applied at both local and national levels, in the global south and the global north. The contexts of the case studies range from new and struggling democracies, like Uganda and Tajikistan, to countries suffering acute political crisis, such as Zimbabwe, to prosperous and stable democracies, like Canada, the United Kingdom, and the United States, and contexts of endemic corruption and patronage, such as Honduras and the Philippines. Many of the countries studied are emerging from a not-so-distant history of colonialism, authoritarianism, or, in some cases, dictatorship, such as Bolivia, Uganda, and Uruguay. The various chapters of the volume offer a rich diversity of experiences, but also reveal many common issues and lessons.

In the remainder of Part 1, two highly experienced practitioner-analysts begin by revisiting the notion of participatory governance, exploring some of its inherent challenges and questioning some of the assumptions of this volume. First, *Dina Abad* analyzes the experience of the Philippines, and discusses how, in the absence of genuine political will, participatory governance runs the risk of becoming an instrument of cooptation, rather than an instrument of empowerment. She further questions to what extent it is feasible, or strategic, in a context of entrenched patronage and systemic corruption, to invest energy in influencing political will. *John Clark* acknowledges lack of political will as a key obstacle to participatory governance, but argues that efforts to build political will must take into account, and seek to simultaneously address, other obstacles inherent to participatory governance at the level of citizens and civil society.

Generating Political Will for Participatory Governance at the Local Level

Part 2 focuses on experiences of building political will for participatory governance at the local level. *Richard Holloway* and his colleagues from the Aga Khan Foundation share lessons based on efforts in three different countries, Tajikistan, Kenya, and Tanzania, to strengthen relationships, dialogue, and collaboration between local government authorities and grassroots level CSOs. *Mary Jacksteit* explores how community members and activists in Washington, D.C. were able to overcome an impasse with a neighborhood governing body, entrenched in confrontational relations and resistant to citizen participation. *Tricia Zipfel* discusses both the opportunities and challenges of translating unprecedented top-level political will for participatory governance into concrete practices and outcomes at the ground level in the United Kingdom. Next, *Harriet Namisi* from Uganda explores how political will can be influenced by *pressure from below*, as a result of grassroots level civic education, awareness-raising, and support to citizen-led advocacy. Finally,

Emmanuel Areño discusses how the use of *social contracts* has helped counter corruption and enhance the responsiveness and accountability of public officials in the Philippines.

Nurturing Political Will for Participatory Budgeting

Even governments who welcome citizen participation in processes of policy dialogue, planning, or service delivery, frequently lack political will when it comes to giving citizens and CSOs a say in allocating public resources. Part 3 looks at three cases of building political will for participatory budgeting. First, *Takawira Mumvuma* shares lessons about how participatory budgeting was successfully introduced in a financially strapped, rural community in Zimbabwe. Second, *Elizabeth Pinnington* explores how political will for participatory budgeting was nurtured, but this time in a relatively prosperous, culturally diverse, urban community in Canada. Finally, *Ronald MacLean-Abaroa*, former mayor of La Paz and Minister of Finance of Bolivia, describes how the adoption of a nationwide *Popular Participation* approach transformed citizen–state relations, by involving ordinary citizens in the allocation of resources at the municipal level and subsequently inviting civil society representatives from marginalized communities to help determine the appropriate use of more than US$1.5 billion in debt relief.

Building Political Will for Participatory Governance at the National Level

Part 4 looks at several examples of building political will for participatory governance at the national level. First, *Janine Hicks* and *Imraan Buccus* share the experience of building political will for the development and adoption of a full-fledged national public participation policy in South Africa. Next, *Anabel Cruz* describes and analyzes the efforts of multistakeholder coalitions in four Latin American countries—Honduras, Nicaragua, Chile, and Uruguay—to advocate for and directly contribute to the adoption and implementation of Right to Information legislation. Finally, *Angela Keller-Herzog,* of Transparency International, offers an analysis of how Advocacy and Legal Advice Centers, in different countries around the world, have succeeded in fostering citizen participation and government responsiveness in the fight against corruption.

Finally, a concluding chapter offers a summary of key findings from all of the case studies. It includes an analysis of principal reasons for political won't, effective strategies for nurturing political will, and key factors of success and lessons learned in building political will for participatory governance.

References

Allison, G.T. and P.D. Zelikow. 1999. *Essence of Decision: Explaining the Cuban Missile Crisis*. New York: Longman.

Atkinson, M. 28 December 2000. Political will puts relief. *The Guardian*. London.

Brinkerhoff, D.W. 2000. Assessing political will for anti-corruption efforts: An analytical framework. *Public Administration and Development* 20 (3): 239–253.

Cammack, D. 2007. The logic of African neopatrimonialism: What role for donors? *ODI Development Policy Review* 25 (5): 599–614.

Chase, Rob and Anushay Anjum. 2008. Demand for good governance stocktaking. *Social Development Department Discussion Paper*. Washington, D.C.: World Bank.

CIVICUS Participatory Governance Programme. 2006. *CIVICUS Participatory Governance Programme 2006–2009 Concept Note*. Johannesburg, South Africa: CIVICUS.

CIVICUS Participatory Governance Programme. 2007. *Results of a Survey to Assess Practitioners' Priority Needs and Preferences*. Johannesburg, South Africa: CIVICUS.

Commonwealth Foundation. 1999. *Citizens and Governance: Civil Society in the New Millennium*. London: Commonwealth Foundation.

Evans, G. 2000. Preventing and containing violent conflict: mobilizing political will. *Introductory Statement to Ministry of Foreign Affairs International Seminar on Preventing Violent Conflict: The Search for Political Will, Strategies and Effective Tools*. Krusenberg, Sweden.

Gaventa, John. 2002. Introduction: Exploring citizenship, participation and accountability. In *IDS Bulletin* 3 (2). Brighton, UK: Institute of Development Studies.

Hammergren, L. 1998. *Political Will, Constituency Building, and Public Support in Rule of Law Programs*. Washington, D.C.: U.S. Agency for International Development.

Hope, K. 15 November 2000. Small steps towards telecoms liberalistion. *Financial Times*. London.

Hyden, G., J. Court, and K. Mease. 2004. *Making Sense of Governance: Empirical Evidence from 16 Developing Countries*. Boulder, CO: Lynne Rienner.

Jentleson, B.W. 2000. Coercive prevention: normative, political and policy dilemmas. *Peaceworks*, No. 35. Washington, D.C.: United States Institute of Peace.

Kpundeh, Sahr J. 1998. Political will in fighting corruption. In *Corruption and Integrity Improvement Initiatives in Developing Countries.* New York: United Nations Development Programme.

Kpundeh, S. and P. Dininio. 2006. Political Will. In *The Role of Parliament in Curbing Corruption* ed. Rick Stapenhurst et al. 41–48. Washington, D.C.: World Bank Institute.

Krafchik, Warren. 2004. *Can Civil Society Add Value to Budget Decision-Making?* Washington, D.C.: International Budget Project.

Malena, C., R. Forster, and J. Singh. 2004. *Social Accountability: An Introduction to the Concept and Emerging Practice.* Washington, D.C.: World Bank.

March, J.G. and H.A. Simon. 1993. *Organizations.* Cambridge, MA: Blackwell Publishers.

Marrin, M. 11 February 2000. Labour's schools policy is just window-dressing. *The Daily Telegraph.* London.

Moore, R.T. 19 March 2000. Political will needed to take action on health-care system. *The Boston Herald.* Boston, MA.

Narayan, Deepa et al. 2000. *Voices of the Poor: Crying out for Change.* Washington, D.C.: World Bank.

Ng, V. 15 May 2000. Johor Strait clean-up exercise can work with political will, commitment. *New Straits Times.* Malaysia.

Paul, Samuel. 2002. *Holding the State to Account: Citizen Monitoring in Action.* Bangalore, ME: Public Affairs Center.

Songco, Dan. 2001. Accountability to the poor: Experiences in civic engagement in public expenditure management – A synthesis paper. Paper prepared as part of the Action Learning Program on Participatory Processes for Poverty Reduction Strategies. Washington, D.C.: World Bank.

Stapenhurst, R., N. Johnston, and R. Pelizzo (eds.). 2006. *The Role of Parliament in Curbing Corruption.* Washington, D.C.: World Bank Institute.

Tandon, Rajesh and Ranjita Mohanty. 2002. *Civil Society and Governance.* New Delhi, India: Samskriti.

Treadway, D.C., W.A. Hochwarter, C.J. Kacmar, and G.R. Ferris. 2005. Political will, political skill, and political behavior. *Journal of Organizational Behavior* 26: 229–245.

United Nations Development Program, 1997. *Governance for Sustainable Human Development.* New York: United Nations Development Program.

United Nations Development Program. 2008. *Tackling Corruption, Transforming Lives: Accelerating Human Development in Asia and the Pacific.* Colombo: United Nations Development Program Human Development Report Unit.

Woocher, L. 2001. Deconstructing political will: Explaining the failure to prevent deadly conflict and mass atrocities. *Princeton Journal of Public and International Affairs* 12: 10.

World Bank. 2004. *Better Governance for Development in the Middle East and North Africa: Enhancing Inclusiveness and Accountability.* Washington, D.C.: World Bank.

World Bank. 2002. *Empowerment and Poverty Reduction: A Sourcebook.* Washington, D.C.: World Bank.

World Bank. 1992. *Governance and Development.* Washington, D.C.: World Bank.

World Bank. 1994. *Governance: The World Bank's Experience.* Washington, D.C.: World Bank.

CHAPTER 2

REVISITING PARTICIPATORY GOVERNANCE: AN INSTRUMENT FOR EMPOWERMENT OR CO-OPTATION?

Henedina Abad

Introduction

Participatory governance has become a major focus of development discourse and practice. International covenants proclaim the right to participate in development as an inalienable human right "by virtue of which every human person and all peoples are entitled to participate in, contribute to and enjoy economic, social, cultural and political development, in which all human rights and fundamental freedoms can be fully realized" (United Nations General Assembly 1986). The concern for good governance, as a means of promoting sustainable and equitable development, has heightened interest in participatory governance in development practice. The premise is that governments, especially in the developing world, are pervasive and dominating. They control the allocation and disposition of the country's resources, meager as they may be. Therefore, governments are critical arenas for reform.

Proponents of participatory governance will argue that governments are most often under the control of the political and economic elite in society, and that the culture of patronage has engendered systemic corruption and inefficiency. However, at the same time, they also hold that governments are not monolithic, and space and opportunities exist for constructive engagements toward meaningful reforms, no matter how incremental they may be. Some development agencies go so far as to proclaim participatory governance as the *missing link* to poverty reduction, improved transparency and accountability in governance, more equitable allocation of scarce budgetary resources, and better delivery of social services. Concededly, while evidence of the benefits of participatory governance has been demonstrated in some local initiatives, or in some agencies or programs and projects, the fact is the mitigation of corruption, the reduction in inequity, and even the strengthening of democratic institutions remain simply aspirations.

In fact, in many parts of the world, like the Philippines and Thailand, these efforts have not only led to worsening poverty and social division, but also to the weakening of democratic institutions. The engagement of civil society organizations (CSOs) with these regimes, in so-called participatory exercises have been *unconstructive* and, even worse, they have transformed many CSOs into conduits for patronage, if not becoming new intermediary patrons themselves. In the process, the experience has not been empowering and liberating. It has only served to deepen dependencies, develop new ones, and legitimize the structures of dominance and inequity.

Critics point to public leaders' lack of political will to bring about profound changes, as the culprit. That may be partly true, but I submit that genuine and sustained change can only come about from the determination and unrelenting action of the intended beneficiaries of the reforms—and those that enable them to perform that role, such as CSOs in whatever arena of engagement they may find themselves in—and not from the concern and beneficence of those in power.

Empowerment Is the Objective

In the context of societies in the developing world, the objective of any exercise in participatory democracy must be empowerment. Empowerment is meant here as a greater meaningful share in political decision making and in the fruits of developments, for those in the margins of society. It not only pertains to CSOs, but, more importantly, is concerned with the primary groups that these organizations serve, such as landless farm workers, the urban poor, subsistence fishermen, and the like.

This may seem basic, but it is worthwhile to go back to the basics. In the Philippines, many CSOs seem to have forgotten this basic principle. It is important to remember that while primary organizations and CSOs are partners in the process of change, their interests may not always converge. In fact, they may differ and conflict. That happens when CSOs advance their own interests at the expense of the people they seek to serve. In the process, they end up only empowering themselves as they take on the role of intermediary patrons. Then a new form of dependency, between the primary organization and CSOs develops. That is why the ultimate test of a CSO's success, in playing a mediating role, is being able to hand over the principal role of engagement in participatory governance to the organic leaders of the primary organizations they serve, and to relegate themselves to their appropriate supporting role.

Admittedly, playing a mediating and enabling role in participatory governance is complicated. This is especially true for CSO leaders who come from a long tradition of distrusting government and bureaucratic politics, and preferring to operate in the familiar and uncomplicated confines of independent nongovernmental work. The difficulties do not end there. Then, there is the trying task of navigating within the bureaucratic maze: finding a space to maneuver for reforms, building tactical and principle-based alliances, and crossing over back and forth in the governmental and nongovernmental arenas. It is not uncommon for CSO leaders to be suspected by their own constituents of having been compromised and swallowed by the temptations of perks and privilege in the echelons of bureaucratic power.

Locating Political Will

Clearly it is important to build political will for participatory governance among public officials and elected representatives, because these are the very people who eventually make the decisions that make reforms possible. Building a constituency for reforms within government is therefore key, whether it be a key public officer who will champion the cause or a group of reformers, and whether the alliance be short term, such as fighting for a bigger portion of the national budget for an agency concerned, or based on a longer-term shared vision of equitable and sustainable development.

However, we all know too well that public officials have many publics to appease, including the President, politicians in Congress, business interests, their own patrons, international donors, and the media. They are subject to the vagaries of power and politics. The laudable reforms they introduce, or the mechanisms they put in place, to facilitate meaningful engagement in governance can be reversed overnight by their successors or by a change in government. Unfortunately, that is the nature of affairs in government and politics.

That is why it is crucially important to build the political will of those who ultimately should benefit from the reform initiatives. They may be agrarian reform beneficiaries, basic education teachers, the elderly, or the landless urban poor. The call is for them to translate their numbers into organized forces that can be warm bodies in mass actions, or control votes in elections and build alliances across the board, with politicians, the media, enlightened segments of the elite and the business community, the academe, and the international donor community. The objective, in collaboration with their allies from within the bureaucracy, is to make the reforms politically costly or difficult to resist, or, if already in place, to reverse them. It is not a guarantee that reforms will happen or will endure, but it gives the reforms a better chance of happening or enduring.

On top of that, whether the exercise succeeds or fails, it gives the intended beneficiaries the opportunity to flex their collective muscles, develop greater experience and wisdom in engagement, and gain a semblance of respect, even if it is grudgingly extended.

The importance of CSOs maintaining close ties with their primary organizations cannot be overemphasized. They should constantly engage them, as ordinary citizens also need to understand and experience the complex process of engagement, not to mention doing so can also liberate and empower them. This is much more easily said than done. Many times, I have witnessed how powerless people become corrupted by the very same power that was intended to liberate them.

Participatory Governance Is a Political Process

This brings me to my final point: participatory governance is essentially a *political* process, aimed at reforming the citizen-state relationship. As previously discussed, building the will to initiate and sustain such reforms must be approached from within, by supporting reform champions and reform advocates, and from without, by empowering the ultimate beneficiaries and their civil society advocates.

It is important to emphasize this point because there is a tendency to treat the process as essentially a technical or administrative exercise, and gloss over the underlying political dynamics or treat its political ramifications as being an externality that should be avoided as much as possible. The consequence is that when reforms stall, the response is to adopt merely technical responses, such as capacity building programs that emphasize the acquisition of knowledge and skills.

I agree that even as the process is essentially political, it does have administrative, technical, legal, and technological dimensions that cannot be ignored, and reformers must be prepared to address them with as much rigor and passion as possible. Politics is messy, dirty, and unpredictable. Understandably, it is much easier to deal with manageable variables, such as skills upgrading, technology provision, or effective communication mechanisms, and to gingerly and carefully avoid the unmanageable *political stuff*. That, I believe, is the crux of the problem.

Participation, like governance, is about power. Writers, such as John Gaventa and Andrea Cornwall, instruct us about how space and power are deeply linked: "Power relations help shape the boundaries of partici-patory spaces, what is possible within them, and who may enter with which identities, discourses and interests" (Gaventa 2006). As such, it is illusory to design participatory strategies without full consideration of power and how it is influenced by the political and economic relations in society.

The Broader Philippine Picture

Philippine-style democracy is handicapped by the continuing dominance of a political aristocracy, whose source of wealth is derived from its con-trol of the state apparatus, and an economic oligarchy, whose economic base may be independent of the state apparatus, but whose access to the state is nonetheless its principal method of accumulating wealth. This structural weakness has led to the underdevelopment of the political and institutional foundations necessary to transform the huge assets into sus-tained and predictable development success.

The result is a situation that over and over again has been caricatured in political commentaries as a small network of families and clans monop-olizing power and economic wealth, while the great mass of people live in poverty and misery. A very thin layer of middle class exists in the pyram-idal structure, but most have gambled the few possessions they have and reluctantly left their families to seek fortune as overseas workers. Over the years, this condition has fostered a culture of political patronage, which breeds and thrives on the insecurity and helplessness of the poor. The deeper the poverty, the greater the dependency, the more secure the hold over power.

Thus, while the poor are politically free to exercise their right of suf-frage, their economic insecurity renders them vulnerable to the dictates of their patron. In a patronage system, elections have little to do with the merit of philosophies and platforms. They are essentially contests among competing patrons, who represent clans and interest groups that mas-querade as political parties. Political clans and personal networks super-sede parties as the main form of political organization. The most enduring and entrenched patrons are those who are able to control the sources of patronage.

This patron–client relationship dominates the election process in the Philippines. In our warped sense of democratic representation, the popu-lar mandate does not favor those who *lead using the power of influence through example,* but rather those with a proven track record or the best potential of delivering benefits or *gifts,* no matter what the character or qualification of the candidate.

Organized groups have sometimes fallen into this trap. They have succumbed to the political tactics of the patron, in order to get support for their advocacies. As a result, their support is given to the *best provider* rather than someone who leads by example.

For the patron-leader, power is not just important; it is his or her reason for being. It is the ultimate goal. Once attained, the next preoccupation is to seek opportunities to expand such powers and retain those powers for as long as possible. The follower is valued only to the extent that he can be useful toward this end. Outside of that, he is dispensable. The common good does not figure into the thinking of the patron-leader. Only personal, clan, or class interests take primacy. As long as the poor represent no more than votes to politicians, politics will be no more than theatre and democracy a farce.

With the prevailing dominant culture of patronage politics, it can be expected that the individual interests of those in power, rather than the interests of citizens, will determine officials' commitment to participatory governance. Is empowerment possible under this setup? To truthfully answer this question, we need to ask and analyze how spaces for engagement were created, in whose interests, and according to which or whose terms.

Civil society leaders must look at the whole picture and not allow themselves to be disempowered by their involvement in participatory governance institutions. The challenge is to create and expand new political spaces for government transparency, citizen participation, and social accountability work. The focus of this work should be on how to effect political and social change to transform the country's elite-dominated democracy into a participatory and deliberative democracy.

Providing political and social space for citizens implies creating an enabling environment that allows citizens to become involved in the deliberation of issues and problems and in finding solutions. First and foremost, citizen participation requires maximum transparency and sharing of information. This means giving people access to information on which to base deliberations or exact accountability from government. Second, spaces need to be widened for the involvement of the poor and marginalized in decision making. A critical consciousness and the political capabilities for democratic engagement also need to be built. Government can only do the first requirement. CSOs, or nonstate actors, must perform the second.

References

Gaventa, John. 2006. Finding the spaces for change. *IDS Bulletin* 37 (6).
United Nations General Assembly. 1986. *Declaration on the Right to Development*. New York: UNHCR, A/Res/41/128.

CHAPTER 3

BUILDING POLITICAL WILL FOR PARTICIPATORY GOVERNANCE: OVERCOMING THE OBSTACLES

John Clark

Keeping Politics in Participatory Governance

To build political will for participatory governance it is essential to look at the interface between its practitioners and more traditional political institutions. It is important to consider what changes in the mechanisms of democracy are needed to provide a more enabling environment for participatory governance. However, it is equally important to reflect on how participatory governance can *strengthen*, rather than erode, representative democracy.

The contents of this chapter were first presented, appropriately, in Glasgow, Scotland. This was appropriate because Keir Hardy, one of its sons, was born in 1856 in Motherwell, just a few miles southeast of Glasgow. He fought hard to extend democracy to all citizens, not just the male elite. He became the first Member of Parliament, an independent, to represent the working class. In 1906, he went on to found the British Labour Party. People of all political positions, no matter how much they may disagree with its politics today, recognize that, from its birth until 1970, the Labour Party introduced many key reforms that opened opportunities and services to marginalized groups, and these reforms have now been internalized by *all* mainstream political parties. In the fifteen years it held the reins of government, it introduced, for example, the National Health Service; universal, free, state education; unemployment benefits; state pensions; the legalization of trade unions; the right to strike; independence for Britain's colonies; and the legalization of abortions and homosexuality.

These achievements are reminders that *representative democracy* has played a pivotal role in harnessing the power of government for ordinary people. However exciting the opportunities are for participatory governance today, it must be developed in ways that strengthen and improve, not seek to supplant representative democracy. Indeed, if this recognition is not embedded in programs of participatory governance, there will not be enough political will for them to really flourish.

The history of the Labour Party also provides other important lessons for participatory governance. Since its heyday in the 1970s, the party has seen a severe membership contraction, from 700,000 members, representing the largest membership organization in the United Kingdom, to just 159,000 in July 2008 (Save the Labour Party 2008; Clark 2003). There is no single reason for this decline, but a large factor is that the party is no longer seen as defining the fault line of political divides in society. In the first half of the twentieth century, this fault line was in essence the inequity of economic power. There was massive inequality along class lines, massive inequity in the ownership of the means of production, and massive inequities of opportunity and incomes. Once all parties had embraced the welfare state, progressive taxation, and equality of opportunity as norms, the distinctive *raison d'être* of the Labour Party was less clear. Conversely, in the 1980s and 1990s, a plethora of organizations arose that more energetically defined the political fault lines of the times.

An equally significant lesson is that democratic systems, especially political parties, can be strengthened and remain relevant in the twenty-first century by learning from participatory governance ways to better connect with citizens and their various concerns. Participatory governance not only *needs* political will, it can also *generate* political will.

No one would have believed at the peak of Labour's membership in 1971, for example, that an organization formed that year concerned primarily with the marine environment would overtake it in membership, but that is precisely what happened. By 1990, Greenpeace grew to 320,000 members by when the Labour Party had slipped to 280,000 members (Clark 2003). Similarly, organizations concerning women's rights, sexuality, consumers' concerns, and many other issues significantly increased their membership. The dominant political concern shifted from a contest over the ownership of the means of production to more diverse debates about what *is* produced, how it is produced, and for what sort of society.

This dynamic can be seen as a seismic shift in democracy. In its earliest manifestation, in Ancient Greece, everyone was directly and equally involved in decision making. All free men could go to the

Forum and vote on issues they were concerned about. This is where the term *demos kratein,* people's rule, came from. Of course, in larger societies such direct democracy is impractical. Hence indirect, or representative, democracy evolved and was solidified in seventeenth-century Britain, through the civil wars and the *Glorious Revolution,* which established the supremacy of parliament over the monarch. The deficiency of this system was that early Members of Parliament lacked any quality control. They could be *bought* by vested interests, or be delinquent in their duties. Political parties were the response. Edmund Burke defined a party as "an organized assembly of men, united for working together for the national interest, according to the particular principle they agreed upon" (Burke 1770). Parties offered a seal of approval, of a collective of members, and a wholesaling of representative democracy. This institution of political parties has served politics well for centuries.

However, today there is no single principle that defines national interests, rather there are hundreds. Individuals identify with different issues, and it is unlikely that a single political party will have a platform that matches a particular person's unique palette of interests. Constituents of democracies increasingly prefer to be represented according to the *issues* they care about, rather than the place where they live. Moreover, these issues do not necessarily reflect *national interests,* but rather *global* interests. This exposes the paradox of all democratic systems: the most challenging political issues of today are increasingly global in nature, yet, in essence, the highest level of democracy remains at the *national* level. Although the United Nations is, to a certain extent, a parliament of national administrations, there is no global parliament of legislators. At the same time, many matters of governance are devolved to local levels or to a growing number of implementing agencies, making the customization of policy to specific situations and the oversight of implementation increasingly difficult.

The importance of participatory governance is that it addresses these democratic deficits. Civic engagement allows citizens more direct say over the policy issues they are most concerned about. It allows citizens to aggregate according to those issues, including transnationally, and it allows citizens to monitor and help adjust the implementation of policies and programs (Held 2002). In these ways participatory governance is crucial in helping to *democratize democracy*. Therefore, it should not be seen as supplanting representative democracy, but instead as refining and customizing it, to make it better and more relevant to the twenty-first century. However, to do so effectively, there are three sets of obstacles to participatory governance to be overcome.

Overcoming the Obstacles to Participatory Governance

The promise of participatory governance is limited by factors intrinsic to citizens, by problems in its interface with traditional democracy, and by the inherent weaknesses of the tools it uses. Each of these obstacles is discussed in turn, and measures that could help overcome these obstacles are suggested.

Obstacles Relating to Citizens and Constituencies

The greatest political problem in well-established democracies is *apathy*. The established theories and institutions of democracy are based on the tenet that decisions concerning government actions and laws, whether at the national or local level, are legitimized, and even improved, through the engagement of citizens in decision making, while recognizing that this contribution requires citizens to be well-informed about issues and the policy choices. Local and national elections, referenda, public consultations, opinion polls, and the like are the hallowed institutions that enable citizen engagement. However, even in countries where democracy is celebrated, and where the government models transparency, the use of these institutions is often disappointing.

Some argue that it is unfair to label this as citizen apathy. They view it as a manifestation of citizen disgust, commenting that citizens do not lack interest, as the word *apathy* implies, but feel disengaged because of disgust or disillusionment with politics as usual. Most people feel powerless to effect any meaningful change by just voting for one party or another, since the mainstream parties have gravitated toward a political consensus that favors the elite. For example, governments of all hues in Anglo-Saxon countries now espouse tax, financial regulation, property rights, trade, and patent policies that favor the very rich. Not coincidentally, 81 percent of political donors in U.S. congressional elections in the late 1990s earned more than $100,000 a year, and only 5 percent earned less than $50,000 (The Economist 2009, 12). The latter group, by far the majority of citizens, may feel alienated from the processes of representative democracy, but are far from apathetic when it comes to support for other nonprofit causes. Indeed, they are just as likely to donate to social, religious, and other charitable organizations as the wealthy (Social Capital 2000).

In this analysis people feel *powerless* to effect any meaningful change just by voting for one party or another. Opinion polls suggest that ordinary citizens *are* interested and *do* care, often passionately, about public issues, such as the environment, the global financial crisis, and their jobs. While this is undoubtedly true, up to a point, it may be a romanticized view of citizens' political commitment in general. While there are plenty of citizens who feel passionately about issues such as global warming, the environment, and the *war on terror,* when it comes to national patterns, only a minority are prepared to take any action at all—whether writing to their Member of Parliament (MP) or local newspaper, joining a protest, organizing a meeting or petition, or any other form of action. In the heady days of political turmoil in the 1960s, the British establishment tried to write off political disquiet by purporting to speak for the *silent majority.* However, then, as now, formal democracy can only listen to those who decide *not* to remain silent.

The majorities of citizens often *elect* not to participate in these processes, and those who do often cast their views without properly informing themselves about the issues. If questioned, they may justify inaction by claiming that all candidates are as bad as each other, but this is a thin excuse. In the United States, for example, the policies espoused by George W. Bush and Al Gore were radically different in the 2000 presidential campaign, yet only 51 percent of eligible voters turned out. Bureaucrats may compound voter indifference by issuing background information that is impenetrable to the average citizen—a particular deterrent to participation in the European Union. However, the greater problem is that most citizens cannot be bothered. They are more likely to vote in TV programs, such as *Big Brother,* for their favorite celebrity than to take part in the formal democratic processes of the state.

Is it not ironic that citizens will sacrifice their lives in wars fighting for democracy, but fewer and fewer can be bothered to use it, even by turning out every four or five years to vote in national elections? Even less use the more time-consuming tools of participatory governance. Hence, as participatory governance becomes more influential, there is an elite drift toward the self-selected few who bother to make their voice heard. More effective outreach is needed to inform a wider base of citizens about the opportunities they have to engage and to showcase how such engagement can truly make a difference, and there should be systematic education about citizenship and governance, but these are only partial solutions. Civil society activists should also make a more determined effort to tune into the concerns of ordinary citizens so as to ensure their platforms truly embrace those perspectives.

In countries where democracy is more fragile, *fear* is the dominant obstacle. Citizens fear that speaking out or identifying with a cause may lead to reprisals, loss of liberty, or possibly worse. While the end of the Cold War saw an ascendancy of civic freedoms, more recently many states have used imprisonment and even torture to muzzle civil society organizations (CSOs) in countries ranging from Ethiopia to Venezuela, Russia to

Syria, and China to Cambodia. The threats to freedom of association and assembly, pillars of international human rights law, must be defended through international action by both civil society and governments. Only this can provide a safe climate for civil society and active citizenship. Moreover, states need to strive to make citizen participation *meaningful*, not just possible. This entails greater transparency with regards to government programs, more attention to civic education, and support for enhancing the capacities of citizens' institutions.

More generally, especially in countries where formal CSOs are relatively new, the sector needs to overcome *mistrust*. It can do this only when civil society, especially its most prominent organizations, are accountable to citizens and demonstrate that they make a difference. In many countries, citizens are skeptical of nongovernmental organizations (NGOs)—the most visible form of CSOs in the field of participatory governance—perhaps because they see NGOs as part of the national elite, rather than institutions of the people. In some countries this distrust is magnified by government officials and others openly bad-mouthing the sector and impugning its motives, especially by claiming that they are driven by the ideas and funds of foreigners. Though it is tempting for advocacy NGOs to rely on international partners for funds and inspiration in their campaigns, they rest on thin ice unless they build substantial indigenous support and look to domestic constituencies for political tactics. This would make their advocacy more convincing and help ensure their legitimacy in the eyes of politicians, the media, and citizens in general.

The indicators of success in these areas comprise: increasing membership and contributions, in cash and time, to CSOs; increasing the density and effectiveness of defenders of associational rights; and broadening civil society support from a narrow elite to the wider society.

Obstacles Relating to the Deficits in Traditional Representative Democracy

Those who are elected within representative democracies are often unwilling to share power and therefore are often quite hostile to policy-oriented CSOs. While *autocracy* is the sharp end of this tendency, a related phenomenon is *technocracy*, the conviction of those in office that only the anointed few truly understand the complexity of policymaking and that advocacy groups oversimplify for effect, and are therefore unreliable (Held 2002; Clark 2003). Those who are elected are prepared to participate in campaigns every few years, but in between elections prefer to keep citizens and their organizations at bay. They like citizens for their votes and donations, but not for their ideas or influence. Hence, those holding elected or administrative office tend to divide civil society into two schools. One school is good, because it provides services and fills the gaps that the public sector is not able to meet. The other school comprises advocacy groups who are seen as critics, who should be avoided wherever possible.

This is a generalization. Of course there are many politicians and officials who are open- minded, and many who welcome every opportunity to join in public debate. Others are nervous to engage because they take the burden of power the electorates have bestowed on them seriously, and are cautious about if and how they share this trust. They will do so *if* they see it enables them to perform their duties better. Hence, participatory governance practitioners need to demonstrate that they can be useful to officials by helping them identify better policy choices and better courses of implementation, especially by demonstrating mutuality of interests. Politicians and administrators cannot be everywhere or know every issue equally. Citizen groups can provide valuable inputs regarding priority concerns, realities on the ground, and the delivery of programs.

If those in office come to value such inputs, and learn to identify and connect with the CSOs who have the intelligence they need, they will find that participatory governance helps them do a better job. To do this they must first recognize that power is not a zero-sum game, but a resource that can grow immensely through such cooperation. It is not simply a case of *political will* versus *political won't*. Many holding office might be prepared to share power more fully once they start to see mutuality of interests at work. The *political would* needs to be explored. The clearest example of this symbiosis at work has been in the field of climate change. Civil society organizations and independent institutes of science built an irrefutable case and the public demanded action, to the point where it became popular, rather than politically suicidal, for electoral candidates to propose policies entailing large spending commitments to address the problem. Previously only Green parties may have argued this case, but now any progressive politician will do so.

Injecting the concerns of CSOs into mainstream politics requires forums for dialogue and consultation that bring civil society, politicians, and scholars together. Good illustrations are the participatory budget exercises of Porto Alegro and many other cities in the global South. Partnerships between diverse stakeholders that result from such forums have frequently helped identify wastage and corruption, for example in Uganda, the Philippines, and India. Such partnerships often entail entrusting community-based organizations to help citizens prioritize and implement local-level investments, as in the Kecamatan Development Project in

Indonesia (Mallaby 2004). Such examples of participatory governance show that concrete outcomes can be improved when it is recognized that holders of public office and holders of public *confidence* have different strengths that can complement each other to realize mutual interests. If both sides can make this leap of faith and learn to collaborate, rather than compete, both will emerge stronger. For participatory governance to flourish, the primary need is not for stronger civil society or for stronger institutions of government but for a more vibrant exchange between these two sectors.

Obstacles Relating to Deficiencies in Participatory Governance

Participatory governance practitioners must step back from their evident successes to see why public officeholders may have legitimate reservations about their work. Recognizing this perspective is an important ingredient for forming stronger collaboration. Interest groups may be *points of light,* but together those points do not necessarily form a complete landscape. Bestowing too much trust in the power of advocacy can lead to *atomizing* politics as government strategy loses coherence and logic, to a scatter of ad hoc responses to a myriad of interest groups. This can result in a drift toward elitism, because pressure groups are often middle-class and capital city-based. For example, the government of Zimbabwe panders to certain interest groups, while ignoring the common good. Citizen groups in Bangkok and Manila have demonstrated their ability to mobilize large numbers of young, well-to-do protestors capable of bringing down governments that, despite all their faults, remain very popular with the rural poor. At least in elections, people of all classes and locations can vote.

Civic engagement is likely to leave important gaps. There are no pressure groups for things we take for granted, such as sewerage and postal services, until those things disappear. Parents in middle-class areas are more likely to muster effective lobbies to improve resources for their local schools than their counterparts in deprived inner-city areas. The regressive distribution of education resources in most political systems is a testament to this. The squeaky wheel gets the oil, and, on the whole, the poor have not mastered the art of squeaking to the same degree as the articulate middle classes. However, when CSOs specifically champion the causes of the marginalized, inequities can be redressed. In Bangladesh, for example, NGOs such as BRAC have demonstrated the power of educating girls through their own schools and have campaigned for gender equity in the public education system. This—together with improved literacy for women, micro-credit programs that enable women to start their own businesses, and employment opportunities in the garment sector—were driven to a considerable degree by civil society and have dramatically enhanced the political agency of women.

Where participatory governance practitioners are disciplined enough to start consultations with a totally open menu, they are able to identify taken-for-granted services that are eroding, or of little interest to the middle classes. Unfortunately, exercises often start with a biased set of assumptions. Activists want to promote particular conclusions and may skew their research methodology accordingly. They may demonstrate that there is a constituency of support for the cause they espouse, but not detail the depth of that support. In other words, they leave out the trade-offs that the constituency considers warranted for the cause in question. Participatory budgeting exercises, for example, might be limited to investment expenditures in particular sectors, often quite narrow ones. These might reveal a substantial public thirst for increased expenditures in those sectors, but not tackle the question of *where* these resources might be found, such as reducing investment elsewhere, trimming recurrent expenditures, or increasing revenues. If public servants do not heed the signals presented by advocacy groups, it may be because they consider the research on which it is based to be incomplete. They may also consider the advocacy group to be biased toward the conclusion of a vocal, middle-class constituency rather than marginalized groups.

To overcome charges of bias, participatory governance practitioners concerned with specific sectors can form broad coalitions with peers interested in different areas, and they can prioritize reaching out to marginalized groups to help construct a more holistic vision of societal needs, experiences, and preferences. Moreover, by involving mayors, legislators, or other elected officeholders, participatory governance practitioners can help raise particular concerns while drawing on the broader overview that people may have. Broadening the scope in this way can enhance confidence in participatory governance and strengthen electoral democracy. It can ensure that attention is given to a hitherto neglected topic, but in a way that helps policy makers assess how deeply people, especially marginalized groups, are concerned about that topic.

Conclusions for Building the Will for Participatory Governance

Building political will for participatory governance goes hand in hand with generating the *participatory* will among its practitioners. Now is not the time to jettison *representative* democracy. No council of CSO leaders is waiting in the wings to assume the mantle of power, and if one existed it would not enjoy the public's trust.

The key challenge for practitioners of participatory governance and civic engagement is to address the deficits and obstacles described above. Doing so effectively, and recognizing that participatory governance is a complement to, not a substitute for, traditional democracy, is the source of the needed political will for participatory governance, and will help ensure that representative democracy remains relevant in the twenty-first century.

This may entail involving elected or appointed officials more regularly in the participatory research and consultations of participatory governance, or advising officials who are conducting their own deliberative processes. It may require working with members of parliaments who share concerns about certain issues of governance, to encourage them to form caucuses on specific issues, perhaps even across party divides. It may mean pressing for reforms in the processes of traditional democracy— such as introducing *at-large* MPs who speak for interest coalitions rather than physical constituencies, or the creation of a transnational forum bringing together legislators that have parallel duties, perhaps even a global parliament.

In these ways, CSOs can realize a strong power of supply and demand, not in the conventional marketplace of goods and services, but in the market of the *3's: interests, ideas, and ideologies.* The currency in this colorful and diverse bazaar is not cash but *commitment*— citizens' contributions of time and money. As with other bazaars, this one is lively but limited. In the same way that one may go to the local market for soap or handicrafts, but not dream of buying a computer or house there, so too citizens look to traditional democratic institutions for the big issues of governance. For all their stuffiness, these provide the formality, the guarantees, and the redress mechanisms for grievances. Participatory governance has an important but somewhat different role in these areas. It is to ensure that the institutions of the state function properly and that citizens' voices are heard. So, while some decisions of the state could usefully be devolved to well-designed mechanisms of participatory governance, in other areas the goal should be to strengthen and open the deliberative processes of the state institution.

To make participatory governance more effective, and to mobilize the political will for it to flourish, it is important to overcome the obstacles described above and to strive to demonstrate that its goal is to supplement and strengthen representative democracy, not to supplant it. Therefore, the acid question is how can participatory governance strengthen and complement systems of political representation; how can participatory governance *democratize democracy?*

References

2009. Special report on the rich: More or less equal. *The Economist,* 4–10 April.

Burke, E. 1770. *Thoughts on the Cause of the Present Discontent,* 6th ed., Dodsley.

Clark, J. 2003. *Worlds Apart: Civil Society and the Battle for Ethical Globalization.* Bloomfield, CT: Kumarian Press; London: Earthscan.

Held, D. 2002. Cosmopolitanism and globalization. *Logos* 1:3.

International Budget Partnership. 2005. *Newsletter.* No. 30, November. Information is available at the Internationalbudget.org Web site.

Mallaby, S. 2004. *The World's Banker.* New York: Penguin Press.

Save the Labour Party. 2009. *Annual Report and Accounts 2008/9.* Information is available at the savethelabourparty.org Web site.

Social Capital. 2000. *Community Benchmark Survey.* Storrs, CT: Roper Center, University of Connecticut.

PART 2

GENERATING POLITICAL WILL FOR PARTICIPATORY GOVERNANCE AT THE LOCAL LEVEL

CHAPTER 4

LESSONS FROM THE WORK OF THE AGA KHAN FOUNDATION IN PROMOTING GOOD LOCAL GOVERNANCE IN TAJIKISTAN, KENYA, AND TANZANIA

Richard Holloway, Shahribonu Shonasimova, Margaret Ngari, and Achim Chiaji

Introduction

The Aga Khan Foundation (AKF) is known for multiyear investments supporting the emergence of local civil society organizations (CSOs). The model for its work is the Aga Khan Rural Support Programme, which has been in operation in Pakistan for twenty-six years. In general, AKF builds specific kinds of CSOs, called village organizations (VOs) or women's organizations for community development, and gradually adds initiatives in agriculture, education, health, savings, and credit. Initially, such organizations were independent, created in collaboration with AKF, and did not have any structural relations with government.

Over time, however, it has been recognized that greater collaboration with local government is necessary to acquaint government with the initiatives of local CSOs, diminish mutual suspicion, encourage mutual collaboration, and focus on sustaining local initiatives by using resources from both CSOs and local government. The AKF thus started to encourage villagers to form clusters or federations of village organizations at the district level, normally the lowest level of local government. Such supra village clusters are considered more likely to be taken seriously by local government, and are also better-placed to make claims on decentralized funds.

Local governments vary greatly in their levels of competence and experience, their comfort in dealing with CSOs, and their familiarity with the management of decentralized funds. Civil society organizations also vary greatly in their representation of villagers and their competence as

51

organizations. The AKF considers *good local governance* to be a situation where both local government and locally representative CSOs work together for the benefit of the local population. It has identified a set of indicators for this and devised a self-assessment tool called the Local Good Governance Capacity Assessment Tool (LOGOCAT), which is still being piloted, but was tried out in the three case studies presented here from Tajikistan, Kenya, and Tanzania.

In all the three cases, there is interest from the players, to differing degrees, to enhance collaboration between CSOs and local government. The AKF is enthusiastic about building political will for better governance in which both sets of actors can participate fully.

The Mountain Societies Development Support Programme in Tajikistan

Introduction

In 1991, the Republic of Tajikistan gained independence from the Soviet Union and has since been undertaking a difficult transition from a command economy to a market-oriented economy. It has made some progress toward the creation of a democratic system of government, and has committed itself to transferring significant powers and responsibilities to local levels of government. Local governance reform aims to develop an effective public administration that can support equitable economic growth, and also contribute to poverty reduction and sustainable development.

The Aga Khan Foundation's Mountain Societies Development Support Programme (MSDSP) is committed to supporting the Republic of Tajikistan in developing an effective and transparent institutional system, for the implementation of participatory development in the country.

Description of the Initiative

Promoting decentralized governance is a challenge for a country accustomed to a command economy, but Tajikistan has made some important progress. In 1994, a new institution of local governance was established, at the subdistrict level. This is the executive/administrative body of the village, accountable to the subdistrict council, made up of village-level representatives. This reform was intended to promote local self-government, and provide a framework for a broader range of actors to contribute to local governance processes.

In 2004, the Aga Khan Foundation's Mountain Societies Development Support Programme (AKF/MSDSP), with financing from the Swedish

International Development Cooperation Agency (SIDA), initiated the Tajikistan Governance and Livelihood Programme (TGLP) as a pilot in ten of forty-three subdistricts in Gorno-Badakhshan Autonomous Oblast (GBAO). Its objective was to promote good local governance, by supporting the active participation of local people and strengthening collaboration between CSOs and local government authorities. A committee, called the Subdistrict Development Committee, was established as a bridge to link representatives of VOs and local government to plan, implement, and jointly monitor agreed upon local development initiatives. The fact that under the MSDSP VOs were already established, had benefited from several years of capacity-building, and been federated into a supra organization, the Social Union for Development of Village Organizations, was a significant advantage for the new program.

Local development projects were determined by village members using a planning process introduced by AKF/MSDSP. Priorities, identified by VOs, were submitted to subdistrict development committees, with representatives of both VOs and local government participating in final decision making. Once a decision was taken, project implementation and monitoring was undertaken jointly, with a tripartite contribution to project costs of 81 percent from donors, 13 percent from government, and 6 percent from VOs. Most projects involved the construction of schools, kindergartens, sports facilities, irrigation, and drinking water.

Capacity-building measures were provided jointly for local government and CSO representatives. One hundred seventy different training courses were delivered to 3,000 members of CSOs and local government in all ten subdistricts. Of those trained, 26 percent were women. Study visits were also organized for local government and civil society representatives. As a result, knowledge and skills among local government and CSO representatives, in the ten pilot subdistricts, improved in topics like project planning and monitoring, financial management, local governance, participatory methodologies, and social partnership. Access of the poor, including women, to basic services—such as education, water, roads, irrigated lands, and income generating opportunities—increased as a result of the project. The most significant result of the program, however, was the increase in trust between local government and CSOs in the target areas.

Overall, fifty-eight different socioeconomic infrastructure projects were jointly identified and implemented, benefiting more than 10,000 households in the ten subdistricts. An independent evaluation of the program concluded that "the model can succeed, and has done so, as it has provided an opportunity to help build the capacity of local government institutions, introduced them to participatory planning mechanisms and

helped facilitate their interaction with local civil society organizations"
(Hussein 2005, 21). Following the success of the pilot phase, a second
phase of the project was initiated in May 2008.

Lack of Political Will

The collapse of the Soviet Union, and the subsequent civil war, left Tajikistan
among the poorest countries in the world and the Tajik Government with a
highly centralized and weak system of governance. Local government institutions lacked capacity and were severely under-resourced. Lack of accountability and transparency discredited them in the eyes of local communities,
and led to donors preferring to provide development assistance to local
communities through CSOs and other channels.

In 2004, the Lower Parliament passed a new law on *Local Self-
Governing Bodies for Settlements and Villages,* which introduced democratic self-government at the subdistrict level for the first time. This was a
radical step in a country where all government officials are appointed
from above, and are accountable to the upper echelons of government.
The law proposed a subdistrict council formed by representatives elected
from the villages, whose Chair, previously appointed from above was chosen by the representatives from among themselves.

The law, however, was withdrawn from the agenda of the Upper House
for further discussion. It seemed that the reform process was stopping
before it started.

At the local level, VOs operated as independent bodies with little or no
links to local government institutions. The MSDSP was financing infrastructure projects through VOs, when it was really the responsibility of
the government to rehabilitate and maintain such institutions as schools,
hospitals, water supply schemes, and village-level recreational facilities.

When the TGLP was initiated, there were serious questions as to
whether involving government would work as envisaged, or whether government would dominate the process of participation. For MSDSP, there
was a risk in working much more closely with government. Village organizations in other AKF countries were still operating independently.

As a result of the Soviet experience, many local government authorities were initially skeptical about greater civil society involvement in
government-led budget planning and implementation processes. However, they have now come to understand and appreciate the role of civil
society in fostering local development. One key factor that has supported
this has been greater clarity amongst all stakeholders as to their respective
roles and functions. Although government can and should lead long-term
development planning processes, stakeholders recognize that there are key

roles for civil society to play, including informing decision makers about the specific priorities of local communities, serving as a vehicle for information exchange between local authorities and the general public, and mobilizing local communities to participate in and contribute to local initiatives. The MSDSP operated along these lines, and encouraged greater collaboration with local government bodies. An important sticking point was, however, the legal nature of CSOs, and what legal rights they had to exist and get involved in development.

Strategies for Building Political Will

The Mountain Societies Development Support Programme advocates participatory processes that allow local authorities, communities, government agencies, and other stakeholders to jointly participate in decision-making processes that make local government accountable to the people. The support of local government authorities was needed to implement these processes.

One of the major objectives of TGLP was to build the capacity of each pilot subdistrict government and development committee to adopt participatory and transparent methods of development programming and management. This was seen as the means to strengthen local government and forge effective partnerships with VOs. This was achieved through many varied trainings for VOs and subdistrict governments. These included trainings on local governance systems, which provided information about the organizational and legal basis of local self-government, the need for reforms, and the content of relevant laws, acts, and decrees. Other topics included ethics of local government staff and their duties to the local population.

In 2005, the President of Tajikistan authorized a Government Working Group on Local Government Reform, to develop a *local government strategy*. This was considered an encouraging sign of commitment by the executive to the reform process. Additionally, in 2007, the President signed a law allowing community-based organizations to form clusters at the subdistrict level, and for these to have a legal identity. Subsequently, in 2008, he signed a law giving a legal identity to community-based organizations at the village level. The MSDSP was delighted to see the groups they had been fostering become legally registered bodies.

How Citizen–State Relations have Evolved

In addition to forming and training Subdistrict Development Committees for joint government-community planning in each of the ten pilot subdistricts, the TGLP supported the creation of *observation teams*. These teams were made up of VO members and charged with monitoring Subdistrict Development Committee plans and the formulation of joint subdistrict development plans.

Subdistrict Development Committees organized meetings at the community and subdistrict levels to discuss problems and identify one or two priority subdistrict level projects. They were developed under the MSDSP, to receive TGLP funding. This process offered a first experience in joint government-community planning, and was later used to develop Subdistrict Development Plans (SdDPs), this time to be implemented with contributions from both government and community sources.

The observation teams participated in and observed all the steps of the planning process to the extent possible. They also witnessed the projects proposed by the subdistricts for subsequent SdDP. During the planning process, the contributions of both the subdistrict government and VOs were discussed, with the expectation that considerable contributions from both would be available for the implementation of the plan.

At the initial stage, however, subdistrict government actors were not so serious about promoting citizen participation, or about contributing resources to local development activities. The MSDSP prepared a special document for collaboration, but the government contribution amounted to only 13 percent. This was due to a lack of budget and management capacity. The regional and district-level governments promised to increase their contribution in the future, and signed a Memorandum of Understanding for the next phase of implementation.

To promote participatory governance, this initiative simply created a mechanism for collaboration and participation, rather than any new formal structures. Village organizations were formally accepted by the government as a credible institution that could identify priority village development needs and implement solutions. The government also acknowledged the added value and credibility of the federation of VOs, the Social Union for Development of Village Organizations. Capacity-building was the entry point and a basis around which the collaboration and engagement of CSOs and local government was established.

Factors of Success and Key Lessons Learned

All Tajikistan Governance and Livelihood Programme activities were carried out within the framework of agreements with the Regional Government, and there were many successes during the initial stage. As a result, the Government of Gorno-Badakshan indicated its full support and was eager to replicate the experience in other subdistricts. It is not easy to assess the initiative's impact on local government, but it is clear that they feel confident, involved, and appreciative of the high profile that the project has brought to government roles and responsibilities at the local level.

The project enabled MSDSP to test an approach in which regional, district, and subdistrict government representatives were closely involved in program implementation. There were long-standing apprehensions about whether involving government would work as envisaged or whether it would jeopardize the process of participation. The MSDSP took on considerable risk in moving from its past approach of keeping a distance from the government, to starting to forge a partnership. Government representatives have not trespassed on the autonomy of the VOs and have abided by the roles and responsibilities specified for the different stakeholders. They have enthusiastically participated in TGLP activities and appear eager to participate in local-level development activities. The various tiers of government at the subdistrict, district, and regional levels all indicated their appreciation for the approach and their willingness to participate.

This has also led to some changes in government-provided services. The government has become a mediator between the villages, in the allocation of scarce resources, using a set of established selection criteria. It has also accepted shared responsibility for monitoring project implementation, doing so at its own cost. In addition, it has agreed to participate in the preparation of the annual development plans for the subdistricts with its representatives playing an active role.

The most significant change, emerging from the government's direct role in TGLP, was that it became ready to lobby for greater resources for village-level development. The government has also assumed responsibility for some existing projects at the village level, especially mini hydroelectric stations, indicating that it would be willing to accept them on its balance sheet and oversee their implementation and maintenance. This new responsibility also better clarifies to government the overall level of investment in its area of jurisdiction, identifies which projects are working well, establishes its role in monitoring local progress, and highlights the need for its technical backstopping and problem solving.

The Coastal Rural Support Programme in Kenya

Introduction

About a decade ago, most communities in Kenya expected NGOs to deliver development. A pattern of dependency and a *hand-out* mentality was quickly becoming common in the communities where NGOs operated. Communities rarely engaged actively in development processes. This was aggravated by the top-down approach that government generally adopted in development initiatives. It was also observed by some development practitioners that in the cases where community groups were involved in planning and implementing projects, they frequently lacked the ability to effectively engage with government.

The Coastal Rural Support Programme (CSRP-K), Kenya's CSO capacity-building component, was therefore designed to help identify and address factors that inhibit the effective engagement of community groups in development, and to address issues relating to collaboration between CSOs and local and central governments. The programme component sought to empower communities in the Kwale and Kilifi districts of the Coast province, to become the drivers of their own development. This was to be done by strengthening communities to negotiate and engage with local and central government functionaries, on issues related to devolved development funds, with special attention to issues of service delivery, good governance, and democratization.

Description of the Initiative

In 2007, the CSRP(K) embarked on a rigorous action research project using the services of an independent researcher specialized in participatory techniques. A self-appraisal exercise was conducted. It identified both strengths and challenges facing communities and mapped out potential response strategies. The communities were then assisted in developing self-confidence in their values and strengths, and brought these qualities to meetings with government representatives. The communities also conducted an assessment of their own organization and leadership, and began to reflect on issues inhibiting their active engagement in development initiatives, such as the skewed nomination of community representatives to devolved funds committees. Through this process, communities were able to clearly see the link between active participation in development initiatives and the level of benefits accruing from the initiatives.

Stakeholder workshops, involving government officials, politicians, and CSOs in various parts of the working area, were then held. They helped identify and bring to the discussion constraints and problems that different actors faced in their efforts to address development priorities. Lack of coordination and duplication of resources were among the most cited challenges. A key outcome of the workshops was the shared realization of the need for multistakeholder engagement among communities, community leaders, politicians, and local and central government authorities.

The harmonization of the relationship between communities, leaders, and local and central government authorities required a carefully chosen team composed of community group representatives, chiefs or provincial administration, and councilors. There were three rationales behind the diverse composition. The first was to overcome the false notion that this kind of community action research was about inciting communities against the government, and to emphasize that councilors, provincial administrators, and civil society leaders all share the common goal of pursuing development for the public benefit. Second, the diverse composition enabled the communities to observe the benefits that arise when different sectors work together, for example, the mobilization of resources on a large scale. Third, this approach sought to build mutual trust and collaboration among different groups of stakeholders, by creating an opportunity to exchange information on a frequent basis, in an environment that promotes openness and inclusive participation.

The CSRP-K encouraged the actors to come together and let the partners take the lead. Dialogue sessions were moderated by a professional facilitator. The program also trained community leaders in negotiation skills and policy dialogue and sponsored workshops to help disseminate information arising from stakeholder consultations.

Lack of Political Will

A lack of political will can be traced to a variety of attitudes and practices, some of which derive from individuals and some of which are organizational. There are government officers who have embraced the idea of partnerships and others who, through their actions, still reflect a patron–client approach in their relationship with communities. Some government officials fear that CSO empowerment may be a threat and go out of their way to scuttle public forums. In such instances, the legal framework is wanting, a factor that does not provide CSOs with an environment conducive for the promotion of their activities. Also, civil servants are often suspicious of the underlying purpose of collaboration and this slows things down considerably.

At the same time, there are no colleges that train government officials on partnering. Where officers have not been exposed to much interaction with actors outside government, they often lack the capacity and skills to operate and engage at the community level, even if they want to.

There are also cases where the capacity and willingness of CSOs to engage with policy makers, and take the initiative in collaboration is lacking. There have been CSOs that are set in their own way of doing things and that lack appreciation for the collaborative approach, just as there are in government. In such cases, where CSOs are unwilling to participate in and engage with development processes, the CSRP-K has faced an uphill battle.

Certain mind-sets, with respect to development within communities, are reinforced by poverty conditions, which make communities skeptical of change. Low levels of literacy have also made communities vulnerable to manipulation by elite leaders, who do not necessarily have their best interest at heart. The transformation of mind-sets is the biggest challenge to be faced, as it determines the pace at which things take place and how effective the process can be. Yet, in any process of change, people usually take time to internalize and accept the change.

Strategies for Building Political Will

There are a number of strategies for improving the relationship and the engagement between communities and government, which have been used by CSRP-K. It has encouraged more open communication and dialogue between citizens and the leaders, which is initially moderated by CSRP-K, and then continues on their own. It has encouraged CSOs to assist government officials, rather than simply receiving assistance from them, for example by providing transport to the field and mobilization of community members for official meetings.

It has supported CSOs holding consultations across government departments and with political leaders on whether a project is really necessary and helped communities, once they have participated in the formulation of community development plans that clearly identify necessary resources, to be clear about what they expect their leaders to deliver. When CSOs and communities do think that a project is needed, it has trained them on how devolved development funds work, and how they can access resources from them.

At the time of campaigns for elective positions in parliament or in local authorities, the CSRP-K encouraged communities to be informed about issues, rather than just personalities. It also assisted women, youth, and marginalized members of society to become involved, speak up, and actively participate in discussions. The program operates in a society that is governed by cultures that tend to marginalize women, and initially, these groups rarely spoke during the meetings.

In some cases, former CSO leaders who had been involved in the collaborative initiatives secured positions in the local government authorities. This made it easier for the communities to interact and work closely with government agencies and officials.

How Political Will and Citizen–State Relations have Evolved

The action research project, initiated by the CSRP-K, created a new climate of collaboration and partnership. Those who were prepared to work collaboratively revealed themselves, and, for the most part, those who rejected such an approach were voted out of their positions. A challenge, however, has been the lack of adequate structures to underpin and support new partnership relationships. There is an abundance of committees, but they do not reach down to the village level. The representation of community interests on these committees is lacking, because the selection of committee members is subject to discretion, and on occasion to partisan interests. These development committees are frequently chaired by provincial or district officers, who at times limit the participation of CSOs. Further, the criteria for selecting CSOs to participate in the development committees are limiting. While District Development Committees are frequently cited as an example of public participation in development planning and implementation, mechanisms for harmonizing district-wide plans have not been effective, because not all areas within districts have CSOs that have been exposed to participatory planning methodologies.

Two suggestions have been made to solidify the new way of working. First, in a bid to strengthen the bottom-up planning process, CSRP-K facilitated the evolution of planning structures that start at the village level, with opportunities for consolidating the plans upwards, while at the same time incorporating technical inputs of various government departments and other stakeholders. These technical teams provide a coordinating structure for development actors at lower administrative levels. They include a Divisional Technical Team, made up of government and CSO representatives and chaired by the District Officer. This is a forum/structure, where stakeholders share proposals from the community and discuss how they will work together. The Location Technical Team serves the same role as the Divisional Technical Team, but at the location level. Through planning activities, these teams interact with the communities at various levels—such as village, sublocation, and location levels—and help consolidate and harmonize plans as they move up the planning ladder.

Second, CSRP-K is promoting the formalization of CSO federations for negotiation and collaboration with the development planning structures, politicians, and local authorities. The idea of CSO federations, called *Supra,* was born out of the need to revitalize the inactive development planning structures and ensure that communities effectively participate in development fora. In order to ensure representation at every level of development planning, village-level CSOs elect representatives to a CSO location committee, which in turn selects representatives to sit on the Division Technical Team and so on, up to the district and constituency levels. The objective of this effort is to enrich the current development planning system and help government officials appreciate and acknowledge the added value that CSOs and community representatives can bring at every level of the planning process.

This structural framework makes sure that there will be community representatives attending development committee meetings and ensures the flow of information from the lowest to the highest level of the government development planning system. The CSO federations do not work parallel to, or in competition with, existing development committees. Instead, they engage the development planning structures, as well as councilors, chiefs, and Members of Parliament (MPs) at respective levels and in various forums. One such forum is the Location Level Leaders' Forum, convened by the Chief and attended by government officers, the area MP, NGOs, and other CSOs to deliberate on development matters in the location, the district, and the constituency.

Factors of Success and Key Lessons Learned

Strengthening the relationship between communities, leaders, and local government authorities requires paying attention to accountability, transparency, and good governance. Community groups cannot hold their leaders accountable, unless they themselves conduct their affairs in a transparent and accountable manner. The partnership approach is empowering. It has also minimized any resistance that CSOs, working on their own, would have faced from local and central government officials and politicians.

The Work of the NGO Resource Centre
in Zanzibar, Tanzania

Introduction

Zanzibar, part of the United Republic of Tanzania, adopted multiparty democracy in 1995, following a long legacy of repressive single party socialist rule since 1964. Zanzibar's experience with local government is equally recent. The current local administration in Zanzibar has both elements of devolution and deconcentration, but is characterized by central government domination at local levels. Administratively, Zanzibar is divided into five regions, each of which is divided into two districts. At the head of each district administration is a District Commissioner (DC) and District Administrative Officer (DAO); both are appointed by the President. In addition, every district has a Planning Officer (PO), a Community Development Officer (CDO), and officers from sectoral ministries assigned to the district. The lowest unit, of which there are 326 in

Zanzibar, is administered by a Sheha, a government employee appointed by the Regional Commissioner in consultation with the DC.

A parallel, but less elaborate system of devolved structures exists side by side with the regional administration arrangement. This is the *hal-mashauri,* or Local Council system. Under Act no 3 and 4 of 1995, Zanzibar established one municipality in Zanzibar, nine district councils, and three town councils falling under the Ministry of Regional Administration and Special Departments. The combination of the above agencies and institutions fit within what is termed as local government in Zanzibar.

Although both the constitution of Tanzania, and the manifesto of the ruling Chama Cha Mapinduzi (CCM) party in Zanzibar, acknowledge local government as an important agent for ensuring people-centered development, the current local government system suffers from important weaknesses. These weaknesses include: poor planning capacity; plans and budgets that fail to reflect citizens' concerns; inadequate autonomy to generate and manage local resources; insufficient financial and human resources, which compromise the ability of Local Government Authorities (LGAs) to fulfill their mandate; lack of regular platforms for engaging nonstate actors and CSOs; and duplication of functions and staffing at each level of government, which result in waste of scarce resources and make it is difficult to hold government accountable.

Description of the Initiative

In 1998, the NGO Resource Centre (NGORC), an AKF-supported civil society capacity-building organization in Zanzibar, launched an initiative to improve the participation of communities and their organizations in local governance. This was done with the belief that this would enhance local governance, reduce poverty, and improve socioeconomic conditions. Since 1998, the NGORC has worked to strengthen the managerial capacity of community-based organizations (CBOs), NGOs, and Village Development Committees (VDCs), enhancing their effectiveness, their support base, and their public image. At the same time, the NGORC has been working with government agencies and officers at village, district, and national levels, seeking to promote and improve the quality of citizen engagement in governance processes. As a result, government counterparts have become more open and willing to work closely with citizens and community representatives, for example, by participating in regular consultations and joint planning exercises.

The NGORC has supported a range of activities to advance the goals of this initiative. First, it offered training and mentoring support to community organizations, equipping them with skills in planning, community mobilization, facilitation, lobbying, advocacy, leadership, recordkeeping, and resource mobilization, thereby improving their capacity to understand the distinct roles of various actors and how to work with them toward common goals. Second, it created platforms in villages for planning and prioritization among communities and local government officers. Third, it facilitated consistent dialogues between community representatives and local authorities, whenever an issue of concern emerged in which government attention or participation was required.

Whenever there were major and strategic community concerns, the VDCs organized *Majadilianos,* which are consultative platforms for community leaders and their members. These meetings created platforms for local government representatives to listen directly to communities on their most pressing problems or their perceptions of the quality of government services. Even though planning and budgeting processes in Zanzibar are very heavily controlled by the government, this initiative offered both government and community leaders the chance to plan systematically and for the government to receive proposals in an organized manner. A directory of local CSOs has recently been developed to help ensure that local authorities are informed about the existence and nature of local groups.

This initiative had the effect of reducing tensions between local CSOs and local government authorities. As a result, there have been more focused and productive discussions between CSOs and local authorities on pressing issues, and, because of increased confidence on both sides, the government has been more willing to offer its own resources to support VDCs in implementing projects that address community needs. At the end of 2007, from a sample of twenty interviewed VDCs, 45 percent indicated that they had benefited from different forms of government support, in the form of funding or the services of skilled employees. As government listens more to community priorities and plans, the peoples' participation in government programs has also increased.

This initiative has served to improve local services, such as water, education, and roads, as local communities and organizations have become more confident in claiming their local entitlements from the state. Village development committees have been involved in many community development initiatives, especially aimed at improving local road infrastructure, water supply, and building and equipping more schools and health centers. About 60 percent of trained VDCs indicate that there is a very significant positive response from government whenever community leaders need their support in planning and implementing these projects.

Some of the more empowered community groups have built links across constituencies. For example, one pushed for a new National Youth Policy for Zanzibar, which was adopted in February 2007. The NGORC also supports ongoing efforts to lobby for a new CSO policy and to enhance citizen access to information. The combined push from Zanzibar's development partners, and an increasingly engaged citizenry, has resulted in a degree of consensus on the need to undertake comprehensive reform of local government in Zanzibar. It is expected that this will include a reform of policies and laws that would expand the space for community participation in local governance.

In order to address legal and policy constraints, NGORC is conducting a study, which has been sanctioned by the government, to systematically document these challenges, with a view toward developing a comprehensive legal and policy reform program. The government is in the process of establishing a national task force to address these constraints.

Lack of Political Will

The 1990s were characterized by political instability, and citizens' organizations like CBOs, VDCs, and NGOs were viewed with suspicion. A few government-friendly CSOs were allowed to operate, but only on condition that they did not *cause any trouble*. Some advocacy CSOs were intimidated and threatened with deregistration due to perceptions that some of their members belonged to the largest opposition party, the Civic United Front (CUF). This also made many organizations avoid any direct engagement with government, as a way of *playing it safe*. Official public policy statements in many government documents, however, were less aggressive than the actual treatment CSOs received from local government agents. Organizations like NGORC, which were part of a foreign organization, had to tread carefully and not be perceived as supporting CSOs unpopular with government.

There were other reasons for government sensitivity and a suspicious relationship with community organizations. Zanzibar was concerned with waking up a historical past in which sectarian interest groups, which promoted parochial and discriminatory ideologies on basis of religion or race, had emerged. In large part, however, government resistance was due to a lack of understanding about the way CSOs organize and work. In some quarters it was assumed that NGOs were organizing communities against the government with an agenda from CUF. It was, and still is, imperative to build consensus regarding the legitimate role of CSOs and communities in democratic governance. Other key challenges faced by participatory governance practitioners include low levels of education and awareness about how government works, lack of government transparency such as lack of citizen access to relevant information and policies, and an unfavorable policy and legal environment, which curtails CSO activities.

Strategies for Building Political Will

While attempting to implement its mandate as a capacity-building institution for community organizations, NGORC realized the futility of equipping communities to participate in local development, without the support of local government authorities. Hence, this initiative began as a way of smoothing the relationship between communities and local government, in order to increase impact in NGORC project areas. Slowly, it became clear that much of the difficulty was due to a lack of mutual understanding about each other's different mandates and circumstances and lack of appreciation of the difficulties that each party was facing. To address this situation, the NGORC supported increased sharing of information between community organizations and the government at various levels, and regular direct discussions between community organizations and the Ministry of Regional Administration, local government, and special departments.

Whereas NGORC had secured the respect of the government as a neutral and competent capacity-builder, the same could not be said of the VOs it supported. There were many instances where local government officers would blacklist organizations that became more assertive in pushing for their rights. In a few cases, NGORC was able to explain the situation to the respective authorities and help the respective organizations repackage their demands in a way that enabled them to reestablish productive discussions with the authorities concerned.

In the context of Zanzibar, the strategy most favored by NGORC and its partner organizations was *proposing*. This entailed building mutual respect with the concerned government units. The NGORC volunteered its staff to offer technical expertise, especially facilitation. This seemed to work better because the local government officers blocked out citizens and organizations that used confrontational strategies to put their messages across. Proposing collaborative solutions also worked well where government felt that NGORC had the technical expertise needed to fulfill their own objectives.

How Political Will and Citizen–State Relations have Evolved

First, the NGO Resource Centre itself evolved as a respected broker of working relationships at different levels of government, especially at local levels. Second, there has been a significant improvement of political will, which can be seen in increasingly collaborative relationships between local CSOs and local governments. At the national level these changes are manifested in several ways. Poverty eradication committees and other government task forces now tend to provide space for community leaders without lobbying. Government local development programs, such as the Tanzania Social Action Funds, Participatory Development in Agriculture

Program, and the Rapid Funding Envelopes were designed to ensure significant community participation at local levels. The government is currently reviewing various laws regarding citizen participation, including a Community Development Policy and NGO Policy, and is doing so with significant involvement of local citizens.

Factors of Success and Key Lessons Learned

Several factors have contributed to strengthening political will for participatory governance. These include both the institutional commitment within NGORC to be a facilitator and honest broker that assists both local government officers and CSOs, and the commitment of communities to work together. Quite often, disagreements arose out of a lack of information or due to the weak capacity of one of the parties in handling an issue at hand. It helps to educate the government and its officers on how civil society works, and to educate CSOs on how the government operates. It also helps if government feels CSOs are usefully contributing to their own development initiatives. Civil society organizations must demonstrate the value that they bring to partnerships, in order to inspire respect from the government. Many community organizations wish to engage the government, but they do not know how to package their message so that it becomes a convincing public argument. Government also requires capacity-building in order to play its role more effectively. In a poor country, where budget constraints limit the training and capacity development opportunities available for government officers, it may help to include them in CSO capacity-building programs.

In the context of Zanzibar, certain reforms will be needed to maximize the benefits of the improving governance environment especially for poor and local communities. A review of the local government policy and laws is needed to entrench effective devolution of powers to decentralized units, called *Halmashauris,* including greater transfer of resources and decision making to local government units at the district level. An enactment of a Freedom of Information law should take place, which enables the transparent management of public affairs, as well as informed citizen participation in governance. The public budget processes should be reformed to enable local planning and budgeting.

Conclusions

Across countries, AKF has clearly seen the way forward by supporting VOs and encouraging them to cluster together to negotiate and collaborate with local government to promote the development that the villagers want, and access local government resources, because in many cases national government resources are decentralized to the local government level. They have also been encouraged to work together to hold government account-able for the proper use of development funding allocated to their districts.

The Aga Khan Foundation realized, however, that a piecemeal approach of seeking to collaborate on specific individual projects was not enough. A much more integrated approach was needed for district development, where the roles of local government and local NGOs were both recognized and valued, and a space for ongoing mutual negotiation and planning was established. This approach came to be seen as an attempt to achieve local good governance. What was needed was to explain what was meant by local good governance. To clarify this it was necessary to assess to what extent these elements were in place, and devise plans to address identified shortfalls. Once there was consensus on the elements of local good gover-nance, collaboration would be possible. Local good governance was seen as involving collaborative relations between three sets of actors: CSOs (includ-ing VOs, interest groups, and CSO clusters or federations); local govern-ment, with whatever autonomy it has been granted; and national government, in the context of its devolved or decentralized programs.

In all three cases described above, AKF saw that its work was on the right track and encouraged more participatory governance, but an ana-lytical tool to monitor progress toward participatory governance and identify where the gaps were, or where progress was not advancing fast enough, was lacking. To this end, AKF developed and piloted an instru-ment in Tajikistan, Kenya, and Tanzania called the Local Good Governance Assessment Tool (LOGOCAT). The LOGOCAT identifies the following seven core elements of local good governance. It identifies ten indicators for each of these elements and proposes a scoring system to assess the situation in any given district against the ideal.[1]

1. *Structures for citizen engagement:* To what extent are there struc-tures in place to promote the engagement of local people with district-level elected councils or governance bodies?
2. *Local government structures:* To what extent do local government structures exist and function well?
3. *Local CSOs at village level:* To what extent do CSOs at village level exist and function well?
4. *Local CSOs at district level:* To what extent do clusters or federations of CSOs at district level exist and function well?
5. *Interaction between local CSOs and local government:* To what extent do forums for mutual consultation and planning between local government and CSOs exist and function well?

6. *Financing of development at local government level:* To what extent do local governments have funds at their disposal for development purposes?

7. *Access to local government resources and information:* To what extent do local people have access to local government resources and information?

Key Obstacles

Experience to date has shown three key obstacles to participatory governance: poor design, poor practice, and poor integrity.

Poor design

Decentralized development is a recent phenomenon from the government side, as is the creation of CSOs from the civil society side. Local governments frequently lack resources, experience, and well operating structures. They are uncertain of how to relate to CSOs, with few or no regulations or instructions from their higher authorities on how to do so. There is not so much an objection to participatory governance, as simply a lack of practice in it, and a lack of structures to facilitate it. There is scope for the building of political will, but it has to come from both sides having greater familiarity with the other.

Poor practice

Decentralized development has been conceptualized, but only partially implemented. Civil society organizations exist and have some experience in local participatory planning for local development and in lobbying for these ideas to be recognized and accepted by the local government bodies, but there is still a long way to go. There are few examples of accepted participatory governance practices, but what exists is often personality driven.

Poor integrity

Decentralized development and associated funding from government is well established, as are organized clusters of VOs with well-developed participatory planning methodologies and ways of promoting these to the local government bodies. Unfortunately, much local government decentralized funding is captured by special interests and corruption, and many CSOs are unrepresentative or subject to elite capture or political clientelism. Building political will can often be interpreted by vested interests as being in opposition to them, which is not always the case. Civil society organizations demonstrating that collaboration can be advantageous to local government, particularly in respect to meeting central government policies, is often able to overcome such prejudices.

Key Recommendations

The case studies presented here suggest three key recommendations for promoting participatory governance. These are to promote better public information, develop the capacities of CSOs and CSO clusters, and to conduct joint capacity-building of CSOs and local government officials.

Promote better public information

It is essential to develop clear public information about how government schemes and programs operate, what opportunities and roles for CSOs and citizens' input exist, and what strategies can be used to hold those in authority accountable. If such information is widely available, then building political will for participatory governance is not seen as a confrontational tactic, but rather as an acceptable and useful part of good governance.

Develop capacities of CSOs and CSO clusters

Frequently there is a need to develop the capacities of CSOs, and CSO clusters, to engage with existing systems. Once they understand how the systems operate, they can work to get their initiatives considered and implemented. Introducing functional competencies to CSOs, and CSO clusters, enables them to use the existing systems to build their case, to light a candle, not simply complain against the darkness.

Joint capacity building of CSOs, CSO clusters, and local government officials

A final, important recommendation is to train both groups of people together so that both learn how to operationalize decentralized schemes with integrity, learn the value of collaboration, and learn about each other's comparative advantages. Such practiced collaboration sets the scene for mutual learning and the building of political will.

References

Hussein, M.H. 2005. *An Assessment of the Tajikistan Governance and Livelihood Programme.* Dushanbe, Tajikistan: Aga Khan Foundation and SIDA.

Note

1. For more information on LOGOCAT, please contact richard.holloway@akdn.org.

CHAPTER 5

NEIGHBORHOOD DEMOCRACY AND PARTICIPATION: FORMAL REPRESENTATIVES AND EMPOWERED CITIZENS MOVE FROM COMPETITION TO MUTUAL INTERESTS

Mary Jacksteit

Introduction and Background

Washington, D.C. is an urban community of a half million people, as well as a world capital. In 1973, a federal law provided for the creation of a nonpartisan Advisory Neighborhood Commission (ANC) in every D.C. neighborhood, to give residents a greater say in local public affairs. The ANCs are based on a representative model in which deliberations and votes take place among commissioners elected by the residents of the neighborhood district. According to the city's Office of Advisory Neighborhood Commissions, ANCs are "their neighborhood's official voice in advising the District government . . . on things that affect their neighborhoods," including traffic, recreation, liquor licenses, zoning, economic development, and sanitation (DC Office of ANCs 2006). City government agencies must give ANCs advance notice of new building permits and other proposed actions impacting their neighborhoods. By law, ANC recommendations are entitled to *great weight* by city agencies. This term has been judicially interpreted to mean that agencies must consider ANC input and explain in writing any decision not to adopt the ANC position (Kopff et al. 1977). Because ANCs enjoy considerable autonomy, there is great variation in how they operate and engage the public and unresolved ambiguity about their relationship to other neighborhood groups.

This case concerns a neighborhood undergoing rapid change due to extensive economic development. Its history includes a draconian *urban renewal,* which took place fifty years ago destroying low- and moderate-income homes and businesses, and displacing thousands of, mostly black,

73

residents. Neither city leaders nor residents want this haunting legacy repeated. Current residents include poor, middle class, and some wealthy blacks and whites.

In 2004, an activist connected with the major social service agency serving low-income residents tried to organize a broad alliance to ensure that development would benefit, not threaten, neighborhood residents, particularly the poor. Neither the ANC, nor the leadership of a long-established neighborhood association, the Southwest Neighborhood Assembly (SWNA), embraced the effort.[1] The activist then sought the help of a nonprofit project called Collaboration DC. This chapter focuses on the efforts to mobilize community involvement to achieve community benefits.[2]

The Initiative

Initially, Collaboration DC conducted an assessment,[3] to determine the feasibility of a multiparty, multisector initiative to bring community, government, and business representatives together, to build consensus on shared goals and strategies relating to the impact of development. Two pressing needs emerged: (1) preparing low-income residents to take advantage of new wealth creation opportunities, and (2) building the capacity of community groups and activists to collaborate in engaging residents, developing a shared vision, and negotiating effectively to meet residents' needs and concerns.[4]

An initial series of multistakeholder meetings identified broadly shared goals of preserving a mixed-income neighborhood and improving the economic status of the poor. Government and business participants were interested in working with a unified group of community representatives, to see how these goals might be achieved, and were ready to move forward with a consensus-building process. The ANC and SWNA representatives, however, expressed strong misgivings about the initiative. They refused to participate further, because of doubts about the legitimacy of any process outside of established channels, and about the involvement of other neighborhood entities, particularly the social service agency, which it did not view as an appropriate representative.

As a result, the multiparty negotiation effort was suspended. Focus was shifted to increasing understanding among community leaders, groups, and residents, including the ANC and SWNA, and building stronger support for the initiative. Neighborhood activists helped recruit twenty-five individuals from diverse income and education levels, both experienced and new to public participation, to be trained in *Negotiating for Community Benefits*. At the end of the training, participants committed themselves to action and evolved into an *ad hoc* task force, the Community Benefits Task Force (CBTF), which remained open to any and all participants. Collaboration DC served as the group's facilitator: organizing, planning, and running the group's meetings, and helping with outreach, to widen participation.[5] The group continued to try to win support from the ANC and SWNA leadership, and some SWNA members and one ANC commissioner participated in the task force.

Within several months, the expanded CBTF tentatively identified and agreed upon the types of community benefits that should be created by development projects. These were intended to be further vetted by residents and then serve as goals to pursue in negotiations with developers and city officials. Collaboration DC began plans for reconvening the multisector group with the inclusion of CBTF representatives, and, hopefully, SWNA and ANC leadership. The ANC, however, publicly and forcefully opposed this development and successfully enlisted the neighborhood's city council member to dissuade government and business from participating. As a result, the initiative came to a halt.

Not long after, the CBTF and Collaboration DC were asked by the ANC chair and a SWNA leader to restart their efforts, but to focus on bringing the community together, rather than seeking to negotiate on behalf of the community. The shift in attitude was motivated by a mixture of institutional interests and community-related values. In explaining the request, these leaders described intense pressure from accelerating development. They also expressed concern that continued neighborhood infighting was undermining everyone's credibility and influence and damaging their ability to protect residents' interests. They acknowledged a need to engage low-income residents, because this group was most at risk from changes in the neighborhood, but largely unheard.[6] They recognized that Collaboration DC had useful skills and expertise, and saw that the task force had brought together diverse segments of the community, and recruited new and capable leadership, including a widely respected minister of a neighborhood church and several well-known, longtime civic activists. It seems these leaders realized that by proposing a revised initiative, rather than just opposing one, they could redirect the CBTF's work in a direction that they preferred, while benefiting from its valuable attributes.

The CBTF agreed to the proposal because its primary objectives were to protect residents, and enhance unity and cooperation in the community, not create further conflict. Since they would maintain their independent identity and build on previous efforts, it was easier for the group to accept this revised mission.

Expanded by additional ANC and SWNA participation, the group resumed monthly meetings and agreed to an early, joint activity to foster unity and highlight an urgent concern: a Community Roundtable on Jobs and Business Opportunities.[7] This event was carefully and purposefully designed. First, in a demonstration of unprecedented cooperation, it was cosponsored by the ANC, SWNA, and the key social service organization. Second, a public role was given to the CBTF, signaling its acceptance. Third, extensive outreach was done to publicize the event, especially to low-income residents, with offers of transportation and other assistance to those wishing to attend. Fourth, it departed from familiar meeting models and featured a *participatory, deliberative process* involving: facilitated small group discussions; cooperative problem solving; and the preparation and broad dissemination of jointly produced findings and recommendations.

After the roundtable, the CBTF changed its name to the Community Benefits Coordinating Committee (CBCC), to reflect its new role as a venue and vehicle for activists and groups to share information, coordinate action, and plan joint strategies. It was understood that the ANC and other neighborhood entities would act autonomously in their own realm of operation, but share information and cooperate, as much as possible, through the CBCC's monthly meetings.

The civility and facilitated structure of CBCC meetings fostered honest, substantive, productive discussion.[8] Experts, and others with useful knowledge and/or experience, were invited to meetings to advise the group. This, along with a higher public profile, attracted new participants.

Important external changes occurred when a new city council member took office. He acknowledged the CBCC's value, as a forum for facilitating interactions between the community and city agencies, and hired its original organizer on to his staff. This strengthened the CBCC's legitimacy.

At the same time, there were changes within the ANC, with two new members joining and a rotation of the chair. Also, the CBCC's cochair joined the SWNA board. The new ANC chair asked the CBCC to facilitate a participatory process to identify priorities for community benefits that could inform the ANC's dealings with developers, incorporating key design elements of the previous roundtable.[9] The CBCC, with advice and support from Collaboration DC, organized two roundtables involving over one hundred residents reflecting the neighborhood's diverse population. Preliminary meetings were held to familiarize low-income residents with the issues and encourage their participation in the larger meetings. The resulting report was endorsed by the ANC, the CBCC, and other sponsor groups, and jointly presented at a city council hearing. It has since been used to guide the ANC's negotiations with developers, and conversations with city officials.

The CBCC has continued to function as a vehicle for linking and coordinating the efforts of community actors. It is collaborating with the city council on projects to establish a new community training center for residents, funded by developer contributions, and to ensure jobs for local residents in the construction of a new baseball stadium in the area. Recent steps have been taken to formalize the group's status as a nonprofit organization.

Why Was Political Will Lacking?

Power and Perception Issues

The ANC commissioners saw the independent community benefits group as a challenge to the official representative mandate of the ANC. Initially, the majority of ANC commissioners met the community benefits initiative with skepticism, and, in some cases, open hostility. Reasons for this skepticism included the group's independence, suspicion of the role of an outside facilitator, and resistance to others purporting to speak for residents. Distrust of *the new* was evidenced as early as the initial assessment, when none of the commissioners agreed to be interviewed.

Using a negotiation framework for analysis, it seems the ANC assumed a *zero-sum* scenario, by which only a finite amount of power was available to the community, and to increase the influence of new actors would be to reduce or supplant the ANC's power. The possibility of the neighborhood's *total power being increased,* by greater resident activism and engagement, did not seem plausible. Though this thinking was not universal among ANC commissioners, it was predominant among those whose views carried the most weight.

As a result, the ANC *saw nothing to be gained,* and possibly much to lose, by accommodating the initiative, especially when higher political leadership could be enlisted to deter it. The ANC's resistance was backed by a local city council member who, perhaps loyal to a longstanding relationship, refused to meet with the CBTF, and communicated her disapproval to other key governmental and business stakeholders.

Few neighborhood groups besides the ANC and SWNA played any significant role working on neighborhood-wide issues, despite a prevalent opinion that these two entities were ineffectual, and too often engaged in unproductive conflict that alienated residents from civic engagement. In contrast to some other ANCs that delegate authority to committees and are open to public involvement, this ANC operated in an insular way. It limited opportunities for citizen participation to comment periods, during formal meetings. These conditions seem to have reinforced a strong sense of ownership of the *community voice* by a relatively small circle of individuals, leading to the rejection of any approach inconsistent with established ways of doing things.

Structural Issues

The Advisory Neighborhood Council System is not designed, and does not operate, to foster and support broad citizen participation. First, the formal framework of Washington, D.C.'s ANCs is a representational model, not a participatory one.[10] In 1973, the ANCs were an innovation for local governance, but the ANC system has remained largely unchanged, and does not reflect the significant growth and evolution that has taken place in the field of participatory governance since then. Assessments of participatory efforts dating from this period, have generally found them to be rigid in structure and limited to a narrow group of participants (Berry et al. 1993, 14).

According to the Office for Advisory Neighborhood Commissions, "the intent of the ANC legislation is *to ensure input from an advisory board* that is made up of residents elected every two years" (italics added). There is no requirement or expectation that the ANCs foster broader public participation. Beyond voting commissioners into office, residents have no right to participate outside of public comment periods at formal monthly meetings. One-way *input* or comments are far from a deliberative approach where there is *empowered participation* (Fung 2004, 5) and a genuine exchange of views and joint efforts to develop solutions (Fung and Wright 2003).

By way of contrast, Los Angeles, California, now mandates its neighborhood councils to "[f]oster a sense of community for all people to express ideas and opinions about their neighborhoods and their government" (City of Los Angeles 2008). Portland, Oregon's Office of Neighborhood Involvement operates with a mission of "enhancing the quality of neighborhoods through community participation" (Berry et al. 1993).

Second, technical support and capacity-building for the ANCs is very modest, and nonexistent in the area of citizen participation. The city's Office of the Advisory Neighborhood Commissions has little staff and works within a narrow mandate. The limited training opportunities that exist focus on the ANCs' legal authority and financial responsibilities, and no training is available on participatory governance or process skills, such as consensus-building, facilitation, or interest-based negotiation. Again, in contrast, the Los Angeles Department of Neighborhood Empowerment runs a Leadership Institute for neighborhood council members and other community leaders, which includes skills for mobilizing citizens.[11] In the absence of a centralized training and technical assistance function, a network for the ANCs might, at the very least, allow commissioners to learn from one another and share best practices, but even that does not exist.

Third, accountability for how the ANCs conduct their representational functions is weak. Beyond the requirement to use Robert's Rules of Order at formal meetings, apparently, each ANC has the discretion to conduct its business according to its own preferences. There is wide variation on matters, such as whether and how neighborhood residents are involved in committees. When this initiative began, the ANC had no committees upon which residents could serve. Neighborhood council systems in other cities (City of Reno 2006) have clear guidelines on and expectations of how functions are to be carried out, and specific instructions on how to hold meetings that promote genuine citizen participation.

Accountability is exercised by the electorate every two years, but there is no ongoing monitoring of how the ANCs conduct their work, aside from formal reporting and financial matters. The city council conducts annual oversight hearings, but these typically involve hearing from ANC commissioners, not the public. In other cities, such as Portland, Oregon, guidelines for how and how often neighborhood bodies must conduct outreach to citizens are very specific.[12]

A fourth structural weakness is that within DC's ANC system there has always been ambiguity about the relationship of ANCs with other neighborhood associations and groups. There are no norms or guidelines on how to fashion cooperative relationships. Los Angeles recommends that their neighborhood councils *map* the assets represented by the community organizations within their areas and use them to mobilize residents (City of Los Angeles 2007). The Dayton, Ohio *Priority Boards*, created in 1975, now include representation from neighborhood groups.[13] At the beginning of this initiative the social service agency that started the original organizing was viewed by the ANC as an *outsider*, even though it served the area's low-income residents and had an office in the neighborhood. Despite a history of civic voluntarism, this ANC district showed a pattern of community groups sometimes competing, but typically disconnected from one another.

Strategies for Building Political Will

Creating New Connections

This ANC district lacked sufficient social networks to support citizen communication, cooperation, and mobilization for the common good, especially across organizational, geographic, racial, and class boundaries.

The importance of social networks, or *social capital*, has drawn a great deal of attention in recent years (Putnam 2000). In designing its strategies, Collaboration DC's underlying assumption was that fostering between individuals and groups was crucial to the community's ability to achieve its goals of economic opportunity and neighborhood preservation. Thus, in addition to educating and inspiring, a crucial reason for holding the initial negotiation training was simply to connect diverse neighborhood people and groups who rarely, if ever, found themselves in the same place. A critical connection occurred early in the training, when low-income, black participants heard more affluent white residents tell them that they would fight to prevent their displacement from the neighborhood. Suddenly the potential of an alliance, bridging race and class, became real. During visioning exercises, people also learned that, despite differences in race, education, and income, they shared many of the same values and aspirations for their community. The seeds of familiarity and trust were sown. Over time these grew into new working relationships.

The training also succeeded in its intention to activate more people in the neighborhood. One relative newcomer to the neighborhood, who had avoided public meetings because of their divisiveness and negative tone, wholeheartedly enrolled in the new initiative, eventually becoming one of the cochairs of the CBTF/CBCC and an elected member of the SWNA board.

There was an underlying assumption—or hope—that ANC commissioners would eventually see these developments as beneficial to the ANC as well as the community. The ANC would gain credibility when it could support its positions with deliberative input from a broad base of citizens. A big boost came from having the new city council member make the CBCC a key venue for engaging with the neighborhood, because of how it brought community actors together to pursue shared goals.

Providing New Ideas for How, and to What Ends, the Community Could Work Together

Through the negotiation training, people learned about a model of civic engagement in which residents and groups join together and *take the initiative* to gain benefits from development. This is a significant shift from the more typical reactivity of neighborhood engagement. They learned skills and approaches for being *negotiators* who create their own options and thereby expand the possibilities beyond what others might offer them. It was these new ideas, and the new working relationships discussed above, that motivated participants to organize themselves into the CBTF, and to hold firm to the belief that their neighborhood had to embrace a new approach for advocating residents' interests.

Moving Forward to Demonstrate a Different Way

When the ANC refused to join the initial multisector effort, the decision to proceed with a community-focused effort was not without risk. At that point, the level of grassroots interest was untested. However, subsequent training produced a critical mass of interested and energized people, who were unwilling to have their shared ideas and ambitions narrowed, or defeated, by the limited existing option of relying on the ANC and SWNA. When support for the CBTF was not forthcoming from the ANC, task force members redoubled their efforts to recruit more people from a broad cross section of residents, drawing in tenant organizers, clergy, and others, all the while keeping the door open to the ANC. They also began to develop concrete ideas about the kinds of benefits the community could work for, such as job training programs in the neighborhood. This way of working was in marked contrast to the previous dynamic of discord among groups and leaders, reactive opposition, and incivility, which made city officials dread seeking community input, and deterred many residents from participation.

The ANC was eventually able to see neighborhood people motivated by the public good, representing the diversity of the community, open to broad participation, and intent on producing and advocating good ideas. The ANC commissioners, while worried about their institutional prerogatives, shared a deep concern about the fate of the neighborhood and began to see that a constructive, proactive strategy was advantageous.

Focusing on the Important Underlying Interests at Stake

Interests, as it is used here, means the concerns and needs that underlie the positions that people take (Fisher and Ury 1981). In the initial training, members of the CBTF learned an approach to negotiating for community benefits that focused on their critical underlying concerns of preserving the neighborhood, as a home for current residents of all income levels, and ensuring that development would contribute to improving the quality of life, particularly for the most disadvantaged. When they encountered opposition, another important interest emerged that also guided CBCC decisions. They felt a strong need to increase, not further destroy, unity and cooperation among neighborhood residents and groups, not just as a civic value, but also because they believed this was practically necessary to achieve their primary goals.

Focusing on underlying interests made it possible for the group to be flexible and willing to change strategy. The CBCC would not be the umbrella group for negotiating with developers, but it would instead support and build up the negotiating power of the ANC, by developing the community's program for community benefits and serving as a venue for cooperation and joint work. This flexibility built trust with the ANC, diffusing suspicions about self-promotion and hidden agendas. From Collaboration DC's perspective, this flexibility reflected an important facilitation principle, *free and informed choice,* meaning that participants, not the facilitator, define their goals and ways of achieving them (Schwarz 1994). Collaboration DC offered a particular model for negotiating community benefits, but was ready to adjust its approach to help the CBTF achieve its goals. Ultimately, the CBTF/CBCC and ANC were able to arrive at a *win-win outcome,* which met the crucial interests of both groups, and of community residents.

Recruiting and Supporting New Community Leadership Committed to Participation and Collaboration

This initiative appealed to people anxious for a new dynamic in the neighborhood, one in which individuals and groups could come together for the greater good, particularly to protect the interests of residents through the changes posed by development. They were smart, idealistic, and collaborative people from varying backgrounds and with different levels of income and education. Some were experienced, while others were completely new to public participation. Several were active in narrower venues, such as tenants groups, churches, and social services, and were attracted to a broad group bringing people together for greater impact. Some individuals were past leaders of the neighborhood association, who were drawn to the new energy coalescing around community benefits. All of these individuals immeasurably enhanced the capability and stature of the task force. In time, the rise of this new leadership was reflected in new ANC and SWNA board members.

Using and Modeling Good Process

Civility, collaboration, inclusion, transparency, and equal participation at CBTF/CBCC trainings, meetings, and roundtables demonstrated a change in how neighborhood people and groups could come together to talk and work. The difference was noticed and appreciated. There was opportunity for real deliberation among residents. The conversation was opened up to all, with dominant voices making room for quieter ones. Through respectful conversation, constructive relationships developed and common ground emerged.

This new process also showed that participatory community meetings could be well run and produce results. People could see that meetings were guided by clear purposes, agendas, and ground rules. They ended on time and led to results. All of this built trust and respect for both the CBTF/CBCC and Collaboration DC among community members and with other important stakeholders, such as government officials. "Good process is intentional and strategic. It embraces a series of complementary strategies and tactics that not only *build support for the effort,* but also have a logic that is focused on *achieving better outcomes*" (Potapchuk and Kopell 2005; italics added).

The Evolution of Political Will: What Made It Happen?

Community Benefits Coordinating Committee and Collaboration DC Able to Bring Diverse Groups Together

The Community Benefits Coordinating Committee and Collaboration DC demonstrated their ability to bring together diverse groups of residents for collective deliberation and solution generation. Particularly important was their commitment and ability to gain participation among *low-income residents,* who had ceased to recognize other groups as representing their interests. For a long time, this segment of the population had been conspicuously absent from government and ANC-sponsored meetings.[14] Several ANC commissioners attended the first roundtable and saw that the CBCC was capable of effectively conducting a community forum, and neighborhood residents could make valuable contributions (Fig. 5.1). Also in attendance was the individual who, a few months later, was elected to the city council to represent this area. The positive impression he received had lasting impact.

Advisory Neighborhood Commission Wanted Help from the Community Benefits Task Force/Community Benefits Coordinating Committee

The Advisory Neighborhood Commission leadership acknowledged that the divided and rancorous relationships among neighborhood activists were damaging to the community's influence. They came to see the value of a venue where they, and other leaders and activists, could come together to share information and improve working relationships.

They also felt pressure to powerfully represent the neighborhood on development issues, particularly with respect to community benefits. This meant being able to articulate neighborhood interests and needs, and present credible neighborhood priorities. But, the ANC was not able to develop these on its own. Researchers of neighborhood councils have

Figure 5.1. Community Roundtable Event Organized by Collaboration D.C.

observed that while neighborhood bodies, like ANCs, are effective in reviewing and responding to requests and proposals, and conveying citizen concerns, they are at a *considerable disadvantage* when it comes to *formulating proposals,* because of the demands of their routine tasks (Berry et al. 1993, 109). This is especially true when, as in this case, there is limited capacity.

Third, the ANC needed to bolster the legitimacy of its decision making, since its recommendations are only advisory. Despite the deference described in the law, D.C. government agencies frequently disregard ANC recommendations. To the extent that public input could bolster the ANC's positions, the weight of the ANC's judgments would be increased. It has been observed that local governments are more responsive when they believe that neighborhood associations are "trusted by neighborhood residents" (Berry et al. 1993, 288).

Community Benefits Coordinating Committee and Collaboration DC were Willing to Adapt to the Advisory Neighborhood Commission's Institutional Concerns

As discussed above, it was an accommodation between interests, and agreement on the underlying goal of protecting neighborhood residents, that made possible the ANC's changed attitude toward the CBTF. The goal of achieving community benefits was more important to the CBCC and Collaboration DC than having the leading role in negotiations, the original strategy.

The Power Calculation Changed

It seems that the initial *zero-sum* power analysis described above shifted after the first phase of the initiative was halted. Once the CBTF revised its role from negotiator to convener, it was no longer seen by the ANC as a threat but instead a potentially valuable resource able to bolster the ANC's negotiating posture, because of enhanced citizen participation. In addition, alignment among key community leaders and organizations, and reduced conflict, could be expected to increase the neighborhood's influence, by enhancing the reputation of the ANC as an effective community player. Later, a significant change took place with the election of a new city council member who valued the CBCC, hired the original CBTF organizer to his own staff, and declared his intention to work with the group in advancing community benefits. Still later, when roundtable findings, endorsed by both the ANC and SWNA, were presented at a city council hearing, by a panel of community leaders, council members were congratulatory of the community's work together. Thus, there were political rewards for the ANC aligning itself with citizen participation, and, overall, the neighborhood's power to influence grew.[15]

Other Factors of Success

Staff support

Salaried staff of Collaboration DC supported volunteer neighborhood activists. Collaboration DC's initial assessment, convening, and training

activity created the first forward movement. Thereafter, its role in facilitating, organizing, and planning was crucial until the CBCC was well
enough established, and its volunteer base broad enough, to become self-
reliant. By then, the CBCC itself had the facilitative capacity and participatory norms that Collaboration DC brought at the start.

Trusted, capable leadership

Highly credible and respected leaders assumed control of the task force when
it was under strong assault by the ANC. Over time, this leadership built trust
and legitimacy for the CBCC with key constituencies and the ANC. Their
willingness to take leadership roles was tied to the inclusive, participatory
values of the CBTF. Their own personal attributes were also important:
openness to others, an ability to listen, and a capacity for cooperation.

Multiple outreach methods designed to achieve broad, diverse, and inclusive participation

The initiative was very intentional about reaching all the various elements
of the neighborhood's population. Communication was carried out in multiple ways: through e-mail, flyers, telephone calls, and personal contacts.
Meetings were sited in accessible, sometimes multiple, locations and scheduled to accommodate working parents. Rides were provided to those need-
ing transportation. Children were accommodated. Churches were
recruited to host some of the meetings and ministers invited to participate.
Food was offered so people could come directly from work. Due to the initiative's limited budget, organizers persuaded local businesses to donate
food and supplies for larger events. One meeting was held at a social service agency to provide a comfortable forum for low-income residents,
mostly women, to learn about the CBCC and talk about their own views
and priorities. This created more confidence for participating in the larger
meetings that followed.[16]

These methods succeeded in drawing a mix of affluent and poor, white
and black, educated and uneducated, and people from different geographic regions of the neighborhood. People found this noteworthy
because it was so rare, and saw it as a very welcome and healthy development, reflecting positively on the CBTF/CBCC and the initiative.

The pressure of development activity

Throughout the time period covered in this case study, real estate development was moving quickly across the neighborhood, sometimes

displacing businesses long relied upon by residents. New construction was visible. Rumors abounded and anxiety among residents was rising. This pressure provided a sense of urgency for the community to pull together.

Lessons Learned

It is necessary to anticipate and prepare for objections and opposition, and to assume you will have to make the case for participation. The importance or legitimacy of direct citizen participation is not necessarily self-evident, even at the level of neighborhood councils. Here, the challenge of, and need for, enlisting the support of the ANC was underestimated. The potential for opposition, the underlying interests fueling it, and strategies to meet it, need thorough advance consideration and ongoing attention.

It is essential to address the power and formal role of elected representatives in ways that do not sacrifice key community interests. The CIVICUS Participatory Governance Programme noted that making participation complement and reinforce, not undermine, representative forms of democracy is a challenge (Malena 2006). It was not the *intention* of this initiative to undermine the ANC, but once this concern was raised, it needed to be taken seriously. It took a period of trial and error, but ultimately a workable accommodation was reached.

One demand that the CBTF was able to successfully resist was that the task force abandon its independence and come under the umbrella of SWNA, the neighborhood association, in exchange for the latter's support. Doing that might very well have ended the ANC's opposition as well. However, members of the CBTF knew that low-income residents did not perceive SWNA as representing their interests, and worried that the oversight of the SWNA board would limit the scope, and drain energy from the initiative. Maintaining its independence has allowed the CBCC to evolve into a credible new community organization.

Optimally, the system institutionalizes participation. Ideally, the rules and governing principles of a neighborhood council system need to:

- Require neighborhood councils to support citizen participation on public issues;
- Provide supportive education, technical assistance, and resources for carrying out public participation;
- Create a norm that neighborhood bodies will seek coordination and good relationships with other community organizations; and
- Impose social accountability and monitoring mechanisms.

The absence of these measures in the ANC system not only poses potential hurdles for community-initiated public engagement, it also represents a missed opportunity to build and institutionalize citizen participation and participatory governance in the District of Columbia. As Berry et al. (1993, 45) suggests, representative neighborhood structures may be "useful starting points" for institutional reforms that expand citizen involvement. ANCs are established by law and have been part of the city's governance structure for twenty-five years. That makes them a significantly more solid foundation upon which to construct participation than executive policies and leadership philosophies that can change, and have changed, in one election.[17]

It follows that such changes in the rules and expectations require expanded staff resources and capabilities in the office that supports ANCs. In turn, that means resources must be committed by city leaders.

Education and training in skills supporting participation and public engagement are essential. This starts with a basic understanding of interest-based negotiation (Potapchuk and Kopell 2005; Briggs 2005). Cooperative problem-solving, conflict resolution, and meeting facilitation are other important capacities for citizens and official neighborhood representatives, as well as for staff responsible for providing technical assistance and training to neighborhood councils and similar bodies. Training not only enhances skills and knowledge, but can also raise expectations and hopes about what citizens can do themselves, and about what government, citizens, and other stakeholders can do together.

Conclusion

This study illustrates that elected neighborhood councils can embrace citizen participation when they understand why and how participation not only gives citizens more voice, but also strengthens their own influence and effectiveness as representatives. Participation must be seen as *serving* their interests, not undermining them.

Here, a neighborhood council and community task force found a way to align their efforts to help their neighborhood. Their arrangement expanded citizen engagement and legitimized a coordinating and public participation function that did not exist before, creating significant, new civic capacity in this neighborhood and, importantly, directly beneficial outcomes for residents. Political will for participation was created at this very local level.

Ideally, resolving tensions between participation and representation should not be an ad hoc process. The neighborhood governance system itself should address the issue, establishing norms, requiring public participation, and providing knowledge, skills, and other capacities to support it. This case exposes the weaknesses in the ANC system and others like it, while also suggesting the potential for expanding participatory governance by paying attention to how neighborhood structures do their work.

This case also demonstrates how experts in participatory process can play a valuable role by teaching, convening, facilitating, and modeling new ways for people to work together to improve their communities. This is especially true in a case such as this one, where the community has an unproductive pattern of conflict and disengagement that results in pessimism about the potential for influencing decisions and events.

Last, this case illustrates that promoting participation can be messy and frustrating. Motivation, then, becomes the challenge. It is worth restating that in this case, during the ANC's slow evolution toward political will, it was not the beauty of a process or the ideal of participation that kept people committed. It was the urgency to protect their neighbors and neighborhood, coupled with a realization that it would take everyone's effort to do so, that keep people committed.

References

2008. *City of Los Angeles, Plan for a Citywide System of Neighborhood Councils*. Available online at the LAcityneighborhoods.org Web site.

Berry, Jeffrey M., Kent Portnoy, and Ken Thomson. 1993. *The Rebirth of Urban Democracy*. Washington, D.C.: Brookings.

Briggs, Xavier de Sousa. 2003. We Are All Negotiators Now: An Introduction to Negotiation in Community Problem Solving—Strategy Tool #5. Available on the WHO.org Web site.

City of Los Angeles. 2007. *The Neighborhood Council System: Past, Present and Future: Neighborhood Council Review Commission Final Report*. Available on the NCRCLA.org Web site.

City of Reno, Nevada. 2006. *Citizen Participation Guidebook; a Guide for Neighborhood Advisory Boards*. Available on the Cityofreno.com Web site.

Collaboration DC. 2007. *Holding a Community Roundtable*. Available on the Collaborationdc.net Web site.

Fisher, Roger and William Ury. 1981. *Getting to Yes*. Wilmington, DE: Houghton Mifflin.

Fung, Archon. 2004. *Empowered Participation*. Princeton, NJ: Princeton University Press.

Fung, Archon and Erik Olin Wright. 2003. Thinking About Empowered Participatory Governance. *Deepening Democracy*. Brooklyn, NY: Verso.

Kopff et al. v. DC Alcoholic Beverage Control Board, 381 A.2d 1372 (DC 1977).

Malena, Carmen. 2006. CIVICUS Participatory Governance Programme 2006–2008: Concept Note. Available on the CIVICUS.org Web site.

Moore, Christopher W. 1986. *The Mediation Process: Practical Strategies for Resolving Conflict.* London: Jossey-Bass.

Office of Advisory Neighborhood Commissions. 2006. *What's an ANC?* Washington, D.C.: Office of Advisory Neighborhood Commissions.

Potapchuk, William and Malka Kopell. 2005. *Community Development: A Guide for Grantmakers on Fostering Better Outcomes through Good Process.* Available on the William and Flora Hewlett Foundation and Community Building Institute Web site.

Putnam, R.D. 2000. *Bowling Alone: The Collapse and Revival of American Community.* New York: Simon and Schuster.

Schwartz, Roger. 1994. *The Skilled Facilitator: Practical Wisdom for Developing Effective Groups.* London: Jossey-Bass Publishers.

Notes

1. For the purposes of the case, actions attributed to the ANC or SWNA are referring to the heads of these bodies, unless otherwise indicated.

2. As project director of Collaboration DC, the author was directly involved in the events described and analyzed in this chapter. The observations and analysis presented here are hers.

3. More than thirty interviews were conducted with a variety of community leaders and residents.

4. Discord and disconnection among residents, leaders, and community groups emerged as a prominent concern.

5. Collaboration DC follows principles of inclusiveness, transparency, equality of participation, and civil discourse. This means that meetings have jointly created agendas, ground rules, written summaries, and a facilitator to ensure equitable participation.

6. Public participation is especially challenging for low-income, single mothers who predominate as heads of households in low-income neighborhoods.

7. Unemployment rates among low-income residents was, and remains, very high. Development activity is creating new construction jobs, positions in new commercial and service establishments, and new small-business opportunities. The challenge is insuring that new wealth-creation opportunities are accessible to neighborhood residents. This requires training and mentoring residents, which is a costly endeavor that developer contributions can help support.

8. Collaboration DC's design and planning materials are combined in a guide, *Holding a Community Roundtable*, available at the Collaboration DC Web site.

9. People with good group process skills were recruited from the neighborhood to facilitate small groups. This created an important future resource for the CBCC.

10. In a representative system, elected representatives act *on behalf of* the public. A more participatory system provides for direct citizen involvement in deliberation and decisionmaking. This calls for leaders who can mobilize and facilitate public engagement.

11. For more information on the Carol Baker Tharp Neighborhood Leadership Institute, see http://www.lacityneighborhoods.com/empowerment_academy.htm. Further information about the goals of the Los Angeles Department of Neighborhood Empowerment can be found at http://www.citywatchla.com/content/view/1859/75/. DC has a Neighborhood College, which ANC Commissioners can attend, but it is not specifically tailored to the ANC, and its year-long program is not realistic for most. Only a small percentage of ANC Commissioners attend.

12. See http://www.portlandonline.com/oni.

13. See www.cityofdayton.org/departments/pcd.

14. Universally, those living in poverty are often excluded from political participation. A 1993 study of neighborhood council systems in the U.S. found that low-income, less-educated people were much less involved than higher-income, more highly educated people (Berry et. al. 1993, 14). Efforts to overcome this require *supporting* people to get involved and organized.

15. Fisher and Ury (1981) urge a broader understanding of power and argue that there is power in developing good working relationships, in understanding interests, in inventing persuasive options, and in good communication. Mediators address *zero-sum* impasses, by encouraging disputants to expand the available resources, so that each party's basic needs can be met. If overall power is increased, power sharing is more satisfactory (Moore 1986).

16. Due to lower levels of education, lack of knowledge of the issues, and limited experience with public speaking, the natural inclination for many low-income residents was to avoid larger public forums. This trend was reported by city officials, ANC Commissioners, and low-income residents themselves. This special meeting was intended to try and counter that dynamic and achieve a higher level of participation by this group in the broader process.

17. For example, the current DC mayor has discontinued the biannual citizen summits held by his predecessor.

CHAPTER 6

BUILDING POLITICAL WILL FOR PARTICIPATORY GOVERNANCE AT THE LOCAL LEVEL IN THE UNITED KINGDOM

Tricia Zipfel

UK Policy Moment

Community participation has had a long and varied history in the United Kingdom. Over the past four decades, in different ways and for different reasons, both Labour and Conservative governments have supported the principle of *community involvement* when promoting strategies to improve and regenerate disadvantaged areas. They have encouraged resident consultation, and sometimes supported more meaningful participation in local improvements. For example, since 1990, the government has funded Tenant Management Organisations in over two hundred social housing areas, where residents form cooperatives to take over running their estates, including management of the budget. But, never before has *community empowerment*, the language now being used, been such a central feature of government policy.

Background

Since 1997, there has been a gradual shift in emphasis, from participation to empowerment, which has accelerated over the past two years. When Labour came to power, Tony Blair immediately set up the Social Exclusion Unit to examine the causes of poverty and social exclusion that blighted significant areas of the country. Over the previous two decades, the gap between the poorest 10 percent of the population and the rest of the population had increased more rapidly than in almost any other *developed* country (Joseph Rowntree Foundation 1995). Much of this poverty was concentrated in clearly identifiable, mainly urban areas within eighty-eight local authorities across England. Along with tax and benefit reforms, to increase income at the bottom end, the government launched the *National Strategy for Neighbourhood Renewal* to address structural problems of poverty and social exclusion, through targeted capital investment in area-based projects, improvements to mainstream public sector services, and strong support for community involvement. For example, the strategy established over one hundred pilot projects, many of which were community-led, aimed at improving services and narrowing the gap between the most deprived areas and the rest of the country.

Lessons from previous regeneration programs were drawn upon, in an effort to get the strategy correct this time. Three key insights were emphasized: timing, complexity, and community. A ten- to twenty-year time frame was deemed necessary to achieve sustainable change and embed it in long-term, systemic changes. It was determined that these complex problems would require crosscutting solutions, with public services working together in a coordinated way, in order to deliver meaningful results. Maybe the most crucial insight was that community involvement had to be at the heart of neighborhood renewal, because without local ownership and support it was impossible to identify what would work or make improvements last.

In launching some early schemes in 1999, government ministers stated that the projects would be *community-led*. Many people welcomed this unambiguous and radical approach. However, in reality, this proved to be much more challenging than anyone had anticipated. Some projects became bogged down in conflicts between residents, who expected to make the decisions, and officials and elected members, who often had different priorities. Timing was also a problem, because genuine participation cannot be rushed through, yet these projects were under pressure to deliver results, meet targets, spend to deadlines, and jump through all the hoops involved in spending large sums of public money. The experience created a steep and often fraught learning curve for everyone involved.

However, eight or nine years on, most of these neighborhood renewal schemes are demonstrating positive results, with better service delivery, improved outcomes for local people, and higher levels of local involvement. Within most of the eighty-eight authorities, the gap between outcomes in the poorest neighborhoods and those for the local authority overall, has narrowed. In the majority of cases, the gap between neighborhood outcomes and the national average has also narrowed in relation to all the key indicators other than health, where despite some improvements, the gap remains large.[1]

This experience has also shown what local communities can do, when given the opportunity and resources, and it has opened up debate about the advantages and the problems of putting community empowerment into practice on the ground.

In 2005, the government began to look at the potential for applying these lessons more widely. A number of consultation and policy documents, from the Department of Communities and Local Government, drew on the experience of neighborhood renewal schemes and local partnerships to set out a reform agenda for local government. The aims were to strengthen the role of local government, by devolving more control and allowing greater flexibility in local decision making; to improve services across the board and strengthen the relationship between citizens and the state, by increasing choice, improving accountability, and developing better working partnerships; to link community involvement and empowerment to local government reform and the need to revitalize local democracy.

This has produced a government agenda that sees local government reform and community empowerment as two sides of the same coin. Many people would describe this as a *unique policy moment*, one that must not be squandered. Others remain skeptical that all the talk of *community empowerment* is just rhetoric. However, *community empowerment* has never before had such a high profile within national policy, or commanded so much cross-party support, which is very significant.

What is Driving These Changes?

The climate for change has been created over many years, through a combination of top-down, government policy commitments and bottom-up pressure, shaped by people's experience on the ground. A number of factors are worth highlighting.

Accepted good practice

More than two decades of government policy to tackle economic decline in many urban areas produced a regeneration industry that has had to take on the views of local people. Professionals have sometimes failed to get beyond the most basic forms of consultation, but working closely with local communities is now generally accepted as essential good practice.

Evidence base

A wealth of independent academic research supports this approach, and demonstrates that community involvement is essential for relevant and sustainable improvements, and leads to good investment of public resources. During the 1990s, the Joseph Rowntree Foundation, an independent charity that has been tackling the root causes of poverty for over one hundred years, managed the largest program of action research and evaluation studies in the country, relating to social housing and area regeneration. Since 2000, the Centre for the Analysis of Social Exclusion,[2] based at the London School of Economics, has produced a body of research scrutinizing strategies to reduce poverty and exclusion. Many other academic institutions manage similar programs. The consistent message from this research is that sustainable change cannot be imposed on local communities. Instead, local communities must be involved in the design and delivery of necessary changes, and need to be partners and coproducers if investment in regeneration is to be worthwhile.

Residents' own experience

Involvement in regeneration programs has also impacted on residents themselves. Many have served on community-level regeneration boards or have worked for area regeneration projects. They are connected with the decision makers and service providers who affect their lives, and their communities are better placed to influence decisions. Although these experiences have not always been positive, they have heightened people's awareness of how decisions are made and increased their appetite for more involvement. Increased capacity is also reflected in the vast array of small-scale projects run by local people, often with little or no funding, and thriving on the energy and imagination of a few determined individuals.

Democratic deficit

More recently, other concerns have increased the focus on participation. In the United Kingdom, as in many other western democracies, there is growing disillusion with politics. Fewer people vote in local and national elections, a problem that is most serious in areas of highest disadvantage. This is becoming a real cause of concern for all political parties. An independent inquiry into the state of democracy in the United Kingdom highlighted the serious implications of this growing *democratic deficit* and argued for sweeping changes (Power Inquiry 2006).

Devolved decision making

The government, partly in response to the Power Inquiry, introduced a range of measures to reform democratic structures and processes at every level. Some changes, such as the question of turning the House of Lords into an elected chamber, might seem remote to ordinary citizens, but the language of reform also emphasizes the need to devolve decision-making powers and responsibilities beyond local government to local communities, sometimes known as *double devolution*. Central government considers this to be a *win-win* solution, though not everyone in local government sees it that way.

Empowerment as an objective

Current debate represents a shift in the way government understands participation and empowerment. Until quite recently, ministers spoke about *participation* primarily in terms of improving services and meeting delivery targets. It was a useful, and many would say necessary, means to an end, the end being defined by government objectives. *Empowerment*, on the other hand, related to individual choice and personalized services, rather than collective power to influence decisions. The desire to empower individual citizens is still an important driver of reform, especially in relation to health services and social care. However, the debate has shifted beyond seeing people solely as *empowered consumers* of public services, to the implications of treating people as *active citizens*, with rights and responsibilities within the public realm, and the capacity to exert influence over decisions and call those in power to account. A range of factors has contributed to this shift. It stems partly from people with direct community experience, both inside and outside of government, being taken more seriously and partly from recognition that the scope for improving services through government targets and consumer choice is limited. Possibly the strongest driver has been key politicians recognizing the urgent need to reconnect with ordinary people to reverse the disillusion with politics, which is threatening representative structures, at a time when governments around the world face major problems, such as climate change, mass migration, and economic instability. These issues cannot be addressed without engaging popular opinion or without achieving significant levels of active collaboration.

Language and scope

The language of government policy documents reflects this shift, talking about empowering local people as a way to: revitalize local democracy and reengage people with the political process; open up decision making, so people can be involved in the choices that matter to them most; tackle poverty and inequality, at a time when the gap between rich and poor is still growing; build capacity within communities, so they are more resourceful and cohesive; and tap the local talents and skills of people who might otherwise become marginalized (Government Policy White Papers 2006, 2008). Improving services and making them more accountable to users is still important, as is the need to increase choice in the public sector. However, the issues driving this agenda are much wider than that.

Individual ministers

Another key factor shaping the current policy on empowerment is the personal commitment and enthusiasm of the Secretary of State for Communities and Local Government, Hazel Blears. She has long been a champion of community involvement and has put her personal stamp on many of the changes now being implemented. In the United Kingdom, ministers tend to come and go, so there is always the question of what happens if she is moved to another department. However, her work has reasonably strong roots. It builds on the neighborhood renewal legacy, and on her predecessor's determination to devolve decision making beyond the town hall into the neighborhood. The reforms she promotes are supported by the prime minister and other government departments. Also, the concept of *community empowerment* tends to have cross-party support and most politicians see this agenda as an integral part of the challenge to revitalize democracy in the United Kingdom.

Current Policy Developments

The government began the reform process in 2005, initially exploring the scope for more localized, devolved governance arrangements linked to increased community involvement. Their policies were set out in a series of consultation documents, two government policy *White Papers* (Communities and Local Government 2008), an action plan (Communities and Local Government 2007), and legislation (Her Majesty's Government 2007). The legislation in October 2007, introduced, for the first time, a statutory duty for local authorities not only to inform and consult residents, but also to involve them in decisions that affect their communities. In the summer of 2008, a number of new proposals were made to further strengthen the framework for community empowerment and citizen involvement in local democracy, including proposals to extend the statutory duty to other services, including the police and other public sector bodies.

The reforms are significant for a number of reasons. The government has clearly stated that it "wants to shift power, influence and responsibility away from existing centers of power into the hands of communities and individual citizens" (Policy White Paper 2008). For the first time, the reforms make citizen engagement a statutory requirement of local authorities, and set out ways in which communities can challenge the authorities if arrangements for involvement are not adequate. They make participation more of a right than simply an option that comes by invitation only, and this has shifted the terms of the debate from the capacity of citizens to participate, to the willingness and capacity of government to support their involvement. The reforms also extend empowerment, beyond a few targeted areas, to all neighborhoods and local communities, in an attempt to mainstream community involvement as accepted good practice. Finally, the government has explicitly endorsed the importance of having "a vibrant participatory democracy in order to strengthen representative democracy" (Policy White Paper 2008), and in 2009, it plans to introduce a new duty requiring local authorities to actively *promote democracy*.

Although better local government is central to these reforms, the focus is wider than just local authorities. Hazel Blears wants the empowerment agenda to be adopted in every part of the public sector and she has the backing of other government departments. But, translating this joint commitment at the centre into coordinated action on the ground is complicated. Most areas have a local strategic partnership (LSP), usually led by the local authority, which brings key statutory services, such as health, police, and employment, together with the voluntary sector, the business sector, and local community. The expectation is that, these LSP partners will coordinate their work with local communities, promote empowerment, and embed change across all of their services. This is a huge challenge for most partnerships, but, if it can be achieved, it has the potential to deliver significant improvements in efficiency and effectiveness.

Implementing Community Empowerment

The new measures being introduced by the government are intended to encourage and enable these changes to take place. They include widening and deepening local empowerment opportunities, underpinning and supporting this work and strengthening local representative democracy.

Widening and Deepening Local Empowerment Opportunities

The new statutory *duty to inform, consult, and involve* citizens and communities came into effect in April 2009. It applies to local authorities and complements similar requirements, which already exist for health and police authorities. There are plans to extend this *statutory duty* to other services during the course of 2009. In addition a *Councillor Call for Action,* and the use of petitions, will enable communities and their local councilors to initiate action where problems are not being addressed. The minister has stated that she wants to see some form of *participatory budgeting* operating, to some extent, in every local authority area by 2012. This is the first time any government has made such a commitment to participatory budgeting. Neighborhood management, tenant management of social housing, and the adoption of *local charters* will be encouraged in order to achieve improved service delivery. These initiatives will require the development of local action plans and the introduction of local service delivery, often in the form of neighborhood-based teams and devolved budgets.

Underpinning and Supporting This Work

In order to promote empowerment across all sectors, the government has established a National Empowerment Partnership and regional partnerships, led by the voluntary sector. Eighteen local authorities have been identified as exemplars of good practice to inspire and guide others, and funding is being made available, to enable public assets, such as land or buildings, to be transferred to community ownership. Funding for community development will also be made available to *community anchor organizations*, which are independent, local, trusted organizations, to underpin community activity, and a range of initiatives, specifically designed to encourage the involvement of young people, will be supported.

Strengthening Local Representative Democracy

The government is encouraging local councilors to become champions of, and advocates for, their local communities. Local authority Overview and Scrutiny committees, through which local government and other public services must publicly account for their performance, will be strengthened, and there will be increased accountability of local police and health services.[3] There will also be support for more visible and accountable leadership through directly elected mayors, and steps will be taken to open up opportunities for more citizens, from diverse backgrounds, to stand for election to public office.

Underpinning these reforms is a new framework for performance management and scrutiny, managed by the national Audit Commission, which inspects local authority performance on behalf of the central government.

A new inspection regime, the *Comprehensive Area Assessment*, will come into effect in 2009. It will bring together seven inspectorates to jointly assess public sector services against a range of nationally agreed upon performance indicators. In response to complaints about too many centralized and inappropriate targets, the government has reduced the number of national targets and simplified the measures against which a local authority's and their partners' performance will be assessed, from 1,200 to 198 performance indicators. Apart from a few required indicators, local authorities and LSPs will be able to determine their own priorities from within this list. It includes measures that relate to building stronger, more cohesive communities, and ensuring that local people have a real say in the decisions that matter to them. Despite increased local flexibility, the Audit Commission has made it clear that the quality of community participation will have a high priority in all future assessments.

Underlying Tensions

The policies discussed above reflect a genuine desire on the part of government to engage citizens in the democratic process, and the proposed changes indicate that central government seems to understand what participation and empowerment is all about. However, there is an inherent tension between reforms needed to strengthen representative democracy, and the development of new forms of participatory democracy. Although these two objectives are complementary, the same mechanisms will not necessarily achieve both goals. To strengthen existing representative structures, while at the same time opening them up to greater scrutiny and challenge from communities, requires quite a balancing act. Perhaps it is asking a lot of many traditional political leaders to accept, let alone encourage, other forms of grassroots community leadership. However, from a community perspective, some of the proposals do not go far enough and lack the kind of teeth that many activists feel are needed to deliver real change on the ground. There are concerns that while this agenda sounds exciting, when it comes to implementing it at local level, it will be fudged.

Although central government is providing bold leadership, it is also holding back in a number of ways. Making the involvement of citizens a statutory duty, represents an important step in the right direction, but it falls short of an unequivocal citizens' right to be involved. It focuses on what local authorities and, from 2009, other services need to do to reach out to their communities, but it leaves those in power to determine *when* involvement is appropriate and *how* it will be done. Also while central government can *encourage* local authorities to devolve power and decision making to the neighborhood level, it is very reluctant to *require* them to do so. Central government has little leverage to insist that, as local governments begin to exercise greater flexibility and control over local decisions, they share this increased power with local communities.

Changes in the way that local communities themselves are funded also pose a potential threat, because they may no longer be in a strong position to fight for a place at the decision-making table. For example, as part of the Neighbourhood Renewal program, Community Empowerment Networks were established in eighty-eight of the poorest areas. They were directly funded by central government to provide a voice for communities in local partnership arrangements. But this funding program ended in 2006, and the decision about whether to invest in a community infrastructure of this kind (or not) is now down to the local authority or LSP.

The new national performance management and inspection framework, managed by the Audit Commission, will hopefully ensure that local governments and LSPs take the empowerment agenda seriously and maintain investment in local communities. But assessing empowerment is not easy and it is not yet clear how effective this form of scrutiny will be. Nor is it helped by the language of empowerment, which can be unclear and open to interpretation. Ministers themselves have sometimes been ambiguous. For example, they have talked about *giving people empowerment,* or setting up *community kitties,* such as small grant programs, rather than using the more radical language of popular participation in setting budgets. This may be a deliberate attempt to avoid alarming local government, but such language waters down the much stronger statements in the government policy White Papers.

The current economic climate presents yet another source of uncertainty. Government finances are tight and public spending is likely to be under pressure for many years. Many of the special programs, that funded community participation over the previous eight years have either come to an end or been merged into core local government funding streams. Inevitably, there are competing priorities for these limited resources, and even for people who support community involvement, the choice between investing in participation or spending money on core services, such as health and education, can be a tough call.

Community Capacity to Respond

Although the main focus of the reforms is on local authorities and other public sector providers, pressure for genuine change must be bottom-up as well as top-down. Central government may be able to provide a positive lead, but local communities and the voluntary sector need to be able to respond and make use of the new opportunities on offer. There are many positive signs, but also some potential pitfalls.

One outcome from more than twenty years of area regeneration and neighborhood renewal is that many communities now have considerable experience of government programs. Some residents have served on project and partnership boards for years and have become *expert citizens*. They are able to hold their own in these forums, and see the empowerment agenda as an opportunity to strengthen and extend community involvement in local governance. Their involvement has been like opening up a beneficial *Pandora's box*. Once people experience being able to make a difference, they tend to want to do more, and are unlikely to simply disappear into the woodwork.

The *tenant management movement* in the United Kingdom is a powerful example of local community control, where a combination of topdown and bottom-up processes have achieved fundamental shifts in power and responsibility. After many years of campaigning for better services, in 1995, public housing residents were given a statutory right to manage their estates. Since then, more than two hundred Tenant Management Organisations (TMOs) have been formed, where residents control the budgets and make the decisions about how their estates are run. Some, like the Bloomsbury TMO, which operates in one of the poorest parts of Birmingham, have established separate resident-based companies to undertake cleaning and maintenance work, thus creating local employment. They have also helped improve a range of other facilities, including a new health centre, a credit union, a redeveloped shopping precinct, an employment resource centre, and the redevelopment of open space, including sports pitches and play areas for children.

Unlike TMOs, which are resident led, most regeneration schemes are run by a partnership that involves the local community alongside a range of other stakeholders. Involvement in multiagency partnerships can be challenging in a different way. Community leaders may be faced with more complex problems that need to be brokered across different vested interests within the partnership, as well as among members of their own communities. They need to look at issues from different perspectives and find common ground with others. One community leader, who became chair of her local partnership board, commented, "I would have preferred to remain a local activist, on the outside of such an initiative and to critique, scrutinize and point out what was not working. But this time I decided to try to do things differently, to get my 'hands dirty', and see whether we, the community, could actually make a difference" (IDS 2007).

Where partnerships work well, trust grows and new relationships develop, but the experience of trying to carve out a role for community leaders is not always easy, especially where a local authority is indifferent or even hostile to participation. Many residents have found the culture of partnerships alienating. One resident said that "partnerships are not just about how we participate as residents and citizens. They are also about how others respond to us . . . The institutions also need to change to be more receptive to greater citizen participation and less centralized in their decision making" (IDS 2007).

Many community leaders are skeptical of the government's ability to influence change at this level, and the demise of so many Community Empowerment Networks has not helped instill confidence. The networks were one of a number of civil society or voluntary sector organizations that provided support and helped build solidarity across communities, ensuring that their voices were heard and taken seriously. However, the role of many, though not all, of these voluntary sector organizations is changing, as they shift their focus from advocacy and organizing to service delivery. The government has encouraged this shift, in an attempt to increase the voluntary sector's role, especially as providers of more specialized services, and to make them more financially secure. As a result, many now work alongside the statutory sector and they are increasingly dependent on income from service-related contracts for their survival. This can compromise their independence and reduce their capacity for community development and advocacy work. It also raises questions about who will undertake crucial community empowerment work, such as building independent community organizations and linking community groups together.

Community engagement in the United Kingdom must also fight against a cultural tendency to rely heavily on government and the welfare state to resolve problems and meet the needs of families and communities. This is beginning to change, as people become less satisfied with top-down solutions and as ideas about active citizenship take hold, but a strong tradition of community-based problem solving is still lacking. Although the level of individual volunteering is very high, many people resist coming together as a community to exercise collective power and responsibility, and tend to rely on their formally elected representatives to act on their behalf.

Unfortunately, formal democratic structures are struggling and political party membership is at an all-time low. People are turned off by politics and politicians. Candidates willing to stand for election tend to reflect a very narrow spectrum of society. They are mainly white, male, and over the age of fifty-eight (Communities and Local Government 2007). Other vehicles, such as the Trade Unions, through which people exercised voice and influence in the past, have seen their role diminished. Therefore, perhaps it is not surprising that when direct funding for Community Empowerment Networks was removed in 2006, the rumblings of anger and frustration within the sector did not amount to an outcry that would make the government pay attention.

However, some significant developments have begun to fill this gap. One example is London Citizens, a broad-based community organization[4] that brings together more than eighty groups, from all faiths and ethnic backgrounds, schools, trade unions, and residents' organizations, to provide a common voice for the citizens of London on key issues that matter to them. It has successfully campaigned for a living wage for cleaners and other low-paid staff, raising their pay to a level that is higher than the government's minimum wage, and reflecting what it actually costs to meet a family's basic requirements living in the capital. It is working to ensure the 2012 Olympic Games benefit low-income communities in east London and is campaigning for the government to give permanent residency to illegal migrant workers, who have been in the country for a period of time. London Citizens uses public hearings to call politicians to account. It argues that local communities should be seen as the *first* not the *third* sector, giving informed consent for government to exercise power in a servant role, and challenges attitudes that treat people as consumers rather than citizens. As Neil Jameson, the lead organizer, puts it "London Citizens is an invitation to power, not to partnership—it's important to build alliances, but they have to be negotiated from a position of strength" (IDS 2007).[5] Many people feel that without this kind of grassroots citizen organization, it will be difficult to take advantage of the opportunities for empowerment in the current policy climate.

Local Government Capacity to Respond

Community capacity is one thing, but the capacity of local government to respond to the empowerment agenda is also crucial. It is difficult to change old habits, and *them and us* attitudes, which have tended to shape relations between the community, civil society, and local government, are deeply entrenched in many areas. However, the situation is more complex than that, and there are grounds for optimism.

In May 2007, the central government sponsored a five-day international workshop, organized by the Institute of Development at Sussex University. The workshop brought together twenty-two *champions of participation* from around the world with twenty-two *champions* from the United Kingdom, most of who worked in local government. The dialogue was inspiring, indicating that they understood community empowerment, were passionate about neighborhood renewal, and local management, and were convinced that better ways exist of working together for change. Some of these officers felt beleaguered and unsupported within their own bureaucracies, but overall, the sense of an appetite for change was palpable.

Delegates from the LSP in Bradford talked about the strong links they had forged with partners across all sectors, which had helped them deliver better outcomes for local people. They had also made community development a priority, helping sixty neighborhoods produce local action plans, providing small grants for community self-help projects, and using participatory budgeting to bring diverse communities together to determine the allocation of funding for environmental improvements across the city. Over a three-year period, more than £1 million was allocated by residents using participatory budgeting methods. The existence of special programs like neighborhood renewal funding, which was available for about six years, enabled many local authorities to be innovative without necessarily having to use their core mainstream budgets. Now that this funding is being cut back, maintaining investment in community and neighborhood-based initiatives presents a major challenge.

Delegates from Newcastle City Council also illustrated a strong appetite for change. They too had introduced participatory budgeting, the *U-decide* program. This enabled more than one hundred residents to become involved in deciding how to spend £30,000 on local environmental projects to make their neighborhood *cleaner, greener, and safer*. At the same time, young people from across the city came together to decide how a further £30,000 should be used for youth activities. Working with council officers, a group of teenagers who called themselves *The Wickid Planners* helped mastermind the entire process. Afterwards, one resident said, "U-decide boosted the confidence of community groups in my area enormously. Now we know what we can achieve, we are planning to bring all our groups together and see what we can do with a bigger, united voice" (Participating Budgeting Unit 2007). It has also impacted on local councilors. After the first *participatory budgeting decision day*, one ward councilor commented that "[i]n my four years involved in politics this has been the best day ever. Participatory budgeting is about empowering people" (Participating Budgeting Unit 2007). Some have been emboldened by this experience and now want to apply participatory methods to other decisions that influence parts of the council's mainstream budget.

Although these stories may not be typical, they are not isolated examples either. There is evidence of a new generation of public sector workers and political leaders who welcome the reform agenda from central government, and who are committed to changing things on the ground. However, there are also many old-guard politicians who find participation threatening, and some bureaucrats who want to protect their turf. They may oppose the idea of participatory democracy in principle, as a threat to representative democracy. Some councilors may fear that community participation will undermine their power and status as elected representatives. Many are reluctant to cede control over budgets and other decisions to local communities, because of entrenched negative views about the latter's ability to handle such responsibilities. Many senior officials share these prejudices, but there are also genuine bureaucratic pressures, including some from central government, to meet targets and spend within time frames, that can make participation difficult.

Challenges for Participation in the United Kingdom

The international *Champions of Participation* workshop compared experience across fifteen countries from around the world. It found a remarkable degree of similarity, despite differences in context, culture, and history. Participants shared similar positive and often inspirational examples of participation, but agreed that the barriers need to be understood if top-down policy reforms are to have an impact on the day-to-day world of local government and community involvement. The workshop identified a number of crucial issues.

Changing the attitudes and behavior of those in power, as well as those who are used to being on the receiving end, is crucial but also complex. Elected representatives and officials can have entrenched views of communities, which make them reluctant to give up or share power. They may not have the skills or confidence to effectively engage with local people, or to cope with the messiness and uncertainties of participation. For the most part, they define the rules of engagement and determine the way participation is done. On the other hand, citizens can feel disillusioned and unwilling to engage. They may be stuck in an adversarial *us versus them* mode, and resistant to sharing responsibility and ownership.

Participation and innovation need to be integral to the way local government operates, rather than merely an add-on. Different ways of working together need to be mainstreamed, underpinned by longer-term funding and a clear political commitment to participation. New public spaces for dialogue and deliberation with local citizens are needed. Central government should encourage participation by creating such spaces and providing the resources. However, in order to engage effectively, local government needs to go deeper into communities, to make sure that new voices are heard and listened to, especially the most marginalized and vulnerable groups, whether defined by place or by identity. It is essential that new democratic processes recognize and respond to minority interests. For example participants from India at the *Champions of Participation* workshop, described how requirements, for the inclusion of women and lower castes in the Panchayati Raj village council system, have led to more elected women representatives in India than in the rest of the world combined! This strategy reflects the importance of having community voices at the table, but it also highlights the need to provide support for these citizens, if they are to be effective activists, rather than merely a token presence.

Citizen engagement in the democratic process has significant implications for elected representatives, as well as for citizens. The emergence of community leaders who derive their legitimacy from a participatory process can be threatening to elected members, who rely on political parties for their nomination and the ballot box for their legitimacy. This agenda requires elected members to be genuinely rooted in the communities they represent and to develop the skills and capacity to listen and work with their communities in a different way.

Citizen representatives also face a challenge. They must work on the inside and the outside of institutions, while providing a voice for their communities. They are crucial *expert citizens*, working long hours on a voluntary basis, but if they end up being derogatorily labeled as *the usual suspects*, they can also be undermined. Not surprisingly, many citizens find working in partnership difficult, even if they are respected as equal partners, which too often is not the case. Building relationships that lead to increased capacity for genuine collaboration and trust takes time and can be difficult, especially if there is a negative history to overcome. Even once established, this trust can be fragile and easily undermined.

For officials who are trying to deliver results, meet targets, and balance budgets, participation can introduce a new level of complexity, due to the many different players and expectations that need to be taken into account. Achieving the right balance is tricky, and local government officials can find themselves caught between the legal and performance requirements of central government on the one hand, and local expectations and demands on the other.

What Would Change Look Like?

Creating the political will for participation and empowerment is a complex process that needs to happen at many levels. In the United Kingdom, government has taken a strong lead, but it is also clear that political will at local level, from politicians and the managers who control resources, is crucial. Local citizens must also be willing to engage politically, even though many of them will have been thoroughly turned off from politics and may feel they have better things to do with their time.

For people who care about this agenda, it is not enough simply to have a set of policy ideals; they must be backed up by practical strategies and action. However, there is no single blueprint for effective participation, no *magic bullet*, so it is just as well that the government says it does not want to be prescriptive. This presents both an opportunity and a challenge for local authorities, local services, and local people, to find solutions that work for them and together shape the types of changes they want to see. But it also means that central government has to remain focused and continue to drive, support, and monitor the changes as they take place.

What Might that Involve?

To create a strong voice and an influential presence in local governance arrangements, whether at the neighborhood or city levels, support and resources are needed to build independent community organizations, through which people can come together, resolve their differences, and agree how, and by whom, they want to be represented. The government has recognized the value of having a local infrastructure in their support for community anchor organizations, such as development trusts or tenant management organizations, which are trusted and have the community development expertise to support involvement. Particularly in more disadvantaged areas, their role of ensuring effective and inclusive community involvement in decision making and governance arrangements will be essential.

Although the culture and behavior of existing institutions will need to change, it is also necessary to create new democratic spaces for citizens to engage with local political actors. These spaces must encourage dialogue and problem-solving, and develop better understanding and trust between people. They should facilitate processes that enable those in power to be genuinely accountable to the wider community and that reinforce this principle as a key feature of a strong democracy.

If access to decision making is to be opened up, and if new people are to have the opportunity to become involved and participate, innovative thinking is needed. In the United Kingdom, participatory budgeting represents an exciting new idea borrowed from overseas, but it will take work to ensure that the talk translates into changes that result in greater transparency and more scope for communities to influence spending priorities. Frontline managers and local elected members must also feel empowered by these changes. They need to identify strongly with their local communities and welcome the opportunity to be more accountable. They need to feel able to take decisions with confidence, deliver results, and help inspire everyone with a can-do attitude to problem-solving.

A lot will depend on whether the new performance management and scrutiny arrangements are effective. The Audit Commission must seek out the views and experience of local people, involve them in the assessment process, and make it clear that the quality of a local authority's approach to participation will be a key aspect of the assessment process. Some people would like to see minimum standards adopted, in order to clarify expectations and provide guidance, as has already been done in Scotland.[6]

More technical expertise and support should be provided to communities and local government practitioners who want to improve the quality of participation. This should include imaginative ways of doing outreach and working with people in an everyday setting, rather than simply through formal meetings and ballots once every few years. Examples of approaches that can be more effective than traditional meetings include: bringing visually stimulating and tactile information to the places where people gather, such as pubs, schools, surgeries, and bus stops; using interactive IT systems, which appeal to younger people and enable those who are housebound to have a voice; training residents as outreach workers, providing and gathering information, and developing leadership roles in the process.

The language of reform already affirms the value of public service and the role of government, a message which is equally important for politicians, professionals, and citizens. The empowerment agenda requires a move away from Margaret Thatcher's model of a minimalist state, reliance on an unfettered marketplace for our well-being, and a preoccupation with the interests of the individual, to a society where people can come together to resolve their differences and tackle the challenging problems that confront society at local, national, and international levels.

Many of the issues that impact on local communities go beyond the responsibilities of local government. Effort is therefore needed to mobilize citizens and communities in relation to the private as well as the public sector. This is increasingly important as more services are contracted out and more power is exercised by global institutions, most of which have little or no interest in local communities and whose management structures are not susceptible to democratic accountability.

Finally, the strong focus on social justice and inclusion that was at the heart of the Neighbourhood Renewal Strategy must be maintained, in order to ensure that the most marginalized groups are empowered and that reducing inequality remains a primary aim of this agenda.

Conclusion

Given the way this agenda has been driven, in the United Kingdom, from the top down, one concern is whether Hazel Blears will remain in post long enough to embed the changes she has championed in her own department and across central government. Although it is difficult to imagine that these policies would be reversed, her determination and personal commitment is a key factor in getting people to take this agenda seriously. However, it can never really take root unless local communities take ownership. They need to seize the new powers being provided to force change to happen locally. They need to assert their right as citizens to participate in decision making, not simply respond to an invitation to do so from the government. The government is creating a policy environment in which this could happen. It has set out new powers and duties, and introduced new mechanisms to increase citizen involvement. It has made it clear that community participation is essential for strong, cohesive communities, effective service delivery, and a revitalized democratic system in which citizens connect with the political process. Strong messages have been sent to local communities, as well as to service providers, government officials, councilors, and political parties, all of whom have a pivotal role to play in creating new spaces for participatory democracy alongside existing representative structures.

The question now is will central government be able to drive through these changes? Will they stay focused long enough for the reforms to take root, and will local government and local communities be able to respond positively and make something new and exciting of this unique opportunity?

References

Barclay, Sir Peter (chair). 2005. *Inquiry into Income and Wealth, volume one.* York, UK: Joseph Rowntree Foundation.

Communities and Local Government. 2006. *Strong and Prosperous Communities.* London: Communities and Local Government.

Communities and Local Government. 2007. *An Action Plan for Community Empowerment: Building on Success.* London: Communities and Local Government.

Communities and Local Government. 2007. *Representing the Future: The Report of the Councillors Commission.* London: Communities and Local Government.

Communities and Local Government. 2008. *Communities in Control - Real People, Real Power.* London: Communities and Local Government.

Communities Scotland. 2005. *National Standards for Community Engagement.* Edinburgh, Scotland: Communities Scotland.

Her Majesty's Government. 2007. *Local Government and Public Involvement in Health Act 2007.* London: Her Majesty's Government.

Hills, John. 2005. *Inquiry into Income and Wealth: Volume two.* York, UK: Joseph Rowntree Foundation.

Institute of Development Studies. 2007. *Champions of Participation: Engaging Citizens in Local Governance.* Brighton, UK: Institute of Development Studies.

Institute of Development Studies. 2007. *Champions of Participation Resource Pack.* Brighton, UK: Institute of Development Studies.

Kennedy, Helena (chair). 2006. *Power to the People: an Independent Inquiry into Britain's Democracy.* London, UK: The Power Inquiry.

Participatory Budgeting Unit. 2008. *Participatory Budgeting in the UK: A Toolkit.* Manchester, UK: Church Action on Poverty.

Taylor, Marilyn. 1995. *Unleashing the Potential: Bringing Residents to the Centre of Regeneration.* York, UK: Joseph Rowntree Foundation.

Notes

1. Outcomes are measured in terms of crime reduction, educational attainment, housing and environment, employment, and health. Levels of resident satisfaction in neighborhood renewal areas have also improved significantly. A full evaluation of the *National Strategy for Neighbourhood Renewal* is forthcoming.

2. CASE was established in 1997 and has advised government on all aspects of its strategy to reduce social exclusion.

3. *Overview and Scrutiny committees* are the mechanism through which local government and other public services have to account publicly for their performance.

4. London Citizens is based on a community organizing model developed by Saul Alinsky in Chicago in the 1960s. Information available at the Hlondoncitizens.org.ukH Web site.

5. Champions of Participation: report and resource pack. Available on the ids.ac.uk Web site.

6. *National Standards for Community Engagement* were developed by the Community Development Foundation in Scotland. More information can be found on the Communities Scotland Web site. In 2002, there were 202 registered TMOs across 53 local authorities and 81 TMOs in development, covering an estimated 84,000 homes. Information available at the Communitiesscotland.gov.uk Web site.

CHAPTER 7

BUILDING PRESSURE FROM BELOW: LESSONS FROM UGANDA

Harriet Namisi

Introduction

Uganda's Political History

Uganda's colonial and postcolonial political history is a difficult one, which offers very limited examples of ordinary people having a say in how they should be governed. Prior to British colonization in 1890, the area of Uganda was occupied by various ethnic groups, such as the Buganda, Ankole, and Bunyoro kingdoms, each of which had their own governance systems. The kingdoms provided for their people's social, economic, and political needs through a very strong associational form of livelihood derived from shared cultural beliefs and social attachments. During the colonial period, civic groups, like trade unions and church-based associations, led people to start agitating for a more just and representative government. Uganda gained independence from the British in 1962, but subsequently suffered decades of political power struggles, marked by military coups, civil conflict, limited respect of human rights, and little tolerance for political opposition.

When President Museveni claimed power in 1986, he presented a new political strategy, according to which real democracy had to be organized at all levels from the village up and on the basis of a decent standard of living so that ordinary people could resist the blandishments of unprincipled politicians. This formed the basis for Uganda's return to sanity and, for the first time in history, gave citizens an opportunity to build trust in the government.

In1986, civil society organizations (CSOs) began mushrooming in Uganda, to address the suffering and vulnerabilities resulting from

113

decades of government failure and civil conflict. The outbreak of diseases, like HIV/Aids, served as another source of disarray, requiring support from groups aside from the government, which was struggling to reinstate confidence, power, and authority in Uganda.

The armed forces and executive arm of the government have continued to be the most powerful institutions in Uganda, rather than the people's power. For any nation to develop the political will to promote democracy, participatory and accountable governance is essential. This chapter looks at *political will* as a value system for political leaders, one that calls for integrity, and accountability, and a commitment to meet the needs of the people. Little emphasis is placed on building citizens' will, because their involvement in national development simply requires sensitization and education, while the politicians need to be persuaded and, in some cases, forced to change their attitudes and behavior. This chapter describes the work of the Development Network of Indigenous Voluntary Associations (DENIVA) in *building pressure from below* to enhance citizen participation and good governance in Uganda.

The Political and Legal Environment

Despite some notable exceptions and gaps, the current political and legal environment in Uganda is generally considered to be favorable to deepening democracy and promoting people's participation. The 1995 Constitution of the Republic of Uganda clearly recognizes the significant role of citizens, and provides a legal framework for building participatory governance. The constitution states that, "every Ugandan citizen has the right to participate in the affairs of government," and commits the state to "mobilize, organize, and empower Ugandan citizens to establish independent and sustainable foundations for the development of Uganda." The National Objectives and Directive Principles of State Policy states that the State shall be based on democratic principles that empower and encourage the active participation of all citizens at all levels in their governance; all public offices shall be held in trust for the people; and all persons placed in positions of leadership and responsibility shall, in their work, be answerable to the people (Government of Uganda 1995).

The constitution also stipulates a decentralized system of governance, "to ensure people's participation and democratic control in decision making." The National Objectives and Directive Principles of State Policy declares that the state shall be guided by democratic principles of decentralization and devolution of government functions and powers to the people at appropriate levels where they can best manage and direct their own affairs (Government of Uganda 1995). The 1997 Local Government

Act and Decentralization Policy have been developed in line with the above provisions. The Local Government Act provides for a system whereby district-level government councils, made up of locally elected representatives, are the highest political authority within their area of jurisdiction and have both legislative and executive powers. However, in practice, due to limited revenue sources, weak collection capacity, and political interventions that counter effective mobilization and collection, local governments still find it difficult to fulfill their duties and to generate adequate local revenue to supplement central government transfers (Ministry of Local Government 2006).

Another extremely important and enabling law is the Access to Public Information Act of 2005, which aims "to promote transparency and accountability in all organs of the State, by providing the public with timely, accessible, and accurate information [and] to empower the public to effectively scrutinize and participate in Government decisions that affect them."

Several CSOs have been actively involved in championing people's participation in Uganda, through empowerment and civic education on various government policies and programs. Global experience shows that such efforts, especially when they are inclusive of poor and marginalized populations, can make an important contribution to achieving sustainable, effective democratic governance (PRIA 2003). However, the government has a negative perception of advocacy-oriented nongovernmental organizations (NGOs), compared to service delivery organizations. Official government speeches frequently criticize such organizations for providing information that could alarm the public. Nevertheless, the Ugandan government has recognized CSOs' good work and development contributions. The national Poverty Eradication Action Plan, for example, recognizes the role of CSOs as key partners in development and indicates that the government "enjoys productive partnerships with civil society in a number of areas" (PEAP 2006).

Pressure from Below Initiative

Pressure from Below (PFB) is a new initiative that promotes citizen participation in governance issues. It refers to a local community initiative, which emerged to question the traditional policy implementation paradigm and strategies for poverty eradication in Uganda (DENIVA 2008).

[1]The initiative aims at strengthening the capacity of citizens to understand and defend their civic rights, and promote responsive governance from their leaders. This concept promotes a bottom-up approach to decision making and resource allocation, leading to *democracy from below.*

In order to achieve democracy and good governance, the world needs to release the energy of ordinary people by promoting a strong civic culture and building on people's own initiatives.

Ordinary people, often referred to as the *grass roots* in the development arena, are the final intended beneficiaries of government policies and programs. However, it is a sad reality that many benefits never reach the ground, where the *grass roots* are found. In Uganda, for example, inequalities continue to grow, with a significant proportion of the national population receiving very limited benefits. Chronic poverty in Uganda is estimated at 20 percent, or more than 7 million (DRT 2005). These circumstances have led to various forms of vulnerabilities, including high mortality and maternity deaths; high levels of illiteracy; civil conflicts; corruption; and resource mismanagement.

Democracy and good governance create well-functioning and accountable political, judicial, and administrative institutions and processes—ones that citizens regard as legitimate, in which they participate, and by which they are empowered. Democracy constitutes an important prerequisite for successful economic, corporate, and socioeconomic governance, as it affirms the fundamental rights of citizens, the accountability of government to the governed, and the relative stability of the polity (Anan 1998).

In the context of the Uganda National Development Plan (NDP), good governance is defined as "the process of exercising the authority derived from the people, based on respect for the rule of law, observance of human rights, and diversity, emphasizing transparent, accountable, and responsive institutions, which foster inclusive participation so as to empower the governed to enjoy equitable and sustainable growth, employment and prosperity."[2] To this end, institutions that are mentioned in the constitution should be protected and kept in check through citizen involvement, hence DENIVA's coinage of the phrase *pressure from below.*

The *Pressure from Below* initiative emerged from a realization of the need to revisit national-level advocacy approaches, which were not having the desired effect, and to focus on enhancing the participation of ordinary citizens and promoting responsive governance at all levels. The aim was to encourage citizens to hold political leadership accountable for their actions. The initiative specifically targeted problems of corruption and mismanagement of resources, locally referred to as *eating*, which was growing rapidly at all levels despite the work of many organizations.[3]

Second, the initiative was developed as a contribution toward building a social network that could, in the long term, provide a democratic challenge to the state, starting with the community-level governance structures. The goal was for CSOs to act as *schools of democracy,* empowering their constituencies, enhancing citizenship skills, and teaching leaders how to organize, motivate people, and promote democratic discussion and participation (Diamond 1994).

The need to coordinate and empower DENIVA's constituency, within the governance thematic component, was earmarked as a basis for creating new alliances and interaction with other organizations. This in turn would empower a wider community and the development of civil society in Uganda (Dicklitch 1998). Therefore, DENIVA insists on *people power* as far as governance issues are concerned, as provided for in the Supreme Constitution. As a result, all program activities and initiatives are carried out with the active participation of DENIVA members, who in turn involve community members.

Pressure from Below targets elected leaders, including members of Parliament and local councilors at the village, parish, and subcounty and district levels. High-level bureaucrats are also targeted, because of the rampant level of corruption, often spearheaded by the technical staff of various departments involved in service delivery. DENIVA works with a range of intermediary organizations in different regions throughout the country, and provides an overall facilitative role, in terms of research and documentation, linking up with national, regional, and international initiatives and organizations.[4] PFB groups work in collaboration with all concerned stakeholders, including local government councilors, technical officers, local CSOs, and national advocacy organizations.

The *mission* of PFB is to facilitate capacity-building for communities by strengthening intermediary organizational management capacities; developing and strengthening strategic alliances; and enhancing lobbying and advocacy abilities through civic awareness. Its *vision* is an organized community with the capacity to demand and challenge local leadership to be responsive to community needs, through community participation and a sense of social responsibility. The main *objectives* of PFB are to: (1) strengthen organizational capacities of formal and informal institutions; (2) raise community awareness of their rights, roles, and responsibilities as citizens; (3) increase civic participation in social economic development; and (4) build the capacities of community groups in lobby and advocacy.

The overall strategy of PFB is raising awareness of citizen rights and responsibilities, and working through various empowerment approaches at the community level. Despite initial concerns about members of poor communities being unwilling to engage, community meetings quickly proved very successful in identifying voluntary leaders willing to take on the responsibility of ensuring further community mobilization and contact between communities and facilitators.

In the Walukuba-Masese division of the Jinja Municipality, for example, a social movement emerged to hold local leaders accountable for poor service delivery and the implementation of poverty eradication programs aimed at improving citizens' livelihoods. To strengthen community governance of this initiative, forty-two community facilitators, two from each of the twenty-one villages, were recruited and trained in participatory planning processes and the importance of citizen participation in community development. Additionally, information on national poverty reduction programs and monitoring and evaluation of selected government service delivery systems was provided. Communities were assisted and encouraged to seek further information and deliberate on how they could best benefit from such programs.

An executive committee of seven representatives was further selected to act as the policy arm of the community. In order to ensure productive interactions between the community and local leaders, DENIVA embarked on building the capacity of the identified community facilitators and leaders with regard to constitutional rights and other key policies and laws, such as the Local Government Act that clearly spells out the respective responsibilities of leaders and communities.

Key Results and Outcomes of the Initiative

Through the use of participatory methodologies, such as consultative meetings, baseline surveys, planning and feedback meetings, audio and written documentation, exposure visits, and the use of the media, the project has had some tremendous results. As far as DENIVA is concerned, the PFB initiative has been particularly outstanding in five areas: education, governance, health, conflict resolution, and water and sanitation. Through various interventions, mainly advocacy, CSOs have achieved key successes, which underscore their significance and justify the call for continued support and empowerment.

Peace and Conflict Resolution

Civil society organizations, especially in conflict-affected districts, have remained at the forefront, ensuring that the voices of the victims of armed conflict are heard. For example, in northeastern Uganda DENIVA, in partnership with Katakwi Urafiki Foundation (KAUFO), has long engaged with the local governments of Teso and Karamoja about the security situation, the plight of internally displaced persons (IDPs), and the concerns of the Karimojong. Through research, community-based dialogues, and radio talk shows, conflict resolution issues have been raised at the district, national, and international levels. As a result of continued CSO advocacy, the Teso-Karamoja conflict was brought back onto the public agenda and has become a topic of discussion in such forums as the NDP, Common-wealth People's Forum (CPF), and Annual National Advocacy Weeks. As the level of rights awareness and availability of information increases, cit-izens have the opportunity to challenge local leadership, especially by denying votes to unresponsive politicians. Some of the councilors in Katakwi, including the chairperson at local council V, lost the 2006 general election due to the administration's failure to prioritize people's plight in relation to peace and security.

Civil society organizations' action has resulted in the recognition of IDPs in Teso. This group, long forgotten and neglected, is now better informed and sensitized about their rights and can confidently demand what is due to them. For example, IDPs are reported to be demanding bet-ter living conditions in the camps, guarantees of security and social serv-ices in return areas, and resettlement packages to enable them to recover from the effects of long displacement and start new livelihoods. In Katakwi, IDPs have demanded the government consult them before for-mulating policies that affect them. As a result, in northern Uganda, CSOs are better known than the government in terms of effective service delivery and voicing the plight of citizen needs (DENIVA 2008).

Right to Education

The Development Network of Indigenous Voluntary Associations has worked with Kamwenge District Voluntary Development Organisation (KADIVDO) and the Kamwenge District Local Government to address factors that deter progress in education, particularly at the primary school level. Apart from gender disparities, in terms of enrollment and dropouts, other problems were identified, such as a weak government inspectorate and weak school governance associations. After only two years, a pilot intervention by KADIVDO, to address factors causing poor performance in eleven primary schools, has resulted in notable improvements. Both the children's ability to learn and teachers' motivation to teach has been greatly enhanced. It is reported that children have even begun to transfer from other schools to attend schools with tremendously improved per-formance. Concrete interventions have included a bylaw instructing all parents to provide lunch for schoolchildren and the introduction of sepa-rate toilet facilities for boys and girls, which has contributed to raising girls' enrollment rates.

Good Governance

In Kakuuto and Jinja, DENIVA has worked with subcounty-level CSOs to form pressure groups to challenge the quality of local government services. Through dialogues, open days, discussions, radio talk shows, and music and drama performances, citizens have been able to educate and sensitize people about their rights, and take their leaders to task to improve the quality of priority services, such as water, health, agriculture, infrastructure, education, food security, microfinance, and poverty services. In Jinja, citizens took pictures of collapsing classroom blocks at the local primary school and, after presenting evidence to local authorities and the municipal engineer, succeeded in having the building reconstructed and the corrupt contractor, responsible for the shoddy work, blacklisted.

Health

In Kakuuto, citizens were mobilized by the Kakuuto Network of Indigenous Voluntary Associations (KANIVA), and successfully demanded better health services. They expressed concern about the critical shortage of drugs in health centers, which forced them to buy drugs expensively from private clinics, and observed that drugs were being siphoned out of health facilities by health workers themselves. Through persistent pressure mounted by DENIVA and KANIVA, local government leaders acknowledged the problem and took action. The district chief administrative officer admitted that some health workers were unqualified, negligent of their duties, and misused drugs. Some offending health workers were fired while others were transferred to other stations. Local leaders negotiated with the Ministry of Health to expand the hospital and provide more drugs. In Jinja, community members succeeded in demanding the return of the local ambulance and driver, which was previously withdrawn from the community and used by town officials for attending weddings, burials and such, at the expense of the community's health demands.

In each of these success stories, recommendations were made and submitted for inclusion in district and national policy processes. To date, the greatest weakness is the lack of progress made beyond immediate solutions resulting from citizens' demands.

Analysis of the Current Situation

Despite the good intentions of the Constitution of the Republic of Uganda, in reality the level of citizen participation in most of the government policies and programs is limited and rarely meets citizen expectations. According to Midgley " . . . the state supports community participation, but does so for ulterior motives. Among these is the desire to use community participation for purposes of political and social control . . . and seeks to direct participatory aspirations through alternative mechanisms, which it has established and which it regards as satisfactory . . . and neutralizes spontaneous participatory activities and restricting them only to established mechanisms" (Midgley 1986).

The lack of information, knowledge, and understanding of the roles and expectations of citizens is another factor that has fueled political won't at the local and national levels. Citizens receive limited information about government services, implementing agencies, amount of resources invested, intended beneficiaries, and monitoring and evaluation requirements. As a result, poor services are delivered or nothing is provided at all, yet no one can ably challenge the agencies concerned, and corruption and resource mismanagement continue unchecked.

Numerous key government programs and policies, such as *Prosperity for All,* have been developed without citizens having any participation or say in their development, leading to lack of responsiveness to citizen priorities and implementation challenges. Lack of public understanding of the 2007 to 2010 Peace, Recovery, and Development Plan for Northern Uganda (PRDP), aimed at enabling Northern Uganda to recover from the social, economic, and political devastation resulting from the two decades of war, resulted in raised expectations and subsequent disappointment.

Gender and Building Political Will

The Constitution of the Republic of Uganda is very detailed about the rights of women. Chapter four on Protection and Promotion of Fundamental and Other Human Rights and Freedoms states that: (1) women shall be accorded full and equal dignity of the person with men; (2) the state shall provide the facilities and opportunities necessary to enhance the welfare of women to enable them to realize their full potential and advancement; (3) the state shall protect women and their rights, taking into account their unique status and natural maternal functions in society; (4) women shall have the right to equal treatment with men and that right shall include equal opportunities in political, economic, and social activities; and (5) women shall have the right to affirmative action for the purpose of redressing the imbalances created by history, tradition, or custom (Government of Uganda 1995).

In order to promote greater gender equity in political representation, legislation has also been passed requiring that women hold one third of council seats at the local government level and one seat per district in the national parliament. As a result, many women are vying for political positions and have become engaged in various initiatives at all levels in the governance structure. However, the gains, as a result of these opportunities, have not been felt in public decision making or in building political will for further reform on issues that directly affect them. The level of participation remains fairly dominated by men and patriarchal ideologies (Nyang'oro 1999).

As a result, there are some important gaps. However, there is strong evidence of legal and political will for promoting gender equity in Uganda. One gap is the failure of the government to pass the Domestic Relations Bill, which seeks to address women's property rights in marriage, sets the minimum age of marriage at eighteen, prohibits female genital mutilation, and seeks to protect women against marital rape. The bill has been lingering in parliament since the 1950s.

Strategies used for Building Political Will

In the context of the *Pressure from Below* initiative, strategies to build political will for greater citizen participation in governance processes have included: research and documentation, community organizing, dialogue and negotiation with local leaders, people's manifestos, forum theatre, lobbying and advocacy, and media.

Research and documentation

Research and documentation, including baseline surveys, participatory research, documentation, and dissemination of information, has been key to all levels of PFB activities. Such research is necessary to analyze the governance setting, understand the nature of available services, become familiar with political and administrative leadership, set priorities, and identify sources of funding. Evidence-based approaches are necessary to provide government officials with crucial information about communities and their priorities, and to generate information and analysis for presentation at the community level. Research findings and hard data are also key to advocacy activities and give credibility to efforts trying to exact accountability from government actors.

Community organization

The executive committee of PFB has weekly mandatory meetings with all forty-two village representatives, to identify community needs in relation to basic services, discuss emerging issues, and agree on possible solutions. Priority needs typically include health, education, crime and insecurity, and roads and transport infrastructure. Needs are prioritized, and volunteers are selected to coordinate further consultations with the communities, identify the local leaders responsible, and arrange for a meeting between the community and relevant officials. Regular community meetings maintain the momentum to exert pressure from below and act as a platform for information about what is happening during the week at the national government, local government, and community levels, or specific households. In this way, all are involved and informed about current perspectives, which are used to determine the next week's action or work plan (Fig. 7.1).

Figure 7.1. A Group of Citizens Attending One of the Community Meetings in the Bukedea District (The woman speaking is expressing her disappointment about the poor health services at the Malera Health Center. Women who are in labor and come here at night are asked to bring their own candles for light, even though there are supposed to be solar panels to provide light.)

Dialogue and negotiation with local leaders

Representatives of PFB promote regular dialogue with various local leaders, including village, parish, and district councilors. The primary aim is accountability from political leaders for their decisions and actions. Representatives of PFB also hold one-on-one meetings with technical and administrative personnel at the subcounty, municipal, district, and ministry levels to discuss more specific issues. Dialogue with authorities focuses on the issues raised by political leaders in their own political manifestos. For elected representatives, these are important opportunities for gaining capital and community support. Through experience community members have found that the year leading up to elections is a particularly important and effective time to negotiate with elected leaders.

People's manifestos

People's manifesto days follow an agenda established by the community, but usually focus on the government's own programs and policies, in order to ensure a relevant and productive debate and to achieve results. *People's manifesto days* typically focus on basic services, such as water and sanitation, health services, infrastructure, access to land, and security. The goal is to encourage dialogue and discussion, and to challenge and hold accountable those in power. Some pressure groups, such as those in the Rakai and Katakwi districts, have grown so strong that they hold members of parliament and line ministers accountable for poor services and unhonored campaign promises. The aim of this tool is to build solidarity with stakeholders and make sure that motives are not purely political, but aimed at ensuring that services are effectively and efficiently delivered to the beneficiaries.

Forum theatre

In order to best deliver messages to leaders during the *people's manifesto days,* communication tools such as music, dance, and drama serve a dual purpose as a form of entertainment too. Following acts that introduce issue areas in an entertaining manner, an interaction session is used for communities to question leaders with whom they are dissatisfied. This can be a difficult time for public authorities, because community members raise their grievances and demand answers. Leaders are frequently forced to apologize for poor services and promise future improvements. However, allegations can also be challenged by local leaders, especially if the intermediary organization has failed to provide accurate and up-to-date information to back up complaints. Music, dance, and drama are cheap, entertaining, and relevant tools for keeping leaders focused and maintaining community interest and participation. They are also important tools for sensitizing and educating the public (Fig. 7.2).

Lobbying and advocacy

Lobbying and advocacy involve maintaining pressure by using methods like persuasion, confrontation, and demands, and sometimes refusing to attend local meetings organized by the authorities, or even refusing to listen to the leaders. Pressure from Below groups seize every available opportunity to lobby, advocate, and advance their interests. They even use platforms created by other groups within their localities. Some groups have the capacity to lobby at the local and national levels, arranging meetings with members of parliament and ministers, in an attempt to resolve outstanding issues, especially in relation to land rights. The advantage of this is that community representatives are able to meet local leaders individually, forcing them to act accordingly. Usually these meetings are also used to assess if the leaders are strong, whether or not they have

Figure 7.2. A Group of Youth in the Katakwi District Expressing their Plight using Music, Dance, and Drama in the Magoro Internally Displaced Person's Camps

integrity, and if they were worth the vote or not. These actions have, in some cases, shaped future political decisions. In other cases, leaders have lost their political positions during elections because the people considered them irresponsible and unresponsive.

Media

Pressure from Below uses the media to expose both achievements and failures in public service delivery systems. The *name and shame platform* is used to expose corruption and rampant mismanagement of financial resources allocated for specific services at district or subcounty levels. All forms of media are interested in picking up these stories, including national newspapers and local FM radio stations. The latter are especially effective, because interactive talk shows are conducted in local languages, allowing locally affected community members to understand and participate during call-in sessions. It is a good strategy, because affected leaders, after hearing the information, usually quickly request being hosted on the same program to respond to allegations or promise action. The media creates a powerful incentive for leaders to respond to demands and quickly exposes the hidden motives of dishonest leaders.

How Political Will and Citizen–State Relations Evolved

The impacts of PFB have been rather complex, leading to both intended and unintended consequences. On a positive note, in many cases, citizen-state relations improved as a result of continuous pressure from the communities demanding quality services. After PFB representatives disseminated information through community meetings, radio talk shows, and people's manifesto days, large numbers of citizens became aware and began demanding change. Local leaders had no choice but to collaborate and share information with communities about implementation plans, budget allocations, and disbursements. These are now permanently displayed on local government notice boards. Monitoring and evaluation reports, prepared by PFB groups and submitted to elected representatives, have been a key source of information used for setting and achieving service delivery goals.

Although it has not passed into law, local governments are demanding that NGOs operating at the district level sign Memorandums of Understanding with local governments in order to operate in the area. This is likely to limit the role of intermediary organizations who promote civic activism. *Pressure from Below* groups have purposefully avoided formally registering as NGOs, thus avoiding formal procedures and controversy, and allowing them to remain purely community based and true to their missions and visions. Some PFB representatives have run for local office, aiming to enhance service delivery and influence the attitudes of other leaders. The results have been positive.

Many NGOs are also now working with PFB representatives, because they are seen as understanding the issues affecting their localities better than elected leaders. The representatives also have the ability to mobilize their communities to participate in development initiatives. In order to avoid compromising their ability to demand accountability from these actors, PFB groups have not entered into formal partnerships with NGOs. Instead, they remain a community movement playing an intermediary role and acting as the communities' *voice* and *eyes*.

On the other hand, PFB groups and the wider community are likely to miss opportunities for participation in government planning and budgeting cycles, because they have adopted a reactionary approach toward government policies and decisions. They do not proactively engage on issues before the implementation stage. This is mainly due to capacity gaps and lack of information and knowledge of the planning and budgeting processes. The lack of an institutionalized structure of CSO-government relationships and collaborations limits CSOs' involvement to the near end or final products of the processes. As a result, to the disappointment of government, CSOs end up making loud noises that sometimes lead to the reversal of certain decisions. This is the reason government is uncomfortable with advocacy organizations, referring to them as *talkers* who criticize government without necessarily providing alternative strategies. Due to the limited capacity of CSOs, which are not always diplomatic or tactful in their interactions, opportunities for collaboration have been lost. As a result, both groups accuse each other of lacking transparency and accountability.

In some districts, local-level government officials have sought to partner with PFB groups, so as to ensure proper monitoring of social service delivery. This happens in districts where the political leadership is objective and willing to work with CSOs as key stakeholders. In the Kamwenge district, the education department is working closely with the district CSO network to monitor school management and performance in the Universal Primary Schools, while the Katakwi district is collaborating with the Katakwi Urafiki Foundation, to monitor peace and conflict resolution processes at the community level. Both collaborations have yielded positive results.

Factors of Success and Key Lessons Learned
Community will and volunteerism
A key factor, which has led to success in creating positive political will, has been the communities' willingness to cooperate with intermediary

organizations and DENIVA, and to take up the initiative as their own. Because the initiative is aimed at addressing issues of direct relevance to the local population, the spirit of volunteerism was overwhelming. The PFB groups were able to mobilize communities without any financial facilitation.

Enabling legal and policy framework

A second important factor is the existing legal and policy framework that, despite some notable exceptions, is generally considered to be favorable and enabling to citizen participation.[5] The first and most important instrument providing a strong legal mandate is the 1995 constitution, which guarantees the freedom of association, expression, and participation of all citizens in peaceful activities, including the right to influence the policies and programs of government. The National Objectives and Directive states that, "the State shall be based on democratic principles which empower and encourage the active participation of all citizens at all levels in their governance; all public offices shall be held in trust for the people, and; all persons placed in positions of leadership and responsibility shall, in their work, be answerable to the people" (Government of Uganda 1995). It also declares that the state shall be guided by democratic principles of decentralization and devolution of government functions and powers to the people at appropriate levels, where they can best manage and direct their own affairs, and that civic organizations shall retain autonomy in pursuit of their declared objectives. The Local Government Act (1997) and Decentralization Policy have been developed in line with the above provisions. Other positive provisions are the Public Information Act, which gives all citizens the right to access information, and the Poverty Eradication Action Plan, which recognizes the role of CSOs as key partners in development.

Lessons Learned

Key lessons learned include the power of information, knowledge, and understanding of rights backed by enabling legal provisions. These provided a strong foundation to all the work done under the PFB initiative. Historically, political and social activism in Uganda has been limited, due to contextual factors. Now, many people are comfortable with exercising their rights, even when it means challenging the government. Public budgets are now easily accessible via notice boards, and central government releases are usually published in the two national daily newspapers.

Citizens, with limited external support, usually in the form of *facilitators*, can make a huge contribution toward achieving poverty reduction in Uganda. Citizens have proven that they are able to influence resource allocation and monitor the expenditures and the implementation of various government programs. Through Public Expenditure Tracking tools, citizens have been empowered to identify gaps and challenge leaders, who can no longer ignore them.

It is also now clear that citizens are a key vehicle for achieving good governance, specifically democracy, transparency, and accountability. They wield significant power and authority over public leaders and offices, because these positions are held in the trust of citizens. Raising the civic competence of ordinary people has rightly been coined as *reawakening the sleeping giant.*

A lot of resources are channeled through local governments, but, due to lack of proper checks and balances, most are misappropriated. The cases of Kakuto and Jinja have proven that once citizens are informed and empowered to be on the lookout for loopholes, health centers no longer run out of drugs, inspectors start visiting schools and submitting monitoring reports, and school management committees become functional.

Another lesson emerging from this work is that it is not easy to avoid getting involved in partisan politics, yet, such autonomy is essential for the authority and integrity of NGOs and other CSOs. This is a big risk for civil society groups operating at the local level, because they have limited skills and knowledge of how to manage political relationships (MWENGO and AACC 1993). Efforts are currently under way to sensitize the groups involved in activism to remain neutral and avoid actions that could lead to political alignment and/or alienation.

Due to the legal restrictions and the constant possibility of government sanctions, NGOs are no longer a significant force in influencing policy. This has made the NGO sector timid and curtailed its ability to contribute to the democratization process. Nongovernment organizations also face important internal and external challenges with regard to leadership, capacity, and financial sustainability. As a result, there is an enormous need to develop the spirit of community networks.

What Could Be Done Differently Next Time?

Despite the achievements made so far, gaps and challenges still remain. One of these is the lack of concerted civil society action involving the media, trade unionists, vendors, academics, professional associations, political party representatives, the women's movement, children's networks, NGOs, and community groups. The level of civic competence among the general population remains low, because attempts to build synergies, between various actors toward a common goal of active and informed citizenship, have not been realized as a result of fragmentation and lack of a united front among different parts of civil society. For PFB to have a lasting impact, sector-wide mobilization and collaboration are necessary.

Building the capacity of local governments to account to the people was overlooked in the initial phase of decentralization. It was difficult to build the will of the leaders to prioritize downwards accountability in line with people's expectations, because this was a new and unfamiliar concept for government authorities. However, it is clearly stipulated in the constitution. Many local leaders had no respect for illiterate community representatives, who made demands on them. On the other hand, citizens were very ambitious and sometimes demanded accountability from officials without knowledge of how best to manage the relationships involved. Strengthened capacities will be an important ongoing challenge, to ensure there is compliance with accountability and democratic principles at the local and national levels.

Mobilizing resources for initiatives, like PFB, can be quite difficult. Many donors are reluctant to fund processes that take a long time to create an impact. There is a need, therefore, to identify more development partners willing to support grassroots democracy, as opposed to huge investments at the national level, which lack a solid foundation and are often disconnected from ordinary citizens.

Finally, in order for vulnerable and marginalized groups—such as women, children and youth, the elderly, and people living with HIV/AIDS or physical disability—to participate in and benefit from democracy, their specific needs must be identified and prioritized. Disaggregated information about the priorities and needs of these groups is needed to sensitize local authorities and to influence the planning, budgeting, service delivery, and monitoring and evaluation processes done by local governments.

Replication

These strategies could potentially be replicated elsewhere, but on the condition that political circumstances are similar and legal provisions are conducive and supportive. The PFB approach requires a significant level of civic participation, in terms of depth and breadth, something that is not always easy to achieve, depending on the country context. Countries with strong social movements could replicate these methodologies, and even, through popular demand, overturn disabling laws and policy frameworks and transform political won't into political will.

Reforms

Uganda only returned to multiparty politics in 2005, and held its first multiparty presidential and parliamentary elections in 2006. As a result, political parties are still very weak and levels of political activism are very low. Local councils are mostly dominated by single-party supporters, with limited pressure from the opposition.

In Uganda, separation of power between the executive, legislative, and judicial branches of government is lacking. The executive branch dominates the national parliament, and, as a result, parliamentarians are not able to independently defend the interests of their constituencies. It remains difficult for members of parliament, whether they belong to the ruling party or an opposition party, to challenge or criticize the government. Those who do so are labeled as *rebels* or dismissed as *night dancers,* which refers to people believed to be possessed by spirits who leave their homes at night, running through gardens, graveyards, or people's homes, causing destruction to people and property.

There is an urgent need to address gender issues by not just promoting the *inclusion of women* in sector policies, but *seriously analyzing the underlying reasons for persistent gender subordination and unequal access to public resources, services, and benefits* (Hollands et al. 1998). The women's movement in Uganda continues to face political won't when it comes to passing legislation to empower women and advance women's rights. The Domestic Relations Bill, which has been stuck in parliament since 1959, is a case in point.

Conclusion

Pressure from Below is just one potential strategy for building the political will of leaders to be responsive to citizens, promote citizen participation, and ensure the effective management and distribution of public resources. This approach has thus far provided some positive results, including enhanced levels of citizen participation and improvement in civic awareness. However, further reflection is required regarding the need to promote better networking among community groups, build capacities for engagement with different political actors, and establish independent systems of accountability to better ensure efficient and effective service delivery. The work of DENIVA has focused on ensuring basic rights in the areas of conflict resolution, education, governance, health, sanitation, and water. Through the use of strategies such as community organization, consultative meetings, participatory research and planning, public feedback meetings, audio and written documentation, exposure visits, and the use of the media, the project has achieved some tremendous results.

Project activities have succeeded in putting the plight of conflict-affected communities in northeast Uganda back on the public agenda. The project has led to enhanced access to water and sanitation in Kakuuto, improved security and access to health services in Jinja, and greater government involvement in the education sector, improved school performance, and stronger parent-teacher relations in the district of Kamwenge.

Decentralization has provided precious space for the manifestation of political will and activism. However, many priority social groups, including women, children, youth, the elderly, and people with disabilities, still suffer from social and political exclusion.

There are important questions for future research. These include: if and how social networks can build and maintain political will for participatory governance in the long term?; how participatory governance breakthroughs at the community level can serve to instigate change at the national level?; and how best can political will be nurtured and maintained in the midst of fundamental political disagreements?

References

Ahikire, Josephine. 2007. *Localised or Localising Democracy: Gender and the Politics of Decentralisation in Contemporary Uganda.* Kampala, Uganda: Fountain Publishers.

Angey, Silvia and Christina Nilsen. 2004. *Civil Society Reviews, Comments and Reports: The Financial Sustainability of NGOs in Uganda: Successes, Challenges and Prospects.* Kampala, Uganda.

Annan, Kofi A. 1998. Partnerships for a Global Community, as quoted in the Good Governance Paper for the National Development Plan, Kampala: Uganda.

Development Network of Indigenous Voluntary Associations (DENIVA). 2008. Enabling Democratic Local Governance Environments for Fighting Poverty and Inequality: A Case of Walukuba – Masese in Jinja Municipality, Uganda. DENIVA.

Diamond, Larry (ed.). 1994. *Political Culture and Democracy in Developing Countries: Textbook Edition.* Boulder, Colorado: Lynne Rienner.

Dicklitch, Susan. 1988. *The Elusive Promise of NGOs in Africa: Lessons from Uganda.* Basingstoke: Palgrave.

Development Research and Training (DRT). 2005. *Chronic Poverty in Uganda: The Policy Challenges*. Kampala, Uganda: DRT.

Hollands, Glenn and Gwen Ansell. 1998. *Winds of Small Change: Civil Society Interaction with the African State*. Proceedings of multilateral workshops on good governance, sustainable development, and democracy in Graz, Austria 1995.

Government of Uganda. 1995. *Constitution of the Republic of Uganda*. Kampala, Uganda: Government of Uganda.

Government of Uganda. 1997. *Local Government Act*. Kampala, Uganda: Government of Uganda.

Kwesiga, J.B. and Namisi Harriet. 2006. Issues in Legislation for NGOs in Uganda. *NGO Accountability: Politics, Principles and Innovations*. London: Earthscan.

Marblestone, Clare. 2005. The History of Uganda. Unpublished.

Midley, J. 1986. Community Participation: History, Concepts, and Controversies. In *Community Participation, Social Development and the State*, ed. J. Migley, 13–44. London: Methuen.

Ministry of Local Government. 1992. *Local Government Perspectives*. Kampala, Uganda: Ministry of Local Government.

Ministry of Local Government. 2006. *Decentralisation Policy Framework*. Kampala, Uganda: Ministry of Local Government.

MWENGO and All Africa Conference of Churches. 1993. *Civil Society, the State & African Development in the 1990s: Report of Study and Workshop on the Receding Role of the State in African Development and the Emerging Role of NGOs*. Harare: MWENGO; Nairobi: All Africa Conference of Churches.

Namisi, Harriet. 2008. Promoting CSO Legitimacy, Independence and Credibility. Background paper prepared for the Regional GO Accountability Conference. Kampala, Uganda.

Nyang'oro Julius E. 1999. *Civil Society and Democratic Development in Africa: Perspectives from Eastern and Southern Africa*. Harare, Zimbabwe: MWENGO.

Participatory Research in Asia. 2003. *Governance Where People Matter*. New Delhi, India: Participatory Research in Asia.

Uganda National Bureau of Statistics. 2005. *Spatial Trends of Poverty and Inequality in Uganda: A Tool for Policy Making 2002–2005*. Kampala, Uganda: Uganda National Bureau of Statistics.

Uganda Governance and Monitoring Project. 2007. *Citizen Mobilization and the Activism for Good Governance: the Bumpy Road Ahead*. Kampala, Uganda: Uganda Governance and Monitoring Project.

Notes

1. This work is funded by the Ford Foundation and MS (Danish Association for International Cooperation) Uganda.

2. The NDP is the overall planning framework for guiding public action on development and poverty reduction in Uganda. It was formerly known as the Poverty Eradication Action Plan (PEAP).

3. The Uganda Debt Network, for example, has implemented successful programs on community resource monitoring and holding leaders accountable for many years.

4. These include First Bicycle Information Organisation, the Katakwi Urafiiki Foundation in Eastern Uganda, Kakuuto Network of Indigenous Voluntary Associations in Central Uganda, the Kamwenge District NGO Network in the west, and Kitgum NGO Forum in the north.

5. For example, some unfavorable and disabling laws include the 2006 NGO Amendment Act, the Anti Terrorism Act, and parts of the Penal Code and Police Act.

CHAPTER 8

Beyond Lip Service: Using Social Contracts to Achieve Participatory and Accountable Governance in the Philippines

Emmanuel C. Areño

Introduction and Background

Models of participatory governance were introduced in the Philippines after the People Power Revolution of 1986 that toppled a dictatorship. The Revolutionary Constitution of 1987 emphasized the importance of people's empowerment and acknowledged the vital role of civil society in achieving nonviolent political change. However, despite these revolutionary events power relations and political practices in the Philippines have changed very little, and by the late 1990s graft and corruption issues reemerged as a key political and development issue. From the village, municipal, and provincial level up to the national level, politics is characterized by patriarchy, patronage, and elite capture. While a few *islands of good governance* can be found at the local level, the Philippines, with its 7,100 islands, is far from becoming a *nation of good governance*. Elections have been regularized since 1987, but they are frequently flawed exercises, where money and political dynasties prevail, often through illicit means. Ordinary citizens, many of whom are living in poverty, are expected to vote and then act as spectators of development. A culture of silence has served to perpetuate power inequities. However, widespread discontent over these inequities has been the trigger for change.

Philippine civil society organizations (CSOs) initiated the use of social contracts, or covenant-type agreements, between citizen-voters, politicians, and bureaucrats, in order to promote transparent, participatory, and accountable governance. Such social contracts have since been used

135

in many areas of the Philippines to proactively promote performance-based, platform-oriented politics and active citizenship.

Social contracts between the *governors and the governed* are rooted in long-standing moral and political philosophies, such as Rousseau, but attuned to contemporary demands for social justice and equitable social relationships. Social contracts in the Philippines take the form of manifestos, covenant agreements, memoranda of cooperation, or resolutions accepted by multiple stakeholders. They are tools for social accountability initiated by citizen groups to hold public officials, politicians, and service providers accountable for their conduct and performance, in terms of service delivery, mandated responsibilities, and public obligations. Social contracts ensure that over time dialogue exists between civil society and government actors. They also guarantee that public officials are aware of and fulfill their social responsibilities.

Social contracts are also intended to encourage active citizenship and provide a forum for citizen participation, leading to a more balanced relationship between politicians and civil society and allowing the voice of the disadvantaged to be heard. Philippine CSOs have used social contracts in conjunction with innovative modes of citizen engagement, emphasizing the participation of a critical mass that can create social pressure. Performance oriented leadership is promoted as citizen-voters begin to choose leaders, not because of *good speeches*, but for their *performance and proven capacities* to lead and govern.

The Social Contract Process

There are five stages of the social contract process: (1) people's agenda-setting; (2) candidates' forum; (3) covenant signing; (4) citizen monitoring of the performance of public officials; and (5) institutionalization of the social contract.

Months before local elections, local CSOs are organized, voter education activities are undertaken, and through a series of village-level consultations, a *People's Agenda* is prepared. The people's agenda is addressed to the political candidates, and written as a bold manifesto of the collective, unified, prioritized concerns of grassroots groups, such as women, youth, farmers, fisherfolk, laborers, and vendors.

The people's agenda is presented to politicians during a *candidates' forum,* which is organized by the coordinating CSO in conjunction with a wide range of multisectoral stakeholders, including churches, peasant or labor organizations, media, sector professionals, and academics. The forum is publicized and promoted through posters and announcements in public places, such as market, churches, and government buildings. It attracts large numbers of citizens and journalists who ensure broad media coverage.

At the forum, political candidates are asked to respond to the people's agenda. Following the forum, candidates are then asked to *sign a covenant*, committing themselves to a clean, honest, accountable, meaningful, and peaceful (CHAMP) electoral exercise. This covenant also stipulates a contract between candidates and the voting public, which, if elected into office, holds them accountable through the use of performance evaluations.

During the election campaign, candidates' promises are documented for use later in exacting accountability. After elections, CSOs coordinate *citizen monitoring* of elected public officials' performance. Results of the monitoring are presented and discussed at public feedback sessions attended by thousands of citizens. These are conducted one hundred days after the assumption of office and every six months thereafter. Again, the media plays a critical role in broadcasting feedback sessions and reporting on the progress of the development platforms, programs, and projects, or inaction of the public officials concerned.

As a result of CSO lobbying, some model local government units have begun to formalize the *covenants* signed during the election process into binding contracts and to institutionalize performance accounting mechanisms through official ordinances. Thereby, these have become regular performance evaluation mechanisms integrated into the public administration cycle and not limited to election periods that happen only every three years.

The Local Government Code: A Revolutionary Law

The Local Government Code (LGC) of 1991 legitimized processes of people's empowerment and participation. Among the salient features of this law are the three Ds: *decentralization* of powers, *devolution* of services, and *democratization*. The latter led to the creation of more democratic spaces and avenues for direct citizen participation through local development councils and local special bodies, such as school boards, health boards, peace and order councils, and bids and awards committees. The law mandates that at least one fourth of the total membership of Local Development Councils must come from civil society.

Under the LGC, *barangays*, or marginalized villages, have been allowed, for the first time, to control and manage their own budgets. The LGC also allows citizens to directly allocate 20 percent of development funds derived from the internal revenue allocations (IRAs) of the *barangays*. These funds support small demand-driven projects, such as small potable water systems, livelihood programs, and day care centers. Funds have also been earmarked for gender and development purposes.

The LGC has created significant opportunity for democratic participation, self-governance, and control of development resources at the local level. However, more than ten years after its adoption, official reports showed that less than 55 percent of *barangays* in the country had actually maximized these opportunities (Philippines DILG 2001). Since that time, little has changed. The major reason is that marginalized *barangays* lack the capacity to assume responsibility, especially in development planning, prioritization, and budgeting. Many still depend on municipal budget officers or other local government technical staff to prepare their annual investments plans, or they simply rehash previous budgets without considering the changing issues and needs of the locality.

In many areas where CSOs are strong, however, greater opportunities for empowerment and participation have paved the way for structured frameworks for productive civil society relationships with the government. The LGC has brought about gradual changes in society and citizens' expectations. Governance is no longer seen as a process purely controlled by elected executives, legislators, or appointed public officials, and the participation of citizens and civil society is considered crucial.

The Covenant for Transparency and Accountability: The Iloilo Caucus of Development NGOs Experience[1]

A pioneer in the use of social contracts is the provincial network of CSOs called the Iloilo Caucus of Development NGOs (ICODE). The key model of ICODE is the *Kwentahan Hindi Kwentohan,* which literally means *accountability not lip service,* and is a performance evaluation and public disclosure and feedback mechanism conducted through citizen enquiry. The Covenant for Transparency and Accountability is a social contract designed to formally bind elected representatives to their promises and ensure regular interactive dialogue between citizens and the concerned government official. The Social Contract process is harmonized with the Philippine Local Public Administration (LPA) cycle in order to facilitate its acceptance by local government administrators (Fig. 8.1).

In 1994, to seize the opportunities for active participation in governance and development presented by the passing of the LGC, ICODE refocused its program on local governance, with a particular emphasis on sustainable development, participatory planning and monitoring, and public ethics and values education.

The Covenant for Transparency and Accountability began as a local initiative on the island of Luzon. When representatives from the small, poor municipality of Batad, in the Iloilo province, were exposed to the experience, they vowed to replicate it in their own municipality and sought the assistance of ICODE.

During the local government elections of 1998, with start-up support from local resource agencies and in partnership with the Parish Pastoral Council for Responsible Voting (PPCRV), a church-based organization

Figure 8.1. Filipino Citizens Participating in the Social Contract Process

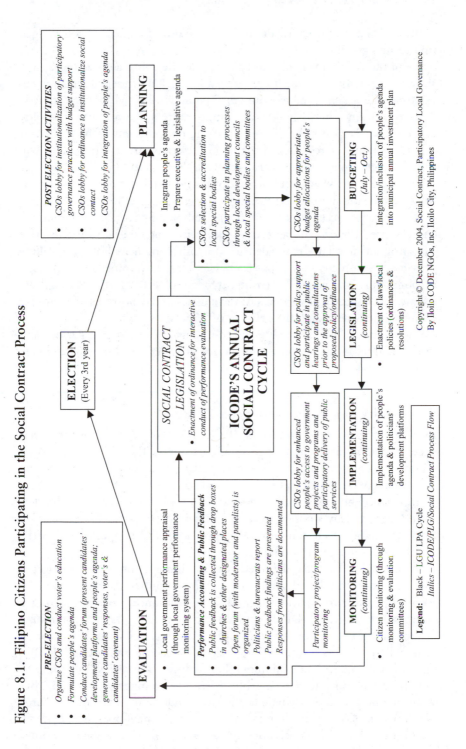

PRE-ELECTION
- *Organize CSOs and conduct voter's education*
- *Formulate people's agenda*
- *Conduct candidates' forum (present candidates' development platforms and people's agenda; generate candidates' responses, voter's & candidates' covenant)*

POST ELECTION ACTIVITIES
- *CSOs lobby for institutionalization of participatory governance practices with budget support*
- *CSOs lobby for ordinance to institutionalize social contact*
- *CSOs lobby for integration of people's agenda*

ELECTION
(Every 3rd year)

PLANNING
- Integrate people's agenda
- Prepare executive & legislative agenda
- *CSOs selection & accreditation to local special bodies*
- *CSOs participate in planning processes through local development councils & local special bodies and committees*

BUDGETING
(July – Oct.)
- *CSOs lobby for appropriate budget allocations for people's agenda*
- Integration/inclusion of people's agenda into municipal annual investment plan

SOCIAL CONTRACT LEGISLATION
- *Enactment of ordinance for interactive conduct of performance evaluation*

ICODE'S ANNUAL SOCIAL CONTRACT CYCLE

LEGISLATION
(continuing)
- *CSOs lobby for policy support and participate in public hearings and consultations prior to the approval of proposed policy/ordinance*
- Enactment of laws/local policies (ordinances & resolutions)

EVALUATION
- Local government performance appraisal (through local government performance monitoring system)

Performance Accounting & Public Feedback
- *Public feedback is collected through drop boxes in churches & other designated places*
- *Open forum (with moderator and panelists) is organized*
- *Politicians & bureaucrats report*
- *Public feedback findings are presented*
- *Responses from politicians are documented*

IMPLEMENTATION
(continuing)
- *CSOs lobby for enhanced people's access to government projects and programs and participatory delivery of public services*
- Implementation of people's agenda & politicians' development platforms

MONITORING
(continuing)
- *Participatory project/program monitoring*
- Citizen monitoring (through monitoring & evaluation committees)

Legend: Black – LGU LPA Cycle
Italics – ICODE/PLG/Social Contract Process Flow

Copyright © December 2004, Social Contract, Participatory Local Governance
By Iloilo CODE NGOs, Inc, Iloilo City, Philippines

with local chapters nationwide, ICODE organized a massive voter education campaign and subsequently facilitated a candidates' forum. The outcome of the election was fair and clean, and the conscientisized electorate showed maturity in their choices of leaders. Many independent-minded, poor candidates emerged as winners. The newly elected mayor toppled a dynasty, but once in office he faced empty coffers and municipal employees in an uproar over the discovery of the nonpayment of benefit remittances. The mayor recognized the need for transparency in dealing with this difficult situation. He recruited ICODE as a technical advisor and, with the help of PPCRV and other CSOs and local champions, a strategy for a *Participatory Local Governance* program was crafted.

The program received support from Diakonia-Sweden, an international church-based donor, who agreed to fund the pilot program for five years. The program was later expanded to four other municipalities in the Iloilo province.[2] The focus of the program was local government transparency, accountability, and active citizenship. Its main objectives were to establish a Municipal Assembly of residents to raise issues and concerns, and make recommendations regarding the delivery of basic services; to set up systems of transparency and accountability and mechanisms to assess the performance of public officials and government service providers; and to capacitate and encourage stakeholders' active participation in local governance processes.

Community Organizing and Capacity Building

In order to meet these objectives, ICODE, which had significant experience in community organizing, sought to apply these principles to the realm of local governance. This involved mobilizing community volunteers to carry out participatory appraisals of the local government's compliance with the LGC and preparing an inventory of key stakeholders, including Barangay Councils, CSOs, and community-based organizations (CBOs), including church-based organizations and cooperatives, for the purpose of constituency building.

A basic gap that was identified was the limited competencies of community leaders to take advantage of the opportunities offered by the LGC for meaningful participation in the local governance process. In order to address this gap, ICODE organized training sessions for community groups on the content of the LGC and, in particular, its provisions for citizen and civil society participation in Local Development Councils (LDCs) and special bodies. The trainings also included strategies and tools for holding public officials accountable. After the trainings, CSOs and CBOs were encouraged to participate in the LDC and to take part in community development planning and annual investments planning processes. Different sectoral groups, such as peasants, urban poor, fisherfolks, youth, women, and cooperatives, were mobilized.

In accordance with the Covenant for Transparency and Accountability, agreed upon during the election campaign, the mayor of Batad, along with other elected leaders, public officials, and civil servants, was called upon to report to the public on the implementation of campaign promises, plans, and accomplishments. Thanks to local CSOs' mobilization efforts, there was significant turnout at these public reporting events, with members of churches, CBOs, schools, and ordinary citizens coming in droves and packing the town plaza.

Key Strategies

The social contract process is based on five key strategies of participatory governance. These strategies are: citizen engagement and participation; public disclosure and transparency; citizens' right to access information; objective and rigorous assessment tools; and continuous and sustained application.

The first, and most essential, strategy is *citizen engagement and participation*. Ensuring the participation of a critical mass of citizens is crucial to attracting and influencing political actors. Civil society organizations involved in this initiative understood the importance of mobilizing thousands of citizen-voters, and the presence of this critical mass earned the respect and attention of politicians. Citizen participation begins with the peoples' agenda-setting process and is sustained throughout the election campaign and subsequent performance evaluation. Through the process, citizens learn about their rights and responsibilities.

Second, the process ensures *transparency and public disclosure* through public reporting, feedback, and discussion sessions. As described above, according to the social contract process, every six months elected leaders are obliged to publicly report on their performance with regard to campaign promises. They are also required to present their executive and legislative plans to the public. These can be used as baselines for performance accounting. Such activities have pressured politicians to constantly review their platforms and have triggered the political will to deliver their promises. Revenue and expenditure reports are disclosed and posted in public places to inform citizens about the status of and efficiency of how public funds are used. On the other hand, CSOs are required to give reports on their programs and projects, especially those using government funds.

Third, citizens have the *right to access public information*, such as local government fiscal plans, project documents, and performance and progress reports. Citizen access to public documents is clearly stipulated in the social contract. Hence, municipal employees, such as the treasurer, and budget and accounting officers are also expected to make information, including revenue and expenditure reports, accessible to the public. Citizen organizations have used this information for budget advocacy.

The role of the media, with regard to public disclosure and access to information, is critical. Publications and media coverage ensure that information is publicly available and reaches a much wider audience.

Fourth, *objective and rigorous assessment tools,* such as public expenditures tracking, poverty indicators monitoring, and evidence-based advocacy, are used to give teeth to the social contract. Civil society organizations have been trained in the use and application of user-friendly participatory monitoring and evaluation tools, tracking systems, and techniques for lobbying and working with local finance committees. Manuals and primers on how to use such tools have also been published and used as guides for replication.

Finally, to ensure *continuous and sustained application of mechanisms,* a number of Philippine CSOs, in partnership with church-based organizations and local government units, have used their creative powers in organizing ordinary citizens to maximize the constitutional and statutory mandates. Popular democratic gatherings and electoral forums have been transformed into avenues for social accountability. By organizing and facilitating candidates' forums, CSOs have transformed traditional political rallies into interactive dialogues between politicians and thousands of citizen-voters. These focus on agendas identified and prepared by the people. Care is taken to ensure that such activities are appropriately attuned to the local context. Initially, nonthreatening approaches, such as voter education and simple candidates' forums, are employed. As the process and local partners mature, more purposive and elaborate methodologies, such as citizen monitoring, performance accounting, and local ordinances, are also applied.

Results and Outcomes of the Initiative

These local initiatives have proved very successful and the process has inspired, empowered, and given hope to previously disillusioned citizens. Voters, who were once timid, have begun to speak up and assert their rights. They have witnessed their collective voices being listened to by politicians. Civil society has successfully negotiated meaningful and guaranteed participation in decision-making processes.

Aside from the corruption prevention function, social pressures have made politicians accede to popular demand for transparency and accessibility, lest they lose electoral support. The use of social contracts has succeeded in arresting a gamut of malpractices, such as embezzlement of public funds, tardiness or absenteeism, and poor planning and budgeting. Even in very challenging contexts, creativity and persistence, on the part of CSOs, has won over citizens and government officials.

Social contracts and participatory local governance initiatives have strong gender equity components, and have sought to promote women's rights and equitable access to political power. Philippine politics traditionally were male dominated. Recent years have seen a modest increase in women's access to elected office at the local and national levels, rising from just 8 percent in 1995 to 21 percent in 1998 and 25 percent in 2007 (Philippines–Canada LGSP 2001). Due to women's equitable access to trainings and exposure visits, a number of women were elected into office as village chiefs or council members. They are also taking on more leadership roles, which used to be male dominated. For example, an alliance on health governance, made up of nine local government units, is now headed by a newly elected female mayor, Elvira Alarcon, who is a staunch advocate of transparent, participatory, and accountable governance.

Analysis of Filipino Political Won't and Will

Despite numerous trailblazing initiatives at the local level, the Philippines has plummeted in the area of government transparency and accountability. Over the past several years, the country has consistently ranked low in Transparency International's Corruption Index, and is still plunging. Philippines' ranking dropped from 131 in 2007 to 141 in 2008, putting it in the company of Iran and Yemen.

The lack of resolution of large-scale corruption at the national level, such as fraudulent election results, procurement scams, diversion of funds, and ghost infrastructure projects, has rendered local efforts insignificant. The classic example was the former president Estrada, who was convicted of plundering billions of pesos, but was pardoned by the current President Arroyo a month after the final verdict. Such acts have led to growing demoralization in the lower rungs of the government and the justice system. It is ironic that local leaders are the ones calling on the national government to emulate what they are doing at the municipal level.

Despite continued calls for more decentralized governance and greater local autonomy, the budget continues to be controlled by the central government and used for patronage by an increasingly unpopular regime. Civil society organizations continue their endless struggle for structural and governance reforms.

Overcoming Lack of Political Will

Lack of political will poses a number of important challenges. For example, in areas where the social contract process did not initially succeed, or where external support was not sustained, initiatives were unable to overcome political won't. Social contracts faltered where politicians were too dominant and well entrenched, or where political win-ability continued to be based on money, fame, or even coercion, rather than performance. In one location, for example, a well-respected mayor who pursued a platform based on performance, honesty, and transparency lost her bid to the wife of a rich congressman, who belonged to a political dynasty. In other cases, CSOs were intimidated, paid off, or compromised by indebtedness to money politics or the *compadrazgo*, or patronage system. In such circumstances, CSOs are no longer effective pressure groups and by default citizens lose. In Iloilo city, which after months of lobbying work finally agreed to experiment with social contracts in June 2008, political won't was due to the complacency of elected officials and the absence of strong pressure groups.

The main obstacle to political will is the feeling of powerlessness and resignation to graft and corruption. Even after the success of the Batad and Bingawan experiences, there are still some who frown at the initiative. One newly elected legislator, who was not part of the historical process, suggested repealing the practice, which she saw as too demanding for elected officials. However, she was met with strong opposition from the incumbents and the CSOs that had championed the cause. Because the initiative was already institutionalized, public demand prevailed and all elected officials are now obliged to render a performance report.

Persistence and creativity

Building support for transparent and accountable governance was a slow process. Initially, only a handful of local chief executives were willing to institutionalize the social contract. Even officers of the DILG were not convinced that it could work. Thanks to the determined efforts of civil society advocates and their local government allies, the social contract process has been implemented and, in some cases, institutionalized. The results have proven that the mechanism can work and is especially effective when integrated into local government management structures. In the end, it was citizens' persistent political will that made reforms for good governance happen.

Due to lack of political will, social contract initiatives require the constant infusion of creative ideas. If mechanisms become a routine exercise, there is a danger that they will become bland and lose their popular appeal.

Institutionalization

A major challenge to countering lack of political will is institutionalizing the social contract process, making it a regular affair, not limited to the election period that happens every three years. Civil society organizations must take the lead in agreeing with local authorities on reporting requirements, and ensuring that unresolved issues are incorporated into the regular legislative and executive sessions' agendas, and dealt with in a timely fashion.

In Batad, when the performance reporting and feedback process became popular among constituents, local champions negotiated for a more incisive statute, a municipal resolution systematizing the signing of covenants by elected officials. The mayor of Batad was poor in rhetoric, but became well respected because of his no-nonsense advocacy for good governance. Eventually he issued an executive order for regular candidates' forums to be facilitated by independent election watch groups from the church (PPCRV) and CSOs (ICODE), and earned the proud title of *Most Transparent Mayor.*

Initial efforts to make municipal resolutions into more binding and lasting ordinances were blocked by conservative legislators, who were fearful of radical reforms. In 2002, the initiative garnered the recognition of a prestigious national awards-giving body, *Galing Pook* or Exemplary Places. This renewed efforts to institutionalize the social contract mechanism through an ordinance; however, again these efforts failed.

In 2004, Bingawan, which had replicated the experience in 2001, had the distinction of institutionalizing the social contract process through an ordinance. The political will of a *converted* mayor, with the support of young progressive politicians hailing from CSOs, made the difference. The ordinance was widely accepted by all political parties and contenders. It became a powerful manifesto that led to Bingawan winning a grant from The World Bank/Asia Foundation, for a project called *Accountability Not Lip Service.* Inspired by Bingawan, other municipalities, including Batad, have begun to pass their own ordinances, or resolutions.

Adopting a nonthreatening approach

The Iloilo Caucus of Development NGOs strategized a nonthreatening approach that encouraged politicians to be open to transparent, participatory, and accountable governance, and gradually compelled them to sign social contracts and covenants. *Anticorruption* terminology was purposefully not used, because it was too intimidating and elicited apprehension and resistance from politicians.

People's agendas were initiated to bring politicians closer to constituents and to inform them of grassroots' priorities. Instead of waiting for the politicians to do the talking and then criticizing, women, youth, farmers, and laborers proactively presented their issues and concerns in the people's forum, which was organized by CSOs. They presented their agenda to the politicians, urging them to respond and prioritize these concerns in their political platforms.

Building citizen competencies

Philippine CSOs, working in participatory governance, frequently identify major challenges, such as a lack of volunteers, especially in the provinces, for monitoring and oversight; a lack of competencies and tools to engage with the public sector; and a lack of localized mechanisms for participatory

Figure 8.2. Covenant Signing is Witnessed by Multisectoral Representatives in Bingawan, Iloilo, 2004

governance. To address these challenges citizen competencies must be developed and large constituencies of mature, responsible, and active citizen-voters, committed to instituting change, need to be built. In order to build capacity from the bottom up, ICODE has undertaken massive *voter education* and active citizenship training at the village and municipal levels. It has gone so far as to develop a School of Local Governance, in partnership with Central Philippine University, aimed at developing knowledge and skills, and promoting interaction among CSOs, the government, and private sector partners. Over the past five years, the training has produced hundreds of audacious advocates calling for reform.

Multistakeholder partnerships

Multistakeholder partnerships are essential for promoting and implementing participatory governance. Developing links with responsible media actors is especially important for ensuring public information-sharing and stimulating public interest. Collaborative partnerships among CSOs, the media, church groups, academia, youth groups, people's organizations, and private sector groups create important synergies. They result in formidable collective strength and a level of influence that no single partner could achieve on their own.

Critical collaboration

Collaborative relations between CSOs and government actors are seen in the nonpartisan posture maintained in local politics. Maintaining a neutral, nonpartisan stance has allowed CSOs to take on the role of technical advisor, mentor, mediator, and development partner. The ICODE has worked with government *allies* and influenced government attitudes through lobbying and advocacy activities. It also has helped local government partners in developing good governance projects, emphasizing the concrete benefits and incentives for citizens and government actors. Through principles of negotiation and critical collaboration, CSOs have been able to *propose* solutions and be proactive in their role as policy advocates. At the same time, CSOs have continued to stand up to government and *oppose* government actions when necessary, for example, in the case of government efforts to establish environmentally destructive coal-fired power plants in various places throughout Iloilo.

Creating social pressures to muster political will

Initially about 50 percent of politicians participated in public forums organized by ICODE and its partners. However, over time absence from such forums raised suspicions of nonperformance, or hiding from anomalies, and elicited negative public reactions, especially in small towns. As a result of social pressure, local politicians' attendance in small town forums is now reported at between 95 and 100 percent. The social pressure of citizen-voters consistently reminds governing politicians about their accountability and covenant commitments. Social pressures must be continuously exerted, lest complacency sets in and politicians give in to the temptation to misuse the power entrusted to them.

How Political Will/Citizen–State Relations Evolved as a Result of the Initiative

Levels of political will and citizen–state relations have improved as a result of the institutionalization of the public reporting and feedback mechanism. Two mayors have attributed the large amounts of money and projects obtained by their municipalities to having transparent and accountable leaders and systems in place. Donors and contractors are more interested when they know their investments are safe from inefficiencies and leakages, under the watchful eye of an engaged public. Newly-elected Bingawan Mayor, Matt Palabrica, expressed gratitude when he realized the effects of more projects and grants from both the national government and international donors, such as the World Bank.

These positive developments have led to CSOs and local authorities becoming agents of social marketing and spreading the word that participatory governance works. Peer-to-peer campaigning has proved very effective in convincing local governments and politicians, from other towns and provinces, to emulate the positive experience of social contracts. One pioneer in the use of social contracts, the mayor of the small town of New Lucena, has become an ardent advocate of the approach and now offers cash awards and recognition to local best practices in participatory and transparent governance.

Braggarts watch out!

The delivery of promises is vigilantly monitored by citizens. During a recent election campaign, one candidate carelessly promised village chiefs that she would buy each one a cell phone unit, when she was elected to office. She eventually won and was forced to shell out for the phones from her own pocket, because such items cannot be paid for with public funds. After a poor performance, she lost badly in her reelection bid. While newly elected politicians may be excused for not reaching optimal performance during their first term, there can be no more excuses during succeeding terms as citizens continually keep track of their performance.

Keeping the covenant: preserving a good public reputation

While generally private matters, or under-the-belt accusations, are not tolerated in public feedback sessions, matters of immorality that are public in nature are routinely raised. In one town, a police motorbike was stolen by thieves, right at the municipal police station. When citizens discovered that policemen were in the station watching pornographic videos at the time of the theft, they publicly voiced their outrage, and successfully pressured the mayor to file for the dismissal of the officers in question. In another case, due to a citizen complaint, a municipal treasurer was dismissed, and later obliged to reimburse the municipality for public funds used for personal purposes. Such actions, even if minor, give citizens a sense of influence and confidence in the responsiveness of the system.

In summary, persistent efforts to promote participatory governance and the use of social contracts in particular, have had many positive results. Citizens now have a greater awareness of local governance affairs, and citizen participation in development planning, budgeting, implementation, and monitoring has been enhanced. The delivery of basic services is faster and more effective, and there is now a greater sense of public servanthood and responsiveness on the part of local authorities. Taxpayers have more trust and confidence in government officials and, as a result, tax revenues have increased. Local government financial management has improved, and there are concrete improvements in socioeconomic development, environmental management, and local legislation.

Factors of Success and Key Lessons Learned
Context matters
Experience has shown that the successful use of social contracts varies depending on context. Social contracts are generally effective at the village and small town level. The rate of success and sustainability is very high in small towns and satisfactory in medium-sized towns. However, success is more challenging in big towns and cities, where it is dependent on the presence of strong CSO representation and media coverage. The following table shows the comparative success of social contracts in different contexts in the Philippines (Table 8.1).

The experience of ICODE reveals a number of important factors of success and lessons learned, with regard to building political will for participatory and accountable governance. Some of these are described below.

CSO capacity
The competence and capacity of CSOs to engage politicians and the government are key. Community level partners benefited from a vast pool of qualified cadres in participatory, transparent, and accountable governance, trained by the ICODE/Central Philippine University School of Governance. Specific competencies are necessary to build self-confidence and earn the respect of politicians and government officials, and strong organized CSO networks are required to mobilize actors and sustain efforts.

The power of numbers
Politicians love, and fear, a large crowd. The role of CSOs in mobilizing critical masses of people was instrumental in their earning the respect and attention of candidates and elected representatives. Social pressure has generated high levels of participation, among targeted politicians, in public disclosure and feedback activities. To best leverage the poor and marginalized, including women, is through the power of the numbers, which can be used to put their agenda into the limelight.

Supporting champions within local government
Key to building political will is having competent, honest, results-driven, and socially progressive individuals elected into office, with a mandate from informed and mature citizen-voters who will support these *champions*.

Table 8.1. Comparative Success of Social Contracts in Building Political Will for Participatory Governance

IMPACT AREAS	Rating*	Indicators
Villages	9 to 10	• High level (55%–65%) of citizens participate in barangay assembly-cum–feedback forum in impact villages of Batad, Bingawan, and New Lucena (ICODE PLG Reports 2004). • High participation in barangay development planning, monitoring, and evaluation. • On the downside, not all villages have strong and organized CSOs. • Except in barangays with presence of good leaders, local CBOs do not have the competencies to sustain the barangay level program.
Small towns (Population below 30,000—e.g., Batad, Bingawan)	10 (fully successful)	• According to municipal records, 95–100% of public officials render reports at regularly scheduled public feedback sessions. • A critical mass of the citizens (more than 10% of the voting population) attend public meetings. • Annual Investments Plan: Significant increase in allocation of municipal budget for purposes of poverty reduction and responsive development. • Special allocation (of PhP 20,000) for the implementation of public reporting and feedback activities.
Big towns (Population 30,000–99,000— e.g., Lambunao, Banate)	8	• More difficult to generate participation from all sectors and villages. • Lack of strong CSOs to sustain activity beyond elections or during regular public administration cycle.
Small cities (Population 100,000–199,000—e.g., Roxas City, Capiz)	7	• Complemented other ongoing participatory governance initiatives.
Big cities (Population 200,000–500,000—e.g., Iloilo City)	6	• Long period of gestation due to bureaucratic snags. • Low attendance of sectoral representatives. • Good media coverage.
Inter-LGU Alliances (ANIHEAD composed of 9 municipalities in Northern Iloilo)	8	• At this point, alliances are still few but very successful, especially in areas with common development interest (ecosystem, socio-economic, culture). • High potential for ripple effects on other local government units.

*Self-rating results from the Local Government Performance Monitoring System (LGPMS) used by DILG, Scale of 1 to 10. 1 = not at all, 10 = fully successful.

They have become champions of participatory governance, and begun to redefine the roles and responsibilities of legislators. Champion leaders and legislators are important to the enactment of resolutions and ordinances.

Ensuring harmonization with local governance cycles

Harmonization of the social contract process with the public administrative cycle is an important practical measure that has gone a long way toward ensuring the support of local government units. Built-in social accountability mechanisms of social contracts have proved beneficial to local government resource management and investment efforts and, as a result, have been institutionalized through internal policies and legislative issuances (ordinances, statutes, resolutions) of participating local government units. These harmonization and institutionalization efforts have helped to fast-track the legitimization of social contracts/covenants, in turn ensuring adequate budget allocations and sustainability.

Rewards and increased revenues

Government units, which have used social contracts or covenants and public disclosure and feedback mechanisms, have realized millions of pesos savings and significantly enhanced their access to resources for social services and development infrastructure. Many have earned recognition from local and international award-giving bodies. Between 2004 and 2008, CSOs and local government partners have received more than 8 million pesos in grants from international donors, because of social contracts, resulting from participatory governance initiatives. Increased public trust and confidence, as a result of social contracts, has also generated increases in tax payments. Where social contracts have been implemented, municipalities have experienced on average between 10 and 20 percent yearly increases in real property and business taxes. Mayor Elvira Alarcon, of Batad, registered a 250 percent increase in tax collection, from 600,000 to over 2 million pesos in one year (Municipality of Batad, 2008).

Potential for replication

Social contracts and agreement frameworks are low-cost tools for guaranteeing the rights of civil society in relation to governance. They are simple, but potent, mechanisms for holding governments to account. They are also straightforward frameworks, which are applicable to different contexts, thus making them easily replicable. Local government executives, legislators, students, and CSOs from nearby towns, and from as far as a 1,000 miles away, have come to Iloilo to learn about social contracts and good participatory governance practices. Some municipalities in the southern

Philippines have emulated the exercises and created their own customized version, which have also won awards from the *Galing Pook* Foundation.

Stakeholders across the world have realized the value-added effects of social contracts and their benefits, in terms of transparent and responsive governance. Partners from India, Bangladesh, Sri Lanka, Thailand, Cambodia, Japan, Indonesia, Sweden, and the United States have visited the Philippines to gain insight on developing new tools for participatory governance and social accountability. Social contract projects are now thriving in communities in Cambodia and Indonesia (ANSA–EAP 2008).

Conclusions

In the Philippines, social contracts are a successful way of combating graft, corruption, and inefficiency. Several Philippine public policy forums, conferences, and learning exchanges have lauded social contracts between citizens and the government as a phenomenal innovation and source of inspiration. In addition to curbing corruption, social contracts have proved extremely effective in improving the performance of local governments and CSOs. By enhancing public trust and performance, they have led to increases in revenues and investment opportunities that surpass all initial expectations.

To become a *nation of good governance,* the Philippines must expand local initiatives and apply them in the national arena, for example in the Office of the President, the Senate, Congress, and national political parties. In December 2008, at a national conference in Manila entitled *Good Governance for Change; Change for Good Governance,* ICODE's social contract was mentioned as an example of a successful initiative that should be brought to scale. Networks of CSOs are now planning for the preparation of a national people's agenda to facilitate strategic engagement among citizens and national and local politicians in the upcoming 2010 Elections.

Social contracts and covenants, particularly those that have been formalized into mutual agreements or local ordinances, have proved powerful tools for generating political will for more participatory, transparent, and accountable governance. A *national-level* Social Contract or Covenant for Transformative Governance is exactly what the country needs to exact accountability of national officials and be liberated from the shame of corruption.

Finally, sustaining the passion of active citizens and civil society advocates is the surest way of ensuring the long-term success of social contracts. Politicians come and go after their tenure of office ends, but citizens remain in the community to carry on the gains that have been initiated. Civil society organizations must never abandon their role as social innovators, promoters of active citizenship, facilitators of citizen-government relations, and catalysts for change.

References

Affiliated Network for Social Accountability in East Asia and the Pacific. 2008. *Putting Social Accountability in the Mainstream*. Manila, Philippines: Affiliated Network for Social Accountability in East Asia and the Pacific.

Areño, Emmanuel. 2008. *Beyond Lip Service*. Paper presented at the 2008 CIVICUS World Assembly in Glasgow, Scotland.

Areño, Emmanuel. 2008. *Iloilo CODE NGOs Report to the British Embassy: Economic Governance Program: Civil Society Tools in Promoting Transparency and Accountability in LGUs through Monitoring of Locally Funded Projects*. Iloilo City, Philippines: ICODE.

Barrios, Xenia Socorro and Rosanna Pandes. 2008. *Hinun-anon sa Siudad: Mechanics and Documentation Report to the Center for Community Journalism and Development*. Iloilo City, Philippines: ICODE.

Batario, Red. 2004. *Breaking the Norms*. Quezon City, Philippines: Center for Community Journalism and Development.

Castillanes, Mara Joy. 2006. Kwentahan Hindi Kwentohan. *Newsletter*, November. Philippines: Pamangkutanon sang People by Bingawan Working Youth Federation.

Galing Pook, Gawad. 2003. Pahayag sa Banwa: The Philippine Case Bank on Innovations and Exemplary Communities of Practices in Local Governance. *List of 2002 Galing Pook Awardees*. Philippines: Galing Pook.

ICODE. 2008. *Good Governance for Change Using Innovative Frameworks and Tools for Claiming Democratic Space*. CSO forum presentations CODE NGO Social Development Week. Quezon City, Philippines.

ICODE. 2007. Report to the *Learning Forum on Institutionalizing Social Accountability in Local Governance Through CDD Approaches*. Convened by the World Bank Institute, Washington, D.C., USA.

Ilago, Simeon Agustin, ed. 2006. Developing Community Capacities for Pro-Poor Budgeting and Local Government Accountability for Poverty Reduction. *Synthesis Report and Case Study Papers*. Quezon City, Philippines: The World Bank.

Jordan, Ella Arao. 2007. *Partnership in Diversity: Best Practices and Lessons Learned: Final Evaluation of Diakonia-Philippine Programme*. Chiang Mai, Thailand: Diakonia Asia Regional Office.

Manuel, Marlon Saligan. 2001. *A Primer on the Local Special Bodies and the Accreditation of People's Organizations and Non-government Organizations*. Quezon City, Philippines.

Municipality of Batad. 2008. Municipal Annual Investments Plan and Budget. Batad, Philippines: Municipality of Batad.

Municipality of Batad. 2006. *Municipal Ordinance Number 2006-035: An Ordinance Establishing the Pahayag sa Banwa.* Batad, Philippines: Municipality of Batad.

Municipality of Bingawan. 2007. *Local Government Performance Monitoring System Report.* Bingawan, Philippines: Municipality of Bingawan.

Municipality of Bingawan. 2007. *Municipal Annual Investments Plan and Budget.* Bingawan, Philippines: Municipality of Bingawan.

Municipality of Bingawan. 2008. *Municipal Annual Investments Plan and Budget.* Bingawan, Philippines: Municipality of Bingawan.

Municipality of Bingawan. 2004. *Municipal Ordinance Number 4: An Ordinance Establishing the Pamankutanon sang Banwa.* Bingawan, Philippines: Municipality of Bingawan.

Philippines-Canada Local Government Support Program. 2001. *Enhancing Participation in Local Governance: Experience from the Philippines.* Manila, Philippines.

Philippines Department of Interior and Local Governments. 2001. *Bureau of Local Government and Development Annual Report.* Philippines: Philippines Department of Interior and Local Governments.

Transparency International. 2008. *Transparency International Corruption Index.* Available at transparencyintl.org.

The Asia Foundation. 2009. *Localizing Counter Corruption in Six Cities in Luzon and Visayas: 2008–2009.* The Asia Foundation.

Villarin, Tom et al. 2008. *Balangay: Resource Manual for Barangay Governance.* Quezon City, Philippines: Institute of Politics and Governance.

Notes

1. The author thanks the following people who were interviewed for this chapter in the period from November 2008 to February 2009: Elvira Alarcon (current Mayor of Batad); Pedro Alarcon (previous Mayor of Batad); Xenia Socorro Barrios (Community Organizer, Municipality of New Lucena); Mara Joy Castillanes (Project Information Officer, Bingawan Working Youth Federation); Elphin Celeste (Barangay Council Member); Elviro Celeste (President, Bingawan Senior Citizens Federation); Ronelo Compas (Bingawan Municipal Councilor); Matt Palabrica (Mayor of Bingawan); Evangeline Palmares (Batad Municipal Council Member); Abner Rubrico (Batad CSO Member); Reynold Sandoy (Batad Municipal Administrator); and Lailanie Vocales Madriaga (Community Organizer, ICODE).

2. Based on this growing local-governance experience, ICODE has since partnered with a range of national and international organizations, for example, in the context of the World Bank-sponsored social accountability programs and the CIDA Philippines-Canada Local Government Support Program. By 2001, ICODE had acted as a consultant to sixteen municipalities in six provinces.

PART 3

Nurturing Political Will for Participatory Budgeting

CHAPTER 9

BUILDING POLITICAL WILL FOR PARTICIPATORY BUDGETING IN RURAL ZIMBABWE: THE CASE OF MUTOKO RURAL DISTRICT COUNCIL

Takawira Mumvuma

Introduction

There are a number of acknowledged preconditions for the successful promotion of participatory governance initiatives. These include political and legal systems and frameworks that allow for the effective engagement of ordinary citizens and civil society participation (Matovu and Mumvuma 2008). Political will is also an important precondition for the success of any participatory governance initiative.[1] It has been observed that political will is necessary to sustain the entire participatory governance process and that the most visible manifestation of this is in the implementation phase, when commitments are concretized into tangible investments (UN-HABITAT 2005). Field experience shows that the introduction of participatory governance initiatives, as part of wider policy reform efforts, are sometimes unsuccessful due to a combination of factors including political resistance, failure to sustain the initiatives, and lack of knowledge about appropriate strategies and tools to firmly establish the initiatives. Experience shows that the key factor underlying the success of participatory governance initiatives is the existence of strong political will, demonstrated by a commitment from leadership at all levels of government *and civil society* (Kpundeh 2000, *italic added*). However, in many African countries, lack of political will is stalling efforts to promote effective participatory governance. One of the biggest current challenges is how to get politicians and other important civil society players to buy into the idea of participatory governance. Mutoko, located in northeastern Zimbabwe, faced such a challenge when it started experimenting with its participatory

157

budgeting initiative in 2001, under a Program to Develop Local Governance in Zimbabwe, funded by the United States Agency for International Development (USAID), under a bilateral agreement with the government of Zimbabwe. The program was implemented by the Urban Institute, a United States-based nonpartisan economic and social research organization, headquartered in Washington D.C., with a local office in Harare.

The objective of this chapter is to discuss how, after some initial delays and resistance, the political will of various stakeholders was galvanized to support the adoption, and consequent practice, of participatory budgeting in Mutoko. The chapter explores the driving force, objectives, implementation, results, and outcomes of Mutoko's participatory budgeting initiative. It then provides an analysis of why political will was initially lacking, and the strategies that were used to build political will. It also looks at the evolution of relations between the local council and civil society organizations (CSOs), as a result of the initiative. Finally, it identifies critical success factors, lessons learned, and summarizes key findings.

Mutoko's Participatory Budget Initiative[2]

What Triggered It?

Prior to 2001, Mutoko faced continuous budget deficits. Whenever the council proposed, or tried, to raise tariffs and charges, there were public demonstrations. Citizens argued that they saw no justification for the increases because they resulted in no improvements to public services. The council failed to consult or inform citizens about its activities (Sigauke 2007). At the same time, there were indications that both elected and appointed council officials were embezzling public funds for personal benefit. Every year, various CSOs, under the leadership of the Mutoko Residents Association and the Informal Traders Association, took to the streets resisting and boycotting increased charges. During this period the informal sector grew sharply in Mutoko, as national economic reforms led to huge job losses and many urban workers returned to their rural homes to try to make a living in the informal sector. Many of these new *arrivals* were more educated and knew how to fight for their rights. As a result, local CSOs, particularly the Mutoko Informal Traders Association, became even more powerful and vocal (Mika 2003). Due to this recurring confrontational relationship with its citizens, the Mutoko District Council was forced to rethink the way it was doing business. The council resolved to adopt a new innovative and participatory approach to its annual budgeting process (Matovu and Mumvuma 2008). Therefore, mounting pressure from civil society, which was demanding responsive budgeting and good governance, was the key trigger for Mutoko's participatory budgeting initiative.

Experimentation with participatory budgeting in Mutoko coincided with the participation of the council in USAID's newly launched demand-driven Program to Develop Local Governance in Zimbabwe. The implementers of this program, in cooperation with local facilitators, became the key external drivers of this initiative, by providing the necessary technical support. There were three main driving forces behind the adoption of participatory budgeting in Mutoko. First, it was driven by demand from citizens for better governance and improved public services. Second, it was driven by the council's desire to put a stop to citizen and civil society protests. The third driving force was the government of Zimbabwe and USAID's joint desire to promote decentralized governance throughout the country.

Objectives

The overall objective of the initiative was to enable Mutoko's citizens to participate in the council's decision-making and budgetary processes, in order to promote transparency, accountability, and local economic development, as well as to improve the well-being of local citizens. The initiative's specific objectives were to achieve greater transparency through the proactive sharing of information; to allow citizens to demand more accountability from the council, through their greater participation in the decision-making and budgeting process; and to establish a simple and effective feedback system.

It was envisaged, that through this initiative, CSOs would become more representative of their constituencies and better able to articulate member's interests.[3] At the same time, the council was expected to become more open to increased input from local stakeholders, thereby improving their service delivery. Ordinary citizens were expected to benefit from improved service delivery, transparency, accountability, and increased participation in council affairs.

Agreeing on a Common Vision and Strategic Plan

The participatory budgeting process in Mutoko was initiated through a series of meetings among key stakeholders. The council implemented an initial local governance visioning process using facilitated orientation meetings, feedback brainstorming meetings, and targeted interviews. A second set of meetings involved the facilitation of broad-based, vision-sharing workshops for all stakeholders. The vision-sharing workshops utilized a range of methodologies to capture the council's and CSOs' concerns and visions. Focus group discussions, public hearings, joint council–CSO meetings, general CSO meetings, and one-on-one meetings with CSO representatives were held. These meetings were further complemented by the training of CSOs and community members in council procedures and budgeting processes, including the costing of projects. These activities resulted in three clear outputs: the council's first ever Five-Year Strategic Plan, a Local Social Contract, and the council's first ever participatory budgeting cycle. To a large extent, these activities succeeded in overcoming the initial mistrust and impasse that existed between CSOs and the council.

Zimbabwean law stipulates that urban municipal councils must be guided by a five-year strategic plan, but this requirement does not apply to rural councils. Nevertheless, the Mutoko Council realized that developing a common vision with the community was not only essential to engender ownership of the participatory budgeting process, but could also serve to reduce conflict and mistrust among concerned stakeholders. As a first step, a first draft of the five-year strategic plan was prepared by the council, with the active participation of a broad spectrum of stakeholders at the village and ward levels. The draft strategic plan was then discussed at various ward development committee meetings, before adoption by the council. Through this participatory process, the council was able to articulate a common vision of what constitutes effective and meaningful participation in local government. They also came up with *key results areas* to be given priority attention under the council's participatory budgeting initiative. These included the following: improving service delivery; enhancing revenue generation and collection; upgrading infrastructure; and promoting investment. This strategic plan now serves as the basis of Mutoko's annual development programs and the resultant annual operating budgets.

Forming a Budget Action Committee

After developing the strategic plan it was decided that the council should form a budget action committee to prepare submissions for the budgeting process. It was agreed that this committee should include the district administrator and council members, as well as representatives from the local business association, the residents association, the informal traders association, the ruling party Zimbabwe African National Union-Patriotic Front (ZANU-PF), and local churches. The committee was tasked with gathering information and making recommendations regarding:

- How to enhance citizen knowledge about the council budget and the services it provides;
- The type of awareness-building activities needed to enable citizens to actively participate in local governance issues;
- How to simplify or *demystify* budget information to make it more easily understood by ordinary citizens;
- How to effectively disseminate budget information to the general public;
- How to design and implement socially acceptable debt collection procedures and systems; and
- The current, and potential, scope and roles of CSOs in Mutoko.

Agreeing on the Participatory Budgeting Cycle

During one of the vision-sharing meetings, group discussions on a participatory budgeting cycle showed a huge deficiency in stakeholder understanding of the process. A participatory analysis of the ideal cycle resulted in the formulation of an agreed cycle for Mutoko that is still in use today, although with some slight modifications. One of the major characteristics of this budget cycle is its inclusive nature, whereby the participation of disadvantaged and marginalized groups of women, children, youth, the disabled, and the aged is key.[4] The cycle is also characterized by its definition of a participatory budgeting timetable that allows for continuous inputs into the operating and capital budgets, built-in monitoring mechanisms, and frequent reviews of the budget by all interested stakeholders. This cycle runs from September to August of the following year, as indicated in Table 9.1.

Developing a Local Social Contract

Civil society organizations, business groups, and the council came together in a new *community forum* being facilitated by both local consultants and external ones from the Urban Institute. Visioning workshops and task forces were organized to develop a *social contract* that was meant to build trust, mitigate conflict, and develop more open and productive relationships. The local social contract spelled out expectations, as well as the respective roles and responsibilities of each stakeholder group in enabling citizens to effectively take part in the participatory budgeting process. The social contract also specified standards of service, charted clear lines of responsibility, and outlined procedures for effective interaction between the council and its stakeholders. Definitions of participation, governance, and instruments of participation were agreed

Table 9.1. Mutoko District Council Participatory Budgeting Cycle

Stage	Date	Activity	Technique	Purpose	Actors	Output
I	September	• Preparation of budget guidelines by the officers • Consultative meetings with citizens • Needs identification	• Committee meetings	• To prepare Committee budgets	• Councilors • Council staff	• Committee draft budgets
II	October	• Final review of the current year budget	• Council meetings • Public meeting/ workshops • Distribution of hard copies of draft budget	• To reach consensus on the consolidated budget	• Councilors • Council staff • Stakeholders • Community	• Participatory draft budget • Agreement on rates, levies, and charges
III	November	• Stakeholder consultation for the coming year's budget • Priority setting • Budget consolidation by the Finance Committee • Advertising of Participatory draft budget calling for objections and petitions	• Media • Public notices	• To achieve budget acceptance by citizens	• Councilors • Council staff • Community	• Citizen consensus, ownership, and support
IV	December	• Finalization and approval of the budget by full Council • Forward budget to Minister	• Full Council meeting • Government gazette	• To get approval of the budget	• Councilors • Council staff • Community • Central Government	• Approved budget

	Month	Activity	Methods	Objectives	Actors	Outputs
V	December/ January	Budget implementation	• Initiation • Monitoring • Reviews	• To improve service delivery • To achieve growth • To attain development	• Councilors • Council staff • Community	• Programs • Projects • Activities
	February	Recess				
VI	March/April	First quarterly budget review	• Public meetings	• To receive feedback • To make evaluations • To sensitize citizens	• Stakeholders • Councilors • Members of Parliament	• Sensitized stakeholders • Preliminary contributions to next budget
VIII	May/June	Capacity building	• Pre-budget workshops • Seminars	• To improve competencies • To raise awareness of civic rights/ obligations • To establish consensus among citizens	• Councilors • Council staff • Community leaders • Facilitators	• Trained staff • Trained actors on budget cycle
IX	July/ August	Stakeholder consultation and second budget review	• Council chamber meetings • Ward meetings • Village meetings • Media • Road shows	• To review needs and priorities • To receive additional contributions from stakeholders • To build consensus on needs and priorities	• Councilors • Council staff • Community • Stakeholders	• Adjusted needs and priorities • Community pledges and contributions

Source: Data from Matovu and Mumvuma 2008, 61–62.

upon, and the social contract came to be regarded by all stakeholders as the participatory budgeting road map for Mutoko. To make sure that the rules of the game contained therein became part of each citizen's way of life, this social contract was signed by the council and all leaders of various civic groups, traditional leaders, and representatives of central government departments.

According to the social contract document, the council was assigned the role of identifying community needs in a participatory manner, providing the necessary services to its citizens, and collecting payment for such services. The council was also expected to provide a conducive environment for citizen participation and to ensure the sustainable development of its locality. The business community was tasked with promoting economic growth and creating employment, as well as providing those services that it could deliver more effectively than the council. It also committed itself to paying its dues promptly to the council. Civil society groups were mandated to assist the council and business community in identifying, understanding, and responding to various community interests and needs. They were expected to pay for services received and to operate within the policy and regulatory framework of the council.

In addition, all parties to the social contract agreed on instruments and processes for inclusive citizen participation, as well as on areas in which the council would reserve control and/or confidentiality. Rules for the recognition and registration of CSOs were agreed upon and codified, including an assessment of the existing relationship between the council and CSOs, and strategies for improving this. In a way, the main aim of the social contract was to empower citizens by clearly specifying the rules of engagement and minimizing the risk of conflict. The fact that the rules contained in the social contract were decided in a very participatory and democratic manner went a long way toward creating much needed trust, mutual respect, and collaboration. This led to enhanced political will for participatory governance and reduced tension and conflict between citizens, and civil society, and the council.

Training

In addition to supporting improved relations between the local authorities and stakeholders, the Urban Institute also organized training for CSOs, by facilitating vision sharing, strategic planning, and social contract processes, aimed at building their advocacy capacity and understanding of local government issues. Ward development committee members were trained in the roles and responsibilities of public administrators, and in budgeting and strategic planning processes. As a result, these committee members developed the capacity to actively participate, along with council members, in quarterly budget performance reviews and to pass this information on to other citizens at the ward level.[5]

Results and Outcomes

The participatory budgeting initiative in Mutoko has been positively received by all local citizen groups, who have started to actively participate, not only in the budgeting process but in council affairs more generally. Encouraged by this positive response, the council has now introduced several reforms that have resulted in making council services more readily available and accessible. For example, a special area was set aside for informal traders to establish their vending facilities, and the main road to the growth point bus terminus was tarred. A key outcome and impact of this initiative was the fact that budget acceptance and ownership has increased, as evidenced by the absence of protests against necessary increases in tariffs and user charges escalations by the council from 2002 up to now. This is due to improved service delivery. In particular, the residential stands, which were previously being corruptly allocated, are now being transparently allocated to deserving applicants after being fully serviced by the council. There is now a better appreciation of what the council does and how services are costed. This has led to a greater willingness to pay for council services and a sharp decrease in residents' default rate on fees and charges owed to the local authority. A greater respect for citizens' needs has been engendered through enhanced dialogue and the clear, agreed upon definition of roles, powers, and responsibilities. Participatory practices have become entrenched in the council's budget formulation, monitoring, and evaluation processes. For civil society actors, the visioning process, which brought together CSOs and local officials in open workshops on governance and financial management, created or rejuvenated civil society's interest in participating in council decision-making and budgetary processes. The initiative has also resulted in the enhancement of the capacity of local civil society actors and community members to understand, question, and formulate budgets. Empowerment, through lobbying and advocacy strategies, has opened various avenues for these organizations to be able to directly interrogate and demand accountability from both elected and nonelected council officials on budgetary issues. As a result, the budgeting process in Mutoko is increasingly becoming more transparent, inclusive, and responsive, as well as results-oriented and people-centered.

Building Political Will

Reasons for the Initial Lack of Political Will

There were two main sources of initial resistance to the participatory budgeting initiative. First, at the central government level there was general suspicion of USAID, after the U.S. government passed the Zimbabwe Democracy and Economic Recovery Act, which, among other things, authorized the U.S. government to fund opposition media, democracy, and governance programs in Zimbabwe. In addition, an earlier similar initiative in a remote district of the country helped to raise political awareness and consciousness amongst the disadvantaged rural population and led to a resounding defeat of the ruling ZANU-PF party in the 2002 local government elections.[6] As a result, the government of Zimbabwe was very suspicious of USAID's proposed local governance program. Second, at the local level, councilors were suspicious of local civil society leaders, who they perceived as seeking to criticize and undermine their legitimate authority. Civil society organizations were viewed as channels for opposition partisan politics or *councilors in waiting*. Councilors were particularly fearful of business leaders, who were viewed as having the monetary resources to dislodge them from the corridors of power. At the same time, this envisaged participatory budgeting initiative ultimately entailed a sharing of political power. It therefore faced some local resistance from both political and traditional leadership, who strongly felt they had the sole mandate to represent their respective constituencies. Councilors, having invested resources to get elected, saw no benefits in sharing political power. On the other hand, it would also appear that the councilors were reluctant to engage CSOs in participatory budgeting, because they feared it would expose their weaknesses and limited capacity to other stakeholders, who regarded them with esteem and admiration (Bvunzawabaya 2006). To make matters worse, civil society representatives were of the view that councilors were embezzling public funds for their personal use. Ordinary citizens, on the other hand, expected immediate tangible outputs, such as the construction of roads, schools, and hospitals, and were initially uninterested and unsupportive when program organizers talked about nontangible outcomes, such as information-sharing and capacity-building.

How Political Will Was Built

Frequently asked questions, with respect to political will, often include the following: Can political will be consciously created? Does it emerge as a result of individual *reform champions,* who may have previously and consciously concealed their reformist tendencies? If it can be created, how then can we identify the likely ingredients for building it? (Transparency International 2000). All three questions are highly relevant to understanding how political will was built for Mutoko's participatory budgeting initiative and to understanding its ultimate success. In this case, there was a conscious and deliberate effort to build political will for enhanced citizen participation and participatory budgeting, and reform-minded champions emerged in the form of the council's chief executive officer and chairman.

A number of strategies and tactics were employed to overcome the initial resistance and to generate the necessary political will for Mutoko's participatory budgeting initiative. At the central government level, a number of roundtable meetings with the donor were carried out to justify and explain the usefulness of the program. In these meetings, USAID representatives were able to reassure government officials that the objective of the proposed program was to help improve the operations and performance of the participating councils. Once convinced of the value of the initiative, the government supplied each consultant with a personal letter of introduction and support for the governance program. This gave the initiative some semblance of national support in the eyes of council officials and local civic leaders. Introductory visits and meetings were also held with the provincial governor, provincial administrator, and district administrator to create the necessary rapport and understanding of the initiative. By visiting the provincial governor, regularly sharing information with the governor's office, and submitting letters of introduction signed by the Ministry of Local Government, the team of consultants was able to build confidence and support, by demonstrating transparency and respect for protocol. The mere observance of these simple but crucial protocols ensured that there was no friction or suspicion in the process of implementing the initiative as both the Urban Institute and USAID were seen to be trustworthy in the local governance program endeavor.

At the local level, despite initial skepticism on the part of local councilors, the initiative was instantly accepted and owned by the chief executive officer, his management team, and the council chairman. Much of this team was made up of fairly new and highly qualified personnel who had taken up office during the recent implementation of a four-year Rural District Council Capacity Building Program.[7] This new generation of officers, which included heads of departments and the chief executive officer, were receptive of new ideas and supportive of change. Their enthusiasm was largely responsible for the fast-track implementation of the participatory budget initiative. Mutoko's vision-sharing and ward development workshops were attended by ordinary citizens, the council team, the local Member of Parliament and his constituency officers, as well as central government representatives and traditional and political leaders from the district, resulting in the signing of a *social contract* by all concerned parties. The collaboration of these various groups helped in generating the necessary support for the initiative Mutoko, which was then 100 percent behind ZANU-PF, the *de facto* ruling party, managed to also galvanize support for the initiative, using the existing political party structures and machinery. Therefore, it would appear that the prevailing political unity and use of existing party and traditional structures played a pivotal role in building the necessary political will for the participatory budgeting experiment.[8] By energizing key figures in both political and civic life, the Mutoko participatory budgeting initiative was able to register some crucial early successes.

Evolution of Citizen–Council Relations

Prior to the advent of the USAID Local Governance Program, the Mutoko Rural District Council was undertaking its planning and budgeting process without any direct community participation. Budget formulation, presentation, implementation, and monitoring and evaluation were regarded as the preserve of elected officials and council management. In most instances, budget consultation was limited to the minimum requirements of advertising in the paper the contents of the participatory draft budget, including proposed rates and tariff charges, and then calling for objections and petitions. The major problem with this was that citizen and civil society participation came at the tail end of the process, reducing it to a mere information-sharing mechanism. In addition, budget presentations at council were predominantly technical and inaccessible to ordinary citizens and civil society players. On the other hand, citizens and local CSOs had developed a culture of taking a backseat as far as civic affairs were concerned. As a result, most citizens were not aware of the council's financial situation, development priorities, and operations.[9] Citizens and local CSOs expected to receive quality services from council, but were uninformed, and apparently uninterested, in council finances. This situation, combined with the fact that communication between citizens and the council was erratic, problem-oriented, and crisis-centered, meant that boycotts and public demonstrations became the predominant form of civic engagement (Nyakudanga 2006).

With the introduction of the participatory budgeting initiative, a systematic approach was adopted, which began by taking stock of all civil society groups in Mutoko. Civil society organizations were initially profiled and then invited to participate in the broad-based, vision-sharing workshops, allowing them to interact directly with both elected and appointed council officials. These workshops encouraged the emergence of a new relationship and mode of mutual understanding and interaction between citizens, and CSOs, and the council.

When Mutoko first introduced a participatory budgeting process that surpassed the minimum legal provisions, it faced the problem of potentially conflicting roles between elected representatives and civil society leaders. As a result, serious conflicts initially emerged between elected officials, civil society leaders, and even with traditional leaders. This was mainly due to the fact that good governance concepts were understood differently, as were ideas about rights, obligations, and roles. This problem was overcome by inviting all stakeholders to participate in a broad-based workshop that sought to openly and collectively define concepts; establish a common understanding of rights, obligations, and roles; identify commonly agreed upon indicators of good governance; and identify participatory planning tools and communication channels. This workshop also provided an opportunity for the chief executive officer, council chairman, and council heads of departments to respond to issues raised by CSO representatives and residents. The high degree of openness that was displayed by council members at this meeting was enthusiastically received and further helped in warming the once strained relationship between the council and CSOs (Bvunzawabaya 2006, 4). At the same, workshop stakeholders put their heads together and developed a participatory budgeting cycle for Mutoko. This development again marked a major positive turning point in the relations between the council and CSOs, which has since been sustained.

Critical Success Factors and Lessons Learned

Critical Success Factors

The successful implementation of Mutoko's participatory budgeting initiative can be attributed to three fundamental factors, namely: (i) the strong support and leadership that was provided by the council chairman, his chief executive officer, and other grassroots actors; (ii) the effective communication between the council and CSOs, which helped to eliminate previous mistrust and antagonism; and (iii) the rigorous technical support that was provided by the chief facilitator of the initiative, the Urban Institute. It is also clear that the strong leadership exhibited from the chief executive officer's office down to the ward development committees, the chiefs, and the local councilors, was key to success of the initiative.

The use of stakeholder and vision-sharing meetings was essential to share information, improve communication, and build trust. Since all of the stakeholders were openly invited to participate, no one could complain that he or she was not given a chance to take part in the local authority's budgetary process. The transparency and openness displayed by the council during these meetings and the commitment to fulfill what was agreed upon during the same meetings, over time, motivated citizens to sustain and increase their participation.

The role played by the Urban Institute was also critical to the success of the initiative. It provided the necessary resources and facilitation, which guaranteed the successful implementation of the participatory budgeting process in Mutoko; particularly the knowledge and skills that were transferred to the local players made a difference.

Lessons Learned

The Mutoko participatory governance initiative offers numerous lessons with regard to building political will for participatory governance. First and foremost, a multisectoral strategic planning approach is critical to building trust and political will, as well as the confidence of local stakeholders in the subsequent process of participatory budgeting. The process of collectively articulating a common vision strengthens local ownership and interest in local governance issues, and, by raising public awareness and expectations, creates the impetus to help sustain political will on the part of the initiative's champions. Second, a locally generated social contract can be very useful in generating political will, by clearly defining the roles and responsibilities of various stakeholders, thereby minimizing the risk of conflict. Third, the process of seeking support for participatory governance in rural settings, calls for the active engagement of existing traditional leadership. Given their popular legitimacy and proximity to citizens, traditional leaders can play a key role in convening and mobilizing support for participatory governance initiatives, for example, by using existing structures such as ward assemblies. Using instruments and processes that respect local culture, values, and norms can help to enhance political will for participatory governance initiatives, such as participatory budgeting. Fourth, external facilitators, including donors as agents of change, are critical in building political will for participatory governance, as long as they are knowledgeable and respectful of local norms, values, and protocols, and are careful to strengthen, rather than strain, existing relationships between ordinary citizens, traditional leaders, and political actors.[10] Fifth, identifying, supporting, and protecting reform-minded champions at the local level from the outset, is an important strategy for nurturing political will and support for participatory governance. Sixth, for political will to endure, participatory governance initiatives must quickly generate positive tangible results, as Mutoko's participatory budgeting initiative demonstrates.[11] Finally, this case demonstrates that lack of competitive, multiparty national politics is not necessarily a constraint to the initiation of successful participatory governance initiatives. Instead, in cases such as this one, it can turn out to be an enabling factor. With or without competitive politics, politicians are bound to offer their support to such initiatives, as long as they are confident that they will help them solve their development problems and enhance their prospects of garnering more political support in their constituencies.

Conclusion

The major conclusions that can be drawn from this case study are that the increasing acceptance and use of participatory budgeting in Mutoko was directly linked to the central government's willingness to support and launch USAID's governance program in Zimbabwe. Without this support, it is doubtful that change could have been achieved. It can also be concluded that the enthusiastic acceptance of the initiative, and the consequent strong leadership provided by the then council chairman and the current chief executive officer, the two key reform-minded champions, was paramount to the successful kick-starting of the initiative and its continued sustenance up to today. Also, in situations were political will is initially nonexistent, it is important to establish strategic alliances and partnerships between government, key political players, civil society groups, traditional leadership structures, and other interested citizen groups at an early stage for participatory governance initiatives to succeed. In the case of Mutoko, this was achieved through the use of various strategies and tactics, such as public hearings, roundtables, vision-sharing workshops, and one-on-one meetings. All this helped build mutual trust between council members and local civil society players, and to overcome the initial suspicions between the donor and government officials. This means that effective communication and openness between government officials and citizens, and civil society, on the one hand, and government and donors on the other, is critical for building political will. Donor support, in terms of knowledge and building skills, also played a central role in ensuring the success of Mutoko's participatory budgeting initiative.

References

Bvunzawabaya, M. 2006. Participatory Budgeting: The Mutoko Experience. Presentation made at the Africities Summit, Nairobi, Kenya.

Kpundeh, S.J. 2000. *Political Will in Fighting Corruption.* Available online at the undp.org Web site.

Matovu, G. and T. Mumvuma. 2008. Participatory budgeting in Africa: A training companion, with cases from Eastern and Southern Africa, from UN-HABITAT, Nairobi, Kenya. *Facilitation Methods,* 11.

Mika, J. 2003. *Sub-National Experiences in Civic Participation, Policy Making and Budgeting Processes: The Case of Mutoko, Zimbabwe.* Harare, Zimbabwe: MDPESA/WBI.

Nyakudanga, O. 2006. Participatory Budgeting: The Mutoko Rural District Council Experience. Presentation made at the Africities Summit, Nairobi, Kenya.

Sigauke, P. 2007. Participatory Budgeting Brewed in an African Pot: A Case Study of Participatory Budgeting in Mutoko. Presentation made at the MDP-ESA Organized Regional Workshop on Participatory Budgeting in Africa, Harare, Zimbabwe.

Transparency International. 2000. *TI Source Book: Building Political Will.* Available at the transparency.org.

UN-HABITAT. 2005. *Urban Governance in Africa: Experiences and Challenges.* A UN-HABITAT background paper presented at the African Ministers' Conference on Housing and Urban Development. Durban, South Africa.

Notes

1. In the context of this paper, political will is defined as the demonstrated credible commitment of political actors, business, traditional, religious, and other civil society leaders to support Mutoko's participatory budgeting initiative (adapted from Kpundeh 2000, 92). Political will refers to more than the will of politicians, given the fact that important players from other interest groups, together with politicians, jointly formed a powerful political constituency that provided strong leadership in supporting Mutoko's participatory budgeting initiative.

2. More information on the initiation, implementation, results, and outcomes of Mutoko's participatory budgeting initiative can be found in Mika (2003); Nyakudanga (2006); Bvunzawabaya (2006); Matovu and Mumvuma (2008); and Sigauke (2007).

3. In Mutoko, such CSOs included ratepayers and residents associations, business associations, church-based groups, transporters and informal traders associations, the war veterans association, and women and youth groups.

4. In real life, however, one of the weaknesses of practicing participatory budgeting in Mutoko is the fact that the process has not been to a greater extent gender sensitive. This is an area that needs improvement.

More effort is necessary to make sure that gender issues are integrated into council policies, budgets, plans, and programs.

5. The same ward committee members actively participated in formulating the council's Five-Year Strategic Plan and in coordinating grassroots inputs before its finalization.

6. Personal communication with the chief executive officer of Mutoko revealed that in Binga, a remote rural district in Matebeland North, the Movement for Democratic Change (MDC) won convincingly with sixteen seats out of twenty-one, after the rural voters were subjected to a rigorous civic education program by a small NGO that was operating in the region.

7. The main objective of this program, which was supported by the World Bank, was to develop the capacity of Rural District Councils (RDCs) in Zimbabwe, and to plan, implement, and manage the sustainable delivery of essential services. The program was made up of three components, namely the institutional, the human resource development, and the capital development components. The institutional development component was meant to support improvements in the capacities of the RDCs to plan and sustain priority services and facilities, as well as financing basic equipment acquisition. The human resources component was designed to build capacity, to provide continuing human resources development assistance to the RDCs, and to respond to specific needs. The capital development component was meant to provide RDCs with access to grant funds, in order to reequip and reinitiate critical services and infrastructure, as well as the provision and creation of incentives for improved RDC performance.

8. During the initiative, traditional leaders cooperated and still are cooperating with the council in rates and levies collection. However, there is a built-in incentive for doing this, as they are paid a 20 percent commission on the total amount of rates and levies collected. Of the total collection, 25 percent is taken up by the council as an administration charge, and the remaining 55 percent is returned to the paying communities to finance local projects of their own choice.

9. Due to a lack of information about the council's mandate, plans, and operations, some CSOs ended up inadvertently undermining the council's vision.

10. It is important to note that in Mutoko, the Urban Institute came to be known as *a friend and development partner* simply because it respected protocol and community norms and values in its local governance capacity-building intervention (Mika 2003, 19).

11. This is supported by Transparency International's observation that "nothing succeeds like success" (International Transparency Source Book 2000, 46).

CHAPTER 10

Building Political Will for Participatory Budgeting in Canada: The Case of the Guelph Neighbourhood Support Coalition

Elizabeth Pinnington

Introduction and Background

Participatory Budgeting

Since 1989, the Brazilian city of Porto Alegre has practiced participatory budgeting, a model of participatory democracy in which local residents deliberate and directly decide how to spend a portion of public funds (Wampler 2007). Different from consultation or grant-making, thousands of citizens in Porto Alegre are involved each year in making decisions about the allocation of up to 20 percent of the public budget, with municipal staff providing technical information and facilitating the completion of projects chosen by residents (Municipality of Porto Alegre 2008). The Worldwatch Institute (2007) reports that by 2007, close to 1,200 municipalities around the world had adapted the Porto Alegre model of participatory budgeting to local contexts. The United Kingdom has mandated that by 2012 every local authority will practice participatory budgeting, and by 2018 children and youth will deliberate 25 percent of the local funds directed to them (UK Department of Communities and Local Government 2007). Participatory budgeting is considered an innovative form of *empowered participatory governance,* which mitigates expert decision-making power and control over public process (Fung and Olin Wright 2003). This model is considered a contribution to deepening democracy, locally and globally, through "the fair distribution of public goods, and the democratic negotiation of the access to these goods among the social actors themselves" (Santos and Avritzer 2005, lviii).

The Canadian Context for Participatory Budgeting

While residents in many Latin American cities tend to become involved in participatory budgeting to address basic infrastructure needs, such as unpaved roads or lack of sewage and clean water distribution, the majority of residents in Canadian cities live with a comparatively developed infrastructure (Lerner and VanWagner 2006). In Guelph's case, for example, residents involved in the participatory budget allocate funds toward social programs, including clothing closets, food cupboards, childcare, and community-building events. In Canada's largest city, the Toronto Community Housing Corporation (TCHC) has 6000–8000 tenants per year deliberate $9 million of the $20 million capital budget to improve their municipal housing spaces (Toronto Community Housing Corporation 2008), including updating security, and creating community meeting places and playgrounds for children. In Montreal, residents of the upper middle-class borough of Plateau Mont-Royal deliberate a portion of the capital budget (Futopulous 2008), increasing citizen engagement and improving shared urban spaces such as parks, as well as negotiating snow removal and other essential services (Rabouin 2008).

Because participatory budgeting happens most often at the municipal level, current Canadian-based experiments must contend with business models of municipal service delivery and marketized bureaucratic systems. During the 1980s, all levels of government in Canada were encouraged to become more *efficient* in their service delivery, taking lessons from business models, which were considered more flexible and creative than government bureaucracies (Inwood 2009). Simultaneous to downloading services to municipalities, higher levels of government encouraged a move toward neoliberal models of public administration, such as New Public Management (NPM), in which governments treat citizens as "clients" and use a market-based approach to service delivery and evaluation (Pierre 1995). An effect of NPM, which favors "expertness, managerial efficacy and allocative efficiency" (Wagenaar 2007, 22), is that hierarchy and social stratification are perpetuated as normal (Foster 2007) and, therefore, marginalized populations stay outside the arena of public decision making while a middle- or upper-class elite maintain control of public process (Frisby and Millar 2002). In this market-based model, an inclusive, deliberative decision-making process can be challenging to learn and support, both on the part of interested residents, as well as institutional officials.

Participatory Budgeting in Guelph: History and Process

Guelph is a city of over 120,000 people, in southwestern Ontario, located 150kms north of the Canada–U.S. border and 100kms west of the country's largest city, Toronto. Due to the presence of a large university, the mean income and education levels in Guelph are higher than both provincial and national averages. The city's median household income is Can$66,000, slightly higher than the provincial average. Roughly 64 percent of residents aged 25–64 have pursued postsecondary education, compared with 55 percent in Ontario and less than 54 percent throughout Canada (City of Guelph 2008). However, Guelph is also home to various low-income and under-resourced neighbourhoods. Over 10 percent of Guelph households are below the Canadian low-income cutoff, which is measured as a greater-than-average amount of income spent on basic household needs, including food, clothing, and housing, compared to an *average* local family (Statistics Canada 2006). Consistent with national trends, single parents and immigrants in Guelph are most susceptible to living with low income (United Way of Guelph Wellington 2007). The Guelph Inclusivity Alliance reports that over 20 percent of Guelph residents are first-generation immigrants. In addition, close to 15 percent of residents indicate that English is not the main language spoken in their homes, which presents additional challenges to participation (City of Guelph 2008).

Since 1999, residents of Guelph have used participatory budgeting to allocate a small portion of the municipal budget, roughly 0.1 percent, combined with donations from other sources. The participatory budgeting process is coordinated by the Neighbourhood Support Coalition (NSC), a civil society organization composed of grassroots neighbourhood groups run by local residents, the vast majority of whom are volunteers.[1] The NSC began in 1997 with five groups who decided to collaborate to improve their service delivery, by sharing information and resources. At that time, the NSC existed primarily to reduce negative health and social outcomes related to living in poverty. Initially, the NSC received partnership support from the City of Guelph, the Guelph Police, and the local branch Family & Children's Services.

The Guelph NSC has since grown to twelve participating neighborhood groups from around the city, representing areas that are considered upper, middle, and lower class in terms of the socioeconomic realities of residents. Residents involved in participatory budgeting say this mixture of participants, from various socioeconomic backgrounds, has posed some challenges to group process, as individuals learn about each others' needs and realities, but has ultimately resulted in a focus on the common good and the allocation of the greatest amount of resources to the most marginalized community members (Pinnington and Schugurensky 2008). Members of the NSC, through being involved in the participatory budget process, report that they are learning to work with municipal staff and council (Pinnington and Schugurensky 2008). On many occasions, NSC members' increased political literacy and social capital has led to residents critically questioning municipal staff, as well as organizing and advocating on behalf of their organization to city council, despite socioeconomic status that might have traditionally been a barrier to political participation. In combination with the political efficacy of NSC members, Guelph's current city council is seen as socially progressive and open to considering requests and ideas from citizens beyond the business and intellectual elite of the community. At the same time, like many Ontario municipalities, the City of Guelph functions with an efficiency model of governance, which inherently tends to exclude lower-income residents. Neighbourhood Support Coalition members, and some city staff, are very cognizant of this challenging dynamic and are actively working together to increase bureaucratic capacity to work across socioeconomic barriers toward greater participation.

In 2008, Guelph neighborhood groups organized over five hundred community-building events, most at low cost or no cost, including family picnics, clothing closets, after-school programs, back-to-school clothing drives, community kitchens, and newcomer welcome programs (Guelph NSC 2008a). The majority of NSC programs and services are delivered by neighborhood volunteers. In 2007, the NSC estimated that volunteers had contributed Can$2,056,320 in service time to the organization, calculated using the Can$12.00/hr/volunteer, Volunteer Canada recognized rate.[2] The majority of NSC volunteers, staff, and community partner organizations' staff are women. Participants link this to a general gendering of care-giving activities, social service provision, and community-building projects, as well as a disproportionate number of women in the community living with low incomes or in social isolation, due to child or elder care responsibilities. Many NSC volunteers have taken administrative, leadership, and staff roles in the organization after having participated in NSC or other community social programming.

The NSC tries to advertise its programming, volunteer, and governance opportunities as widely as possible, including: through the City of Guelph's Web site and quarterly recreation guides, regular event updates in local newspapers, neighborhood newsletters, door-to-door canvassing, direct mailing, phone calls, and informally at neighborhood group events and drop-in centers. The NSC's *Terms of Reference* describe the organization's vision as: "A Guelph community of healthy children, strong families and vibrant neighborhoods that embraces diversity, creates opportunities and promotes a high quality of life for all residents" (Guelph NSC 2006). Neighborhood group representatives are elected from their volunteer base and, in an effort to share power and the workload of committee involvement, typically serve on NSC committees for specified terms, normally two years.

In the early years of the NSC's existence, funding was divided equally between participating neighborhoods. City of Guelph staff, partnering with the NSC, noticed that certain neighborhoods regularly had a surplus by year-end, while other groups struggled to make ends meet in responding to the volume of their communities' needs. After a year of discussion, in 1999 the NSC began using participatory budgeting, when members chose to deliberate and allocate funds by consensus, based on the needs they heard from one another.

Participatory budgeting occurs at the NSC Finance Committee, which is made up of twelve elected representatives from the neighborhood groups. Agency partners, such as Family & Children's Services and the United Way, as well as municipal staff, participate in the finance committee's meetings. Agency representatives and civic employees do not have voting rights. Their role is to provide information, such as information about municipal political processes, and to facilitate access to low-cost resources, such as meeting space. The NSC works to reduce barriers to participation in all its committees, by providing funds for childcare, elder-care, and transportation, as well as food at meetings and translation services in nine different languages (Lerner and Van Wagner 2006). The committee meets once a month. Typical agenda items include the following: information sharing; discussion of funding opportunities; deliberations and allocations of small amounts of funds (up to Can$1,000); and orientation of new members.

There are at least three key differences between the Porto Alegre model of participatory budgeting and the process used by the Guelph NSC. First, NSC members are very proud of the fact that they finalize all decisions about resource allocation through deliberation and consensus, rather than a majority vote. Second, after allocation decisions are made, neighbourhood groups deposit and manage funds from their own organizational bank accounts, reporting back to one another on a regular basis, rather than spending being monitored by public officials. Third, while citizens of Porto Alegre invest mostly in infrastructure, Guelph NSC groups spend the majority of their money on social services and community-building programs, aimed at addressing barriers to civic life, such as poverty, unfamiliarity with the city, and isolation.

Family and Children's Services of Guelph and Wellington County indicates that NSC programming is contributing to a reduction in open child welfare cases in high-risk neighbourhoods (Harvey 2008). Guelph Police report that neighbourhood group programs and services correlate with a reduction in crime rates, particularly in what are considered high-risk areas of the city (Guelph Police Chief 2008). Research on NSC members' civic learning, shows that they develop significant social and political capital by being involved in the participatory budgeting process, by learning about municipal bylaws and processes, and through the act of collaborating with diverse residents from around the city (Pinnington and Schugurensky 2008).

Lack of Political Will for Participatory Budgeting in Guelph

The NSC has enjoyed nine years of collaboration with the City of Guelph, primarily through partnerships with key staff in the Community Development Department. The city is the major funder of the NSC and also provides free meeting space and publicity, insurance, and three staff who work exclusively with neighborhood groups. Janette Loveys-Smith, who was manager of Community Development for six years for the City of Guelph, was one of the key catalysts for participatory budgeting at the NSC. In an interview about the tension between neoliberal models of municipal service delivery and participatory process, she stated: "[municipal staff] have to legitimately respond to people, citizens wanting in the door, wanting to be part of the making of decisions—whatever they are—of city resources" (Loveys-Smith 2007, personal communication). Loveys-Smith supervised three District Community Coordinators (DCCs), who provided a range of support to neighborhood groups, including help with grant writing, networking, and access to city facilities, as well as administrative support. All three DCCs are committed to participatory governance and were hired for their values and skills relating to participatory process (Loveys-Smith 2007, personal communication). While her immediate supervisor was supportive of her work, Loveys-Smith perceived that her philosophy and unconventional actions, related to sharing power with citizens, were not always well understood or supported by fellow administrators in the City of Guelph, including in the Community Development Department.

In early 2008, Loveys-Smith lost her job due to an unanticipated departmental *restructuring* (Hallet 2008), which happened swiftly and largely without explanation. Lerner and VanWagner (2006) posit that the success of participatory budget experiments in Canada is contingent upon support from government staff who advocate for the initiative. Without its institutional champion, many NSC members and concerned residents wondered what the future of participatory budgeting in Guelph would be. The loss of Loveys-Smith is considered to be the first indicator of the lack of political will for participatory budgeting in the City of Guelph.

Around the same time, the NSC realized that, in order to continue viably serving its communities, the organization needed increased funding from the municipality. The NSC claims that it tried to follow proper municipal budget process, including accessing council committee meetings during the development phase of the municipal budget (Guelph NSC 2008). However, city staff claim they have no official record of the NSC applying for more funds (City of Guelph 2008a). The NSC maintains that they were told that the committee agendas were full, and, therefore, the organization could not make their presentation to elected officials (Guelph NSC 2008). Whether or not this situation is an example of a breakdown in communication or subversion of the NSC by senior city staff, the lack of access to public process is considered the second indicator of a lack of political will for participation.

In an unconventional move, the NSC went to the city council on budget approval night to make its request for more funds. City councilors recognized that the NSC had not followed proper public process and redirected the NSC back to the appropriate committee to have their request heard. What followed is considered the third example of lack of political will for participation in the City of Guelph. Senior city staff actively discouraged NSC members from making a budget request. The NSC was told that city staff wanted at least two months to write a report about *service efficiency*, including an investigation of overlap or competition with municipal services (City of Guelph Recreation and Community Services Department 2008, personal communication). While two months is a fairly quick turnaround in municipal reporting, the NSC through consensus decided that it did not want to proceed with its allocation of funds to members, until it had received a response about the funding increase, as this would make a difference in their ability to invite interested new groups to the participatory budgeting table. While the NSC waited for a response from council, its member groups' funds were dwindling dangerously at year-end.

Second, when the NSC tried to register as a delegation at the appropriate council committee meeting three weeks in advance, they were again told by the city clerk's office that the agenda was full. The NSC appealed directly to councilors, to be granted a space at the meeting. Meanwhile, another local civil society organization reports being given space on the same committee's agenda, by the city clerk's office, on the *day of* the meeting (Guelph Civic League 2008, personal communication). Finally, three senior city staff from the Community Development Department openly stated to NSC members that if asked by council, they would indicate that they were unsupportive of the NSC funding increase due to a lack of understanding of the organization and its budget process.

Strategies for Building Political Will for
Participatory Budgeting in Guelph

Build Relationships with Senior City Staff and Councilors

Almost immediately after Loveys-Smith lost her job with the City of Guelph, several NSC members and a University of Toronto researcher and Guelph resident, who had been working closely with the NSC, began meeting with senior city officials and councilors. Many of these meetings were informal, taking place in local cafés, at the beginning or end of council meetings, and at breaks during NSC meetings, in which staff was in attendance. The purpose of these meetings was twofold. First, NSC members wanted to gauge the level of continued city support for the NSC's participatory processes, in order to decide on the future of its relationship with the municipality. Informally, many NSC members had heard Loveys-Smith talk about the difficulty she faced in supporting the idea of participatory budgeting to colleagues, especially those in more senior positions. In an interview about participatory budgeting in Guelph, she recalled: "I have sat in many [city] management meetings and heard 'You can tell that group not to do that, right?' I respond, 'No, actually, I can't'" (Loveys-Smith 2007, personal communication). Indeed, NSC members found some senior city staff more supportive than others. Members reported back to one another, both at NSC meetings and through informal networks, about their thoughts on their relationship with the city.

Second, NSC members and supporters chose to build relationships with city councilors. Coalition chairs sent e-mails to their ward councilors asking for their support for the NSC funding request. The chair of the NSC Finance Committee wrote to the mayor. The university researcher shared, with members of council, papers and study findings related to participatory budgeting, as well as community engagement, from research in Guelph and in other parts of the world. Neighbourhood Support Coalition members also attended council and municipal committee meetings, as a group, to show support and commitment for their request. They found many councilors very supportive of both the participatory budget, as well as the distinct community engagement work that neighborhood groups were doing around the city. Certain councilors generously gave of their time to research participatory process, to enable themselves to support the NSC's request, when it came before council a second time.

Raise Awareness with City Officials about Participatory
Process and the Benefits of Community Engagement

During many of the meetings NSC members had with senior staff and councilors, including presentations to council and municipal committees, they took the opportunity to explain the benefits of and differences between participatory process and top-down service delivery. As noted above, reporting and accountability structures in Canadian municipalities are highly results oriented and tied to efficiency, which is seen as an effective way to transparently manage public funds. Unfortunately, this municipal reporting structure, which focuses on financial return for use (Thibault, Kikulis, and Frisby 2002), does not account for volunteer hours contributed to an initiative (Quarter, Mook, and Richmond 2002). Nor does it adequately recognize qualitative products of citizen participation in decision making and program delivery, such as health benefits (Reid, Frisby, and Ponic 2002) or civic learning (Lerner and Schugurensky 2006). While this structure makes sense for financial efficiency, it often leads to decisions that favor privileged citizens, who have greater capacity to pay user fees for municipal services, such as recreational activities, and more access to public deliberations, due to greater literacy of political process (Frisby and Millar 2002).

Members of the NSC spent time discussing with senior city staff their view that NSC services were not competing with city programs, due to their community engagement focus. Therefore, NSC members argued that they deserved an increase in city funds to continue to promote residents' access to participatory programming, including the budgeting process and neighborhood centers. All three DCCs, who had been working under Janette Loveys-Smith, devoted a considerable amount of time and energy to working with more senior staff, explaining their view of participatory process as *sharing power with* rather than *having power over* residents.

In a culminating event, the NSC invited key senior staff, all city councilors, and the mayor to attend their annual participatory budgeting process for 2008. Two senior staff and one councilor observed the entire four-hour process. At the end of the meeting, both municipal staff indicated having a much greater understanding of the challenges faced by certain neighborhood groups, as well as the benefits of participatory process in distributing funds. In her closing remarks, the city councilor stated, "Now you have a new champion." Members of the NSC were thrilled with this feedback.

Use Local News Media to Highlight the Issue

Throughout early 2008, NSC members and DCCs in the City of Guelph used the media to promote the coalition's participatory budget process. A quarterly community services guide, published by a local newspaper, featured a two-page magazine article about the NSC and their participatory budget. Members of the NSC also advertised their participatory budget date, including an open invitation for observers, in a free community newspaper distributed to most homes in Guelph. After the 2008 participatory budget, the NSC finance chair was contacted to do an exclusive interview with the local daily, highlighting the organization's participatory process and explaining why they were so deserving of an increase in tax-based funding.

The media attention has resulted in two major outcomes. First, at a recent NSC finance meeting, community members discussed having a media strategy for the upcoming year, to increase their local profile, and document their participatory budget for a wider audience. Second, raising the public profile of the NSC through the media is a strategy to create support from elected officials, many of whom have been quite vocal, both during their campaigns and during their subsequent terms in office, about their desire to support local participatory governance initiatives.

Partnering with other Organizations also Working to Support a Participatory Approach to Governance

During the NSC's bid for increased municipal funding, for 2008, which coincided with the NSC experiencing a lack of trust in senior city staff, coalition members partnered with other local organizations for support. In particular, a local citizens' group, that actively works to increase residents' awareness and access to public process, was very helpful in providing information about municipal procedures to NSC members. In addition, this same civil society organization appeared twice as a delegation before council in support of the NSC's participatory budget and its request for funds.

A second organization, a local social service agency, was also helpful during the same time period. Family and Children's Services of Guelph and Wellington County, which already worked closely with many NSC member groups, provided statistics to senior city staff about the number of open child welfare cases in each neighborhood, as well as information about NSC programs contributing to a reduction in these cases. The agency had recently participated in a university study about their innovative partnership with NSC volunteers, which they saw as creating a proactive environment for vulnerable children and their families to seek resources from trusted fellow community members. A Family & Children's Services staff person was present at the NSC participatory budget meeting in 2008, and provided information to municipal staff and councilors about how she saw NSC participatory governance empowering local families. Afterward, a senior city staff person commented on how *eye-opening* that conversation had been for her.

Outcomes and Future Directions

The four initiatives outlined above have led to both short- and longer-term outcomes. In the short term, the city council unanimously voted to grant the NSC the additional Can$50,000 they requested from the already-approved 2008 municipal budget. Coalition members were very pleased to receive this additional funding, which resulted in two new neighborhood groups joining the participatory budgeting table. Both new groups received funds for growth and development projects. In addition, each of the ten existing groups received an increase in funding from their 2007 totals. This enabled them to continue offering essential core initiatives, grow service levels, and provide innovative programming in 2008, in response to demographic growth in the city and changes in the needs of the neighborhood.

Media attention on the participatory budget process, its uniqueness in North America, and its history in Guelph, have led to increased community awareness about the NSC, its functions, and its inclusive governance processes. This attention has led senior city staff and councilors to continue to ask questions about the NSC process and offer to work in a more collaborative, rather than directive, style with NSC members. While traditional municipal governance structures are still in place in Guelph, NSC members and city councilors are committed to working together to deepen discussions about participatory process, and to build willingness and capacity among senior city staff, and in municipal systems, to enhance, rather than co-opt, empowered participatory governance.

Based on feedback from community members who took part in the 2008 participatory budget, the NSC is now working on drafting an official *Terms of Reference* for the process. One senior city staff member, who attended the participatory budgeting process, has suggested that this *Terms of Reference* serve as the basis for a motion to city council. She proposes that participatory budgeting be raised from its current informal status to an officially recognized public process, which would remain in place regardless of staff or council turnover. Members of the NSC also see the *Terms of Reference* as an orientation tool for new volunteers, as well as a way of sharing their allocation process with a wider audience. As word spreads through academic and government communities, citizens' groups and professionals, from around the world, are contacting the City of Guelph and the NSC for more information about their participatory budget process.

It is important to note that a key underlying factor in the NSC's ability to face a lack of political will was the sophisticated capacity of ordinary community members from very diverse socioeconomic situations, for participatory governance. Though there has been significant turnover in involved residents, the collective institutional memory of the NSC, as well as cumulative learning about process, has contributed to their ability to ask pointed questions of city officials, and resist being directed by city staff. During the 2008 participatory budget debrief, members celebrated what many saw as the smoothest, quickest deliberation they had done to date. One community member commented, "We succeeded the other night. I think that means we're getting better and more skilled."

References

City of Guelph. 2008. *City Profile.* Available on the Guelph.ca/business .cfm Web site.

City of Guelph. 2008a. *Emergency Services, Community Services and Operations. Meeting Minutes, March 17, 2008.* Available on the Guelph.ca Web site.

Foster, C. 2007. *Blackness and Modernity: The Colour of Humanity and the Quest for Freedom.* Montreal: McGill-Queen's University Press.

Fung, A. and E. Olin Wright, eds. 2003. *Deepening Democracy: Institutional Innovations in Empowered Participatory Governance: The Real Utopias IV.* Available on the ssc.wisc.edu Web site.

Frisby, W. and S. Millar. 2002. The actualities of doing community development to promote the inclusion of low income populations in local sport and recreation. *European Sport Management Quarterly,* 2: 209–233.

Futopulous, H. 2008. Opening Plenary: Participatory democracy, active citizenship and local governance. Presented at the Learning Democracy by Doing: Alternative Practices in Citizenship Learning and Participatory Democracy Conference. Transformative Learning Centre, OISE/UT.

Guelph Inclusivity Alliance. 2008. Presentation to Guelph City Council. Guelph, Ontario: Neighbourhood Support Coalition.

Guelph Neighbourhood Support Coalition. 2008. Presentation to City of Guelph Emergency Services, Community Services and Operations. Guelph, Ontario: Neighbourhood Support Coalition.

Guelph Neighbourhood Support Coalition. 2008a. Presentation to the City of Guelph Council Meeting. Guelph, Ontario: Neighbourhood Support Coalition.

Guelph Neighbourhood Support Coalition. 2006. *Terms of Reference.* Guelph, Ontario: Neighbourhood Support Coalition.

Guelph Neighbourhood Support Coalition. 2003. *Goal Statement, Joint Agreements, and Sponsorship Agreements.* Guelph, Ontario: Neighbourhood Support Coalition.

Guelph Police Chief. 2008. Presentation at the Neighbourhood Support Coalition Community Information Meeting. Guelph, Ontario.

Hallet, D. 2008. Community services shake-up. *The Guelph Tribune.*

Harvey, E. 2008. Presentation to the Guelph Neighbourhood Support Coalition Finance Committee. Guelph, Ontario: Neighbourhood Support Coalition.

Inwood, G.J. 2009. *Understanding Canadian Public Administration: An Introduction to Theory and Practice.* Toronto, Ontario: Pearson Education Canada.

Lerner, J. and D. Schugurensky. 2007. Who learns what in participatory budgeting? Participatory budgeting in Rosario, Argentina. In *Democratic Practices as Learning Opportunities,* 85–100. R. van der Veen, D. Wildemeersch, J. Youngblood, and V. Marsick eds. Rotterdam, The Netherlands: Sense Publishers.

Lerner, J. and E. Van Wagner. 2006. Participatory budgeting in Canada: Democratic innovations in strategic spaces. In *The Transnational Institute New Politics Publications.* Available on the tni.org Web site.

Municipality of Porto Alegre. 2008. *Regimento Interno do Orçamento Participativo 2007/2008.* Available on the 2.portoalegre.rs.gov Web site.

Pierre, J. 1995. The marketization of the state: Citizens, consumers and the emergence of the public market. In *Governance in a Changing Environment,* 55–81. Peters, G.B. and D. Savoie eds. Montreal, Canada: Canadian Centre for Management Development.

Pinnington, E., J. Lerner, and D. Schgurensky. 2009. Participatory budgeting in North America: The case of Guelph, Canada. In *Journal of Public Budgeting, Accounting & Financial Management,* 21:2/3.

Pinnington, E. and D. Schugurensky. 2008. Learning democracy by doing: Participatory budgeting in Guelph, Canada. Presentation at the Learning Democracy by Doing Conference. Ontario Institute for Studies in Education, University of Toronto.

Quarter, J., L. Mook, and B.J. Richmond. 2002. *What Counts: Social Accounting for Nonprofits and Cooperatives.* New Jersey: Prentice Hall.

Rabouin, L. 2008. Participatory budgeting in the borough of Plateau Montreal. Presentation at the Learning Democracy by Doing: Alternative Practices in Citizenship Learning and Participatory Democracy Conference. Transformative Learning Centre, OISE/UT.

Reid, C., W. Frisby, and P. Ponic. 2002. Confronting two-tiered recreation and poor women's exclusion: Promoting inclusion, health and social justice. *Canadian Woman Studies,* 21(3): 88–95.

Santos, B. and L. Avritzer. 2005. Opening up the canon of democracy. In *Democratizing Democracy,* xxxiv–lxxiv. B. Santos ed. London: Verso.

Santos, B. 2005. Participatory budgeting in Porto Alegre: Toward a redistributive democracy. In *Democratizing Democracy*, 307–376. B. Santos ed. London: Verso.

Statistics Canada. 2006. Low Income Cut-offs for 2006 and Low Income Measures for 2005. Information available at the stattcan.ca Web site.

Thibault, L., L.M. Kikulis, and W. Frisby. 2002. Partnerships between local government sport and leisure departments and the commercial sector: Changes, complexities, and consequences. In *The Commercialization of Sport*, 119–140. T. Slack ed. London: Frank, Cass Publishers.

Toronto Community Housing Corporation. 2008. *Participatory Budgeting Backgrounder*. Distributed to attendees of the 2008 THCH participatory budget, at the North York Civic Centre.

United Kingdom Department of Communities and Local Government. 2007. *An Action Plan for Community Empowerment: Building on Success*. Available on the communities.gov.uk Web site.

United Way of Guelph Wellington. 2007. Available on the unitedwayguelph.com Web site.

Wagenaar, H. 2007. Governance, complexity, and democratic participation. How citizens and public officials harness the complexities of neighborhood decline. *The American Review of Public Administration*, 37(1): 17–50.

Wampler, B. 2007. *Participatory Budgeting in Brazil: Contestation, Cooperation, and Accountability*. Pittsburgh, Pennsylvania: Pennsylvania University Press.

Worldwatch Institute. 2007. *State of the World 2007: Our Urban Future*. New York: W.W. Norton.

Notes

1. Unless otherwise noted, information on the Guelph NSC is based on City of Guelph, 2008; Guelph Neighbourhood Support Coalition, 2003, 2006, 2008; and observations of NSC Finance Committee meetings from 2007–08.

2. 1428 different volunteers $\times$ (10hr/12mos) = 120 x \$12.

CHAPTER 11

FROM COMMAND TO CONSENT IN BOLIVIA: HOW AND WHY TO GAIN POLITICAL WILL FOR CITIZEN PARTICIPATION

Ronald MacLean-Abaroa[1]

Introduction

Emerging from centuries of colonial rule, and more recently from four decades of civilian and military dirigisme, the Bolivian government initiated a social and political innovation known as *Participacion Popular,* or Popular Participation (PP). Next to the reestablishment of democracy, PP is Bolivia's most important governance innovation. It is a unique exercise in citizen participation, institutionalized by law and promoted from the top and center of the political system.

Along with the advent of local democracy in 1985, PP constituted the single most important and largest redistribution of national income and political power to the local level in Bolivia's history. The 1994 Law of Popular Participation (LPP) extended municipal status to all parts of the country, reallocating funds and power. The LPP devolved much of the responsibility for health, education, and infrastructure to the municipalities. Twenty percent of the national income, known as *coparticipacion,* was earmarked as *Popular Participation Funds,* to be credited daily to every municipality's bank account in proportion to its population.

However, the most significant and enduring effect was the adoption of traditional mechanisms for participatory governance. The law officially recognized traditional neighborhood associations and granted them a key role in identifying priority needs and deciding how funds should be spent. It formalized the rights and responsibilities of traditional community organizations to plan, prioritize, and manage the allocation of investment funds, thus creating legal structures and mechanisms mandating citizen

189

involvement. The LPP also formally established *vigilance committees* to ensure that prioritized neighborhood projects were considered in municipal development plans, and provided transparency to the budgetary process (Pierce 1997).

This chapter traces how participatory governance practices in Bolivia have helped to create a new sense of citizenship and new links between citizens and government across the country. At a time when local democracy was taking its first shaky steps, PP transformed the relationship between citizens and authorities, creating greater social stability and a new vision of a future that was ultimately advantageous to both the *governors* and the *governed*. Despite the initial fears of those in power, PP brought positive change to the social fabric of the cities, generating significant political will for participatory governance. With enhanced citizen participation, a sense of community began to flourish and, more importantly, a sense of hope for the future. Popular Participation achieved such acceptance as a viable process for collective decision making, that it was readily transferred from local to national governance. In 2000, the PP model was successfully adopted as the mechanism for a nationwide participatory dialogue about the use of $1.5 billion in *forgiven* external debt.

While the political will to adopt participatory governance practices was initially grounded in self-interest and a need, on the part of governors, to assuage political pressures, the PP and National Dialogue initiatives have resulted in significant concrete benefits for governors and the governed. Based on the Bolivian experience, this chapter explores the crucial question of *why rulers should share power with the ruled*.

A Country of Diversity

Bolivia's nine regional departments are geographically and culturally diverse, with a tradition of economic rivalry (Pierce 1997, 5). In the 2001 census, more than half, or 62.05 percent, of Bolivia's population defined themselves as indigenous (Census 2001). Although Spanish is the official language, many Bolivians speak only indigenous languages and dialects, and indigenous peoples make up a large proportion of the urban and rural poor. During colonial times, Bolivia was one of the richest and most densely populated countries in Latin America. However, by the end of the twentieth century it had become the poorest, and the recipient of a large amount of international aid. Bolivia's population, estimated at seven million in 1989, has been steadily moving east, as the center of economic power shifted from the tin and silver mines of the Andes to the agricultural land of the tropical east, where new discoveries of oil and gas have been made. Each change in economic fortunes has led to new demands for increased regional autonomy, which threatened to loosen the fragile links holding the nation together.

Contrasting Traditions of Governance

National government, as Bolivians experienced it, with over 200 years of *caudillo* rule, whether military or civilian, was paternalistic, top-down, and autocratic. This experience is similar to other postcolonial republics.[2] Central institutions and authorities were ineffective, and extended only to those urban areas designated as municipalities. In the sparsely populated rural areas, local forms of government prevailed for everything from the administration of justice to the allocation of land.

Among the indigenous, agrarian cultures, there was a long tradition of participatory governance through collaborative communal work, sharing of authority, and peer accountability, effected through a range of structures and entities appropriate to local needs. Traditional authority among indigenous Bolivians is rooted in consensus, participatory decision making and a practice of *don,* and *reciprocity* by which authority rotates within the community, and is conferred to those elders who share their wealth with the community, in the form of agricultural surplus during festivities at the end of the crop season. In reciprocity, they are granted *don,* which is honor, prestige, authority, and power. Redistributed wealth is collectively appropriated, and social and economic balance is restored.

These traditions date to pre-Columbus times, and were arguably strengthened during the hardships of colonial times. Extreme poverty and domination, first by the Spanish colonizers, and later by the republican rulers, necessitated survival strategies that emphasized self-reliance, shared and rotating leadership, and peer accountability. These practices were readopted during the mining unions' revolts, after the Chaco war in the late 1930s, which led to the Bolivian revolution of 1952, when the mines were nationalized. During the periods before and after the revolution, the miners took control of mining operations and imposed discipline by a scheme of shared authority and accountability, through *vigilance committees.*

Confrontation and Upheaval

During the periods of military dictatorship from 1936 to the National Revolution of 1952, and again from 1964 to 1982, relationships between the people and the state were confrontational. Divisions between Bolivia's different regions, and between urban and rural societies were deepened. In the cities, influence and corruption, not the needs of the poor, drove infrastructure development. Local people learned that direct action, such as strikes and blockades, were the only ways to exercise power. They organized themselves into what were popularly known as *neighborhood juntas* to collectively defend their interests and pressure the government. In turn, those in power viewed any grouping of citizens with distrust. By 1981, Bolivia's political situation was considered so unstable, and its rulers so corrupt that international aid donors, such as the World Bank, withdrew.

The end of military rule, marking the rebirth of democracy in 1982, unleashed unprecedented hyperinflation, followed by a radical economic package that brought in market reforms in 1985. The mood for change and reform cut across party lines, with the Congress-appointed president, Victor Paz Estenssoro, introducing and extending the reforms originally developed by Hugo Banzer, winner of the electoral majority.

Adding to the economic and social upheaval was the collapse of the world market for tin, which saw up to 30,000 miners lose their jobs. Many of these economic migrants, *relocalizados,* who were predominantly indigenous people, joined others leaving impoverished rural areas, and moved to cities, eager to find jobs, better living conditions, housing, and public transportation.

This mass migration put great pressure on the fledgling democracy, at the national and city level. To counter this, the government introduced an innovative attempt at state collaboration with local communities. The *Fondo Social de Emergencia (FSE),* or Social Emergency Fund, allocated investment resources to needs identified during consultation with citizens, such as retraining and infrastructure. Despite the sheer numbers of people arriving in the main cities at one time, the scheme, which operated from 1987 until the change of government in 1989, achieved surprising success. The FSE initiative broke new ground and sowed the seed for the later development of PP.

Description of the Initiative

The Law of Popular Participation (LPP), promulgated in 1994, represented a bold decision by the national government of Gonzalo Sanchez de Lozada to resolve fundamental problems that had plagued the first years of Bolivia's return to democracy. These centered on calls for increased regional autonomy, which would inevitably widen the rapidly growing gaps between rich and poor, and urban and rural. Only 7 percent of national income was directed to rural areas, while funding to cities favored the east over the west (Pierce 1997, 5).

The Law of Popular Participation redrew the political map of Bolivia, extending municipal status to all parts of the country. At the same time, it mandated the participation of local groups in the budgeting and expenditure of a share of national income, distributed on a per head basis. This enabled a rebalance of power and funding, and reallocated national resources on a much more equitable basis, transferring many responsibilities from central to local government. Local actors were empowered and new relationships between citizens and their local and national governments were created. Extensive public debate and an unprecedented communications campaign preceded the passing of the LPP, and extensive education programs followed.

The Law of Popular Participation set a formal, legal framework for the distribution of 20 percent of national income to the 311 municipal entities, 193 of which had been newly created.[3] It formalized the role of traditional community groups, such as *juntas vecinales,* as *Organizaciones Territoriales de Base* (OTBs), or Territorially-Based Organizations.[4] The OTBs were mandated to *propose, ask, control, and supervise* the work of each mayor's office and the resources pertaining to it. They were also charged with participating in and assisting with projects and maintenance, protecting the environment, promoting equal access for men and women to representation, as well as roles in health and education authorities (Pierce 1997, 15).

Municipalities worked on five-year planning horizons. During the first year of each five-year municipal term, OTBs, assisted by professional facilitators paid with coparticipation funds, engaged in a six-month participatory planning process. They elaborated a yearly budget, and a five-year projection budget, in which they listed their public works preferences, chosen after negotiation amongst OTB members. Once an approved budget plan for expenditure was presented, the national government would make automatic daily payments into the municipal bank account. The coparticipation account was held separately, and all citizens could enquire about the account.

In order to ensure that payments continued, OTBs were required to present annual accounts. The LPP required that each OTB appoint a vigilance committee from within its membership, to oversee that funds were expended as planned, with not more than 10 percent allocated to administration. The vigilance committee could legally challenge the mayor, if it felt there was evidence of wrongdoing.

The Law of Popular Participation was one of a series of initiatives known as *Plan de Todos*, Plan for All, introduced by Gonzalo Sanchez de Lozada, who was elected as president in 1993. As Minister of Planning, Sanchez de Lozada was a key architect of the 1985 economic reforms that encouraged donors, like the World Bank and USAID, to renew aid to Bolivia. Most of this aid was tied to achieving improvements in health, sanitation, and education for the poor and disadvantaged, who were increasingly flocking to the cities.

Despite a number of achievements in the first years of democracy, between 1985 and 1993, Bolivia continued to be a nation divided. Initially, it seemed that democracy was doing nothing to diminish the prevailing poverty. According to the 1992 census, 70.5 percent of Bolivia was poor, including 95.1 percent of the rural population and 52.6 percent of the urban population, while ranking below its neighbors in measures such as years of schooling and infant mortality. Ninety-three percent of government investment funds were directed to the cities, almost all of which went to the three metropolitan areas of La Paz, Cochabamba, and Santa Cruz. This was reflected in internal inequalities. In 1992, the infant mortality rate was 100/1000 in rural areas, and only 62/1000 in cities. Of urban dwellers, 81 percent had access to potable water, compared with only 19 percent of rural families (Pierce 1997, 4).

Sanchez de Lozada stood unsuccessfully for election in 1989. In 1993, he campaigned on proposals for decentralization, and increased public participation in government. In order to govern, Sanchez de Lozada formed a coalition with some of the parties of the left. Sharing their concerns about the social impact of the economic reforms introduced in 1985, in 1991 he created a think tank, the *Fundacion Milenio* to investigate *finding a way to decentralize power without destroying the capacity to govern.* He co-opted some young social scientists, close to the Spanish school of public administration in Santa Cruz, who were already committed to finding ways to implement the decentralization process, involving ordinary citizens in decision making, and empowering them with a higher degree of political participation. Simultaneously, the World Bank had financed a program of decentralization during the Paz Estenssoro administration (1985–89), developing a model of fiscal decentralization. These two groups of people met under *Milenio,* and combined the social and technical aspects of their work to produce the PP scheme. They proposed a model of municipal decentralization, resolving an issue that had been fought over and debated since the early years of the republic (Grindle in Santiso 2001, 119).

Results and Achievements

Local government reform, based on PP, achieved the most significant redistribution of political power and national income in Bolivia's history. As a result of PP, local governments became more relevant political actors, and ordinary citizens were better informed about their rights and responsibilities.

For the first time, all citizens of Bolivia had the mechanisms, both political and economic, to better participate in their own governance (Pierce 1997, 14). To the surprise of many in positions of power, sharing governance was equally advantageous to the governors. The process of negotiation involved in setting budget priorities, and engaging with authorities to ensure that they were honored, generated a new and more positive governance relationship. A sense of community began to flourish, which benefited the citizenry and authorities.

Before PP, democratically elected mayors faced constant pressure to address every issue affecting citizens. Hundreds of requests and complaints were directed upwards to those in authority, who often lacked the resources to give a satisfactory response. Under PP, this social pressure began to recede. Citizens were required to first negotiate budget priorities for their city and community among themselves, before presenting them to the mayor. This defused the pressure, and dispersed it horizontally.

The mayor and council did not receive requests for expenditure and action until the community agreed upon priorities and decisions were confirmed. Those in power gained time and space to focus on the most important issues. Because both the governors and the governed needed each other to implement the plans they so elaborately discussed and drew up, this mutual dependency developed into mutual trust.

Analytical Section

Lack of Political Will

Paternalism, powerlessness, and poverty

As in most postcolonial republics in Latin America and elsewhere, two hundred years of *caudillo* rule, military and civilian, left a strongly paternalistic, top-down, and autocratic tradition of government in Bolivia. During this period, few political institutions developed, or earned respect, there were enduring clashes over visions of the ideal society, and confrontation was considered the only effective communication tool. This caused constant shifts in values and national priorities, a pendulum that swung between *left*, and *right*, resulting in a chronically debilitating political instability, which deepened the mistrust between the governors and the governed. Effective authority was an elusive trait and a scarce political commodity. The idea of the *strong* leader was more of an ideal than a fact, an ideal that often degenerated into despotism and abusive forms of rule. Dictators, both benevolent and brutal, succeeded one another with little benefit to the majority of citizens.

The advent of democratic government was a time of hope for the Bolivian nation, prompting unprecedented cooperation between opposing political parties. However, the ideal of participatory democracy, or power-sharing with citizens, was unthinkable, because neither the power-holders nor the disempowered had any models of how this might be achieved, or tools that could be tried. Economic modernization and market reforms were politically unpopular, and governance deteriorated. Mass street demonstrations by displaced minorities and interest groups threatened social stability and the political system. Those governing were faced with evidence that suggested emerging democracies were as corrupt and unworkable as the dictatorships that preceded them, while the governed were confirmed in their belief that confrontational methods were the only way to achieve change.

Bolivia's first democratically elected mayors only had top-down, authoritarian models for governing their municipalities, which were similar in style to national dictators. Appointed mayors of the past, were not required to respond to an electorate or be accountable to a council. The mayor's monopoly on formal power, in the absence of clear rules, citizens' charters, or council oversight, made local governments prone to despotism, arbitrariness, and corruption.

These traits tended to prevail through the initial years of the young municipal democracy, when elected mayors still had extensive discretion, along with their councils, in deciding the content of their investment budgets, and the types of public services provided to their citizens. Unelected groups, such as *civic committees*, trade associations, and unions had the knowledge and influence to promote their own interests, as did municipal employees. It was not a coincidence that staff presented the mayor with the most expensive projects at the top of the list, which were often located in remote parts of the city. They involved new urban developments that benefited private interests, which bribed the municipal officials to redirect public works their way.

The urban poor learned during the years of dictatorship that the only way to get attention was to make demands that were extreme and often violent, and to demand immediate satisfaction. They learned to distrust politically appointed authorities, who might suddenly be sacked. This distrust persisted well into the democratic period. When economic crises were overcome, people demanded better living conditions, and NOW. If their needs were not met, they did not reelect the mayor. During the initial years of municipal democracy, few mayors were able to renew their mandate, creating the need to devise new forms, ways, and means of government to achieve a mutually agreed understanding of governance.

The curse of the autocrat

The *curse of the autocrat* is where the autocratic exercise of power does not translate into enduring political support, because there are no mechanisms by which this can be built, and no evidence that this would be advantageous to both rulers and the ruled. The *curse of the autocrat* is the political divorce that occurs once a candidate is elected to office, and becomes isolated from the electorate. The collective and participatory *us* of the political campaign, reverts to *us* the people against *them* of the new authorities. This results in growing mutual suspicion and mistrust, which mitigates against the development of any participatory governance, as councilors represent their political parties or respond to the mayor rather than to the electorate, and citizens feel alienated from their representatives and powerless to determine city priorities.

As mayor of La Paz, I became the first democratic mayor, but also the last authoritarian by the legacy I inherited. I felt the *curse of the autocrat*, before *Participacion Popular*. Many of the new arrivals in La Paz, and those in the city of El Alto, the fast-growing adjoining slopes of the city, were effectively immigrants in their own country. They had little concept of citizenship. The idea of community was undeveloped, and their view of *neighborhood* was so narrow that it might only include a handful of families, or a few blocks around. When they saw others benefiting from municipal works, they became infuriated at *losing* to other neighborhoods, and turned their frustration on the representatives they may have recently voted for. There was a constant suspicion of corruption, and sense that the authorities were favoring someone else, generating renewed pressures upon them.

Whatever I was able to achieve as mayor, it only served to whet the appetite for greater demands from the community, with no understanding of resource limitations or the wider needs of the population. Governance became a nightmare. There was not an easy solution, or any solution at all, given the scarcity of funds *and* time.

Although some traditional organizations flourished in the city and participated in donor-supported development projects, there was no mechanism for incorporating such groups into the governance of the city (Tyson 2008). Everything started with and stopped with the mayor.

Strategies for Building Political Will

The political will for PP initially came from the *top*, from high-level political leadership. Its enduring success, however, depended on it being quickly and comprehensively embraced by actors at the *bottom*, by ordinary citizens and community-based organizations.

President Sanchez de Lozada recognized that strong leadership would be needed to generate the political will to implement and maintain such a radical change. His personal commitment was crucial, as was the unprecedented and extensive information and education campaign about PP. Bolivians' hopes for democratic involvement were raised many times in the past, only to leave them disappointed, so there were negative expectations to overcome on all sides. The president himself headed the technical team that drafted the law. It dedicated 300 hours of sessions to the law, while Congress held 450 meetings around the LPP (Grebe in Pierce 1997, 3).

To explain the bill to the electorate, the president, his cabinet, party officials, and the press embarked on a *U.S.-style* education and promotion campaign, which fostered much public debate. This dissemination campaign "the likes of which Bolivia had never before seen" was continued and enhanced after the passing of the law (Campbell 1994). Preliminary publicity included seminars, assemblies, workshops, and talks around the subject of PP, and even a *Miss OTB* contest in one area to attract public attention. By 1995, three thousand municipal employees had received training, and even the military was trained to support the establishment of PP (Pierce 1997, 13).

Three key mechanisms became the catalyst to foster political will for PP, by the governed and by the governors. These were: (i) a carefully designed system of decentralization; (ii) the honoring of traditional decision-making mechanisms; and (iii) a strong legislative framework.

Decentralization

From the first days of democratic government, decentralization was a top agenda item for governments of all political persuasion. Redressing inequalities across the country and addressing calls for greater regional autonomy were seen as essential to maintaining Bolivia as a viable nation. However, during twelve years of debate, successive governments were unable to find an effective and equitable formula for decentralization.

Sanchez de Lozada was committed to a decentralization process that significantly increased the number of municipal entities. Although this would result in the reduction of resources directed to some powerful regional centers, it would also atomize sources of dissent and build new strongholds of support for government policies. The decentralization process mandated by the LPP, and promulgated by Congress in 1994, extended municipal status and the powers associated with it to all regions of the country, including the right to hold elections. For 80 percent of the new municipalities, the funding they received under PP was the first distribution they had received from the national treasury (Pierce 1997, 7).

These national resources added to whatever resources that could be collected locally. The LPP empowered all municipalities to impose property taxes, fees, and licenses (Pierce 1997, 8).

Honoring traditional decision making

The Law of Popular Participation provided for a range of preexisting local groups to be recognized as the OTB representing a community, including indigenous communities, campesino or peasant communities, and a variety of neighborhood groups, or *juntas vecinales,* including capitanes, jilacatas, mallcus, secretarios generales, and all preexisting local titles. By recognizing these different local structures, the law incorporated each community's local traditions of governance, reviving elements of the former rural and community tradition of peasants' participation in consultative decision making. It also incorporated the trade unions' more recent tradition of social control, employing the political lexicon adopted from the Trotskyites and Socialists beginning in the 1930s.

Strong legislative framework

Trust in the legal framework for PP was built through its careful design to generate mutual dependency, by incorporating rights and obligations on the part of both governors and the governed. The national government was obligated to ensure regular payments to municipalities and to respond to concerns in a timely manner. For instance, a vigilance committee could lodge a complaint if they suspected that the municipal bank account was being misused, and the Ministry of Sustainable Development was required to investigate such complaints within a week. Evidence of wrongdoing would be referred to the Senate, and municipal funds frozen. This encouraged honesty in government, because citizens and the mayor depended on each other to ensure that public works were funded and completed. This tended to engender mutual trust, and stable relationships.

How Political Will/Citizen–State Relations Evolved as a Result of the Initiative

Initially, PP was seen as a threat, by those holding both formal and informal power, such as unelected corporate groups and civic committees, which previously held the knowledge and influence to ensure their favored projects had priority. Popular Participation challenged established concepts of authority and hierarchy, on which most political relationships were built, and at first it attracted criticism from both sides of the political spectrum. *Vigilance committees*, evoked the system of urban political control employed in Castro's Cuba and prompted memories of the commando militia used after the 1952 revolution to subdue the urban middle class. This caused PP to be viewed by some as a *communist* measure. At the same time, the most populist of groups, the CONDEPA political party, which was a forbear of *Movimenta al Socialismo* (MAS), or Movement to Socialism, the indigenous party currently in power in Bolivia and led by Evo Morales, also opposed the PP initiative. However, this somehow eroded their self-appointed role as *defenders of the poor* and *the people's voice*. However, political support for PP began to grow once those at the center of the new system, the locally elected authorities, realized that the improved governance and greater stability generated by Popular Participation was of advantage to them.

Unsurprisingly, it was the newly established and largely rural municipalities that first took advantage of PP, setting up OTBs and preparing municipal plans. These districts often did not have a previous relationship with, let alone funding from, the state, so the new distribution of investment funds marked the start of new and positive relationships. Although the largest cities already had some infrastructure, it was typically lacking in country areas, where people were eager to have input in the spending of new coparticipation funding. Rural areas already had established and functioning forms of local governance, which could quickly be recognized as OTBs and give local people the power to decide whether to build a new town hall, spend money on drainage projects, or withhold payment from teachers, "who arrive in town on Tuesday and leave on Thursday nights" (Campbell 1994).

Some cities were slower to see the potential of PP, and some administrations, notably the CONDEPA party mayor of La Paz from 1993–1994, refused to introduce PP. However, for others, including myself, resuming the role of mayor in 1995, PP provided a promise of a much improved governance environment.

When I first became mayor of La Paz in 1985, there was evidence of corruption and neglect everywhere. While some development work had been done on the outskirts of the city, roads in the center were in disrepair and public transport infrequent. This increased the hardships and length of the working day for many people, especially women (Tyson 2008). Key issues were how to better respond to the basic and real needs of the poor? How to enhance their voice and representation, beyond the electoral vote, while at the same time resisting efforts from the well connected, or corrupt, to profit from the municipal budget for their own private gain?

My plan to reform the municipality, the office of the mayor, its institutional setting, and ways of conducting government business attracted the support and funding of the World Bank. Increased citizen participation, designed to encourage a common vision for the city, also aimed at restoring power to ordinary people, by removing the conditions and incentives for corruption to flourish. Citizens were invited to share their opinions on spending priorities, and interns from the Massachusetts Institute of Technology were commissioned to do a cost-benefit analysis of small versus large projects. In order to bring decision making closer to the community, La Paz was divided into four quarters, each of which had an element of self-governance. Donor support contributed to the production of a *Citizen's Manual* and civic education programs. However, something was still missing. Until PP, there were no mechanisms to involve citizens, in a meaningful and ongoing basis, in the development of their city, or to develop any sense of community and a common future.

Once PP was introduced, the improvements in local governance were dramatic. Residents and neighbors got together to negotiate their budget priorities, and the mayor only became involved once numerous issues had been debated and decided upon. New understandings developed, not only of the respective roles and responsibilities of citizens, the city, and the state, but also of the needs of different communities within the city. As mayor, I gained essential time and space to devote to the needs of citizens, to have constructive involvement with their planning process, and at times to suggest projects they might want to consider. The trust engendered by the mutual dependency of the PP process translated into enduring political support.

By giving communities the first say on what to invest in, the selfish interests of powerful minorities were weeded out early in the process. Inequalities also surfaced early on, as did the need for collaboration to redress disparities between the infrastructure and endowment of different parts of the city.

Very importantly, the poor, who lacked trust in the authorities, and the political class in general, were able to forge pragmatic alliances with those in power, in order to pursue common goals over an extended period of time. Working at first with facilitators, they quickly took to the idea of participatory budgeting, and realized it was in their interest to sustain political stability in order to achieve the delivery of a five-year plan.

This was the beginning of the community construction of the *we* as an urban group, beyond immediate individual needs, and concerns. Equally important was the development of a sense of *future*. Neighbors were asked not only to select which public works and services would be implemented this year, but also to pick what would be done over the next five years. Suddenly, urgent needs seemed to be able to wait for a year or more, when compared with someone else's demonstrably *more urgent* needs. Better-off parts of an urban district, after participating in a planning process with others who were less well-off, were able to relinquish their immediate demands in favor of *other* demands or needs. Gradually, a network of solidarity, mutual benefit, and trust began to emerge.

Early on, OTBs and vigilance committees regularly invoked the rights of censure they were accorded by the LPP. Over time, citizens came to appreciate a certain measure of stability, and acquired a sense of tolerance and patience that was previously lacking in their political behavior.

The building of political will did not always proceed as quickly or as smoothly as intended, although the overall trend persisted. Critics of PP pointed out that funds were distributed to all municipalities when some still needed to set up their vigilance committees, and before administrative and legal training had been fully implemented. However, by March 1997, all municipalities had vigilance committees and 92 percent of the total possible number of OTBs had been legally recognized (Pierce 1997, 10). La Paz suffered from corruption scandals after I left in 1997, while bankruptcy disrupted the development of PP in Santa Cruz. Ultimately, in each case, the problems were overcome by the development of a new community culture that recognized the *we* instead of the *us and them*. New dynamics of governance brought the state closer to the citizens. This new relationship was based on transparency and participation, and the new political culture that evolved eventually diminished the remaining traces of patronage and clientelism.

In the early years of municipal democracy, mayors were routinely voted out of office after the first year of being elected, while in the municipal election of 2005, ten years after PP came into existence, seven of the ten mayors of the main municipalities were reelected, signaling widespread approval of their work. As the process matured, municipal democracy became increasingly stable and less contentious, signaling a remarkable improvement in the quality of local governance.

National dialogue

The successful and effective National Dialogue, held in Bolivia in 2000 to determine the appropriate use of $1.5 billion debt relief, marked a fitting conclusion to the advances and achievements of the fifteen-year journey from authoritarianism to PP in Bolivia.

In 1999, after four terms as mayor of La Paz, having run the city both before and after the Participacion Popular governance reform, I became the Minister of Finance of Bolivia in the Hugo Banzer government, which was elected in 1997. I was the first former mayor to be in charge of national finances, with a background in decentralization and demand-side governance under my belt. For once, someone who had been *on the other side of the table* in the decentralization process was in charge of the most centralizing of jobs in the national government.

Although the mechanisms of PP were still in operation at the community level, top-level political will for its continuation was diminishing. The incoming government had all but abandoned the idea of PP, in its efforts to distance itself from the previous administration. The most populist political parties had also rejected it for its erosion of the paternalistic and clientelistic practices, which they preferred. More conservative parties in the new government were suspicious of the political implications of PP, and considered the transfer of 20 percent of the national income to the municipalities to be irresponsible, demagogic, tainted with socialism, and/or prone to corruption.

At the same time, there was an increase in civil opposition to government policies, with demonstrations against the forced removal of coca crops in the Chapare region, and the concession of public utilities, such as water and electricity, to multinational corporations. In the city of Cochabamba, this led to violent street protests. Once again there was a political need for some form of citizen involvement, this time at the national level, to regain a degree of stability and good governance.

As minister of finance, I embraced PP without reservation, having experienced some of the initial fruits of the improved governance it provided. I assembled a team of *municipalists* from the so-called *Mesa Municipal*, a group of local government analysts and professionals, with previous experience with PP and a commitment to municipal development. I also summoned a well-known sociologist with radical ideas on indigenous governance, and a scholar on *don and reciprocity,* and later reestablished an undersecretary for PP at the Ministry of Sustainable Development.

In 2000, a global movement advocated for a *Jubilee,* or forgiveness by the developed world creditors of the debt owed to them by highly indebted poor countries. The scheme called for national governments to redirect these funds to the alleviation of poverty in their own countries. Bolivia had already taken part in one such exercise, known as Heavily Indebted Poor Countries (HIPC) in the late 1990s. The HIPC 1 assembled corporate interest groups, and business and union representatives to decide how and where to invest the funds.

For HIPC 2, principles of PP were used to decide on funding priorities. Input was requested from democratically elected municipal governments, instead of unelected corporate interest groups. Mayors and council members, including those in opposition, were invited to provide their input. To represent civil society, every municipality was invited to elect one representative from each of two social groups, women and indigenous persons, which are traditionally discriminated against.

As it came to be known, the *Dialogo Nacional 2000,* or National Dialogue 2000 began with local dialogues in each municipality, using the by now familiar participatory mechanisms of PP. Citizens and authorities met with open doors to discuss their communities' investment priorities, and most importantly, identify the most disadvantaged citizens whose needs should take priority. They then appointed representatives to attend the National Dialogue.

In May 2000, 1,260 mayors, councilors, women, and indigenous peoples assembled in La Paz, for a week, to present the recommendations of the National Dialogue 2000 to the national government. For the first time, the central actors were local government authorities and members of civil society.

They recommended that the $1.5 billion of forgiven debt be invested primarily in projects favoring indigenous peoples, women, and children, in other words, the poorest of the poor. They went beyond the per-capita distribution of resources used by the PP, and developed a formula to favor the poorest, using an unsatisfied basic needs index to invest the funds over ten years. This allocation mechanism doubled the amount of resources to be dispersed to poor municipalities, with proportionately less for the more affluent cities.

The National Dialogue led to the Law of the National Dialogue, (LND), which requires the use of the participatory model of PP every three years, to allocate forgone debt among municipalities. The National Dialogue also formed the basis for the Poverty Reduction Strategy of Bolivia, and the National Development Strategy. This may be the first time in memory that a nationwide process of citizen participation was adopted by law, and made into a permanent mechanism of national investment planning, also given the force of law.

Factors of Success and Key Lessons Learned

The experiences of PP and the National Dialogue suggest a number of important factors of success and lessons learned in building political will for participatory governance. One of the first factors of success in generating political will for PP was the national government's acknowledgment of the need to address the social dimension of a political agenda that was designed to liberalize the economy by introducing market-inspired reforms.

Second, extensive efforts, led by the president, were made to ensure that citizens were well informed of what was proposed in the PP bill before it was passed, and understood how to make use of its provisions after its passing. A dramatic illustration of the effectiveness of this public outreach and education campaign was that, by 2005, 62 percent of municipalities, many of which did not even exist until the passing of the LPP in 1994, had already established systems, appointed employees, engaged professionals, and were actively preparing to contest their first elections (Pierce 1997, 12).

A third critical factor was having the political courage and strong leadership to develop and implement a bold and innovative model of political and economic decentralization, which potentially threatened some powerful entrenched interests. The broad-based support that was generated through an extensive and inclusive nationwide communication and education scheme was sufficient to counter and overcome the expected resistance and objections from those, like the major cities, who lost some of the (excessive) advantages they had previously enjoyed.

A fourth factor was the effective use of social accountability mechanisms, to check the authority and discretion of the mayors and councils and avert the possibility of corruption in managing the significant resources transferred to the local governments. The decision to incorporate the tried and trusted traditional governance practices of indigenous peoples, along with the old socialist union practices of self-government, ensured that the social controls required by PP would be understood, and favorably viewed. The requirements for presentation of annual budgets and preparation of annual accounts ensured that councils and citizens were mutually dependent. The lesson, particularly for those holding power, was the benefits of the trust generated by mutual dependence and mutual accountability.

Conclusions

Popular Participation is still considered one of the most advanced models in the Americas, for the active participation of citizens, sanctioned by the political will of national laws, and by the executive and legislative branches of the national government. It is not too ambitious to claim that the ascendency of Bolivia's first indigenous president, Evo Morales, five years later, can be traced to the political will to implement *PP* and the *National Dialogue 2000*.

Through PP, and subsequently the National Dialogue, political will was achieved in favor of citizens' participation. Those in authority perceived the advantage of governing with the people, in a concerted and legislated way, improving the governance of the municipalities, and later the country as a whole.

Although its swift and successful adoption in Bolivia was enhanced by preexisting social mechanisms, the principle of citizen participation is, in my opinion, widely applicable. The Bolivian example should encourage other authorities to invite greater citizen participation in prioritizing their local government's investment budget. It offers those in power and elected office a stronger source of legitimacy, political goodwill, time, and *space* to govern. Also, this better governance can translate in the successive reelection of local authorities. For authorities, this is the core argument to advocate for political will for participatory governance, and political success.

Popular Participation represented an enormous leap forward for the ordinary citizens of Bolivia, who had been rendered virtually powerless under former political regimes. It also represented a huge leap of faith by the elected national government, in entrusting the population with the management of 20 percent of the national income. It was a rare example of central government willingly adopting a local government policy, rather than imposing its policy models on subnational entities.

Much still has to be perfected, and many problems remain with the political model of PP, particularly with respect to the efficiency with which the financial resources are being disbursed and the quality of public infrastructure works. However, the main accomplishment of PP is its political success.

Popular Participation has managed to establish a functional bond between citizens and authorities, by which they have created a mutual dependency conducive to a shared responsibility, and an appreciation for stability that was previously lacking. It has created better understanding of the limitations of resources and a greater sense of community. It has brought *time* and *space* to the governance of the municipalities, rewarding good authorities with repeated reelection to office, and inspired public policies at the national level.

Most importantly, by having done all of the former, and more, PP has created the political will to allow for greater citizen participation in processes of political decision making. By doing so, and by demonstrating that power-holders do not need to fear letting citizens speak, PP has made participatory governance attractive to those holding political power.

References

Campbell, T. 1994. Notes on Proposed Bolivian Participation Law, LATAD, 13 March 1994.

Grindle, Merilee. 2000. *Audacious Reforms, Institutional Invention and Democracy in Latin America*. Baltimore, MD: Johns Hopkins University Press.

INE Bolivia. 2003. Caracteristicas Sociodemograficas de la Poblacion Indigena. *Instituto Nacional de Estadistica*, La Paz, Bolivia: Ministerio de Hacienda, Republica de Bolivia.

Pierce, M.H. 1997. Local Level Democracy and Decentralized Development: The Case of Bolivia's Popular Participation Plan. Draft prepared for delivery at the meeting of the Latin American Studies Association, Guadalajara, Mexico.

Santiso, C. 2001. Improving the odds: Institutional innovation and governance reform in Latin America. *European Review of Latin American and Caribbean Studies,* 71: 117–124.

Tyson, J. and R. MacLean-Abaroa. 2008. *The La Paz Municipal Development Project 1987–1996: A tool kit for bank task managers.* World Bank Institute.

Notes

1. The author wishes to acknowledge and thank Janet Tyson for her assistance in editing this chapter.

2. *Caudillo* is a Spanish word usually used to designate an authoritarian political-military leader.

3. The exact number of municipalities varies, according to sources, between 305 and 311. The figure of 193 comes from Campbell 1993.

4. To be officially recognized as an OTB, citizens' groups were required to submit an application, outlining their laws and regulations to the local municipal committee. Unless there was a challenge or dispute, the process could be completed in sixty days.

PART 4

BUILDING POLITICAL WILL FOR PARTICIPATORY GOVERNANCE AT THE NATIONAL LEVEL

CHAPTER 12

BUILDING POLITICAL WILL FOR REFINING PUBLIC PARTICIPATION POLICY IN SOUTH AFRICA

Janine Hicks and Imraan Buccus

Introduction and Background

In South Africa, 19.5 million people are living below the poverty line (Meth 2004). Habib and Kotze (2002) argue that poverty, inequality, and the attendant problems that come with a neoliberal paradigm are the hallmarks of South African society. South Africa has a distinctly compartmentalized civil society, made up of non-governmental organizations (NGOs) and social movements. According to Swilling and Russell (2002), there are approximately 58,000 organizations in the sector. Of these, most are welfare oriented and more prevalent in the poorer urban areas. Fifty-three percent are classified as less formal, community-based formations. Civil society's relationship with the state is a plural one, and some NGOs enjoy a cordial relationship with the state and attempt to make use of the many existing constitutional and legislative provisions for public participation. Social movements, on the other hand, have tended to disown the processes of the state and contest the officially defined terrain of public participation. Instead they engage outside of the official framework, mainly through protest.

South Africa is a multiparty, representative democracy, under a constitution that is sovereign and that entrenches human rights. State power is mostly centralized in the national sphere, with only limited power devolved to provinces and local municipalities. The South African Constitution, and some legislation, complements the power of elected politicians with forms of public participation.

In the national and provincial spheres, this takes the form of public consultation by legislatures. In the municipal sphere there are even more requirements for public participation, outlined in white papers and legislation governing local authority systems and structures. In addition, the public service sector has committed itself to being more transparent, responsive, and accountable to citizens in implementing government policy.[1]

The requirement that national and provincial legislatures consult is reflected in Section 59(1) of the 2006 Constitution, which states that "The National Assembly must—(a) facilitate public involvement in the legislative and other processes of the Assembly and its committees." Section 118 makes similar requirements for provincial legislatures. Notably, the constitution makes it clear that decision-making power resides with parliament alone, reflecting the reality that public participation is limited to informing the deliberations of parliament.

Significantly, the obligations of the local sphere, to consult, are more developed. Section 152(1) of the constitution states that "local government must encourage the involvement of communities and community organizations in the matters of local government." This implies going beyond just consulting communities as an aid to deliberation. In this regard, the Municipal System Act, 2000, section 16, obliges municipalities to "develop a culture of municipal governance that complements formal representative government with a system of participatory governance."

Although the existence of a strong constitutional and legislative framework augurs well for public participation in South Africa, it is necessary to assess how this manifests itself in practice. Is there genuine political will among power-holders for participatory governance? Despite its discourse of public participation, the state's practice of public participation instead reveals a tendency to consolidate authority and political party power, and close access to decision making.

Demonstrable indicators of real political will would include efforts by the state to introduce adequate policy frameworks and practical guidelines for public participation, endow established units with sufficient authority and resources to drive public participation processes, and, contrary to current practice, create meaningful platforms and opportunities for public dialogue, input, and influence in decision-making processes. At present, public participation exercises remain cosmetic and peripheral. Dislocated from decision making, they do not yet reflect a genuine attempt to solicit community input to inform policymaking, thus losing out on the opportunity to produce more relevant, responsive policy, with a better chance of successful implementation.

It is also necessary to examine to what extent citizens and civil society organizations (CSOs) engage with the state and take up opportunities for public participation. What level of capacity, and indeed interest, exists within CSOs and social movements? Many CSOs claim to speak on behalf of the *voiceless,* that is, the marginalized and poor, and to represent their interests in public decision-making processes. Increasingly, however, government agencies are rightfully asking on what basis such representation can be claimed. Very seldom are opportunities created for affected groups themselves to obtain information on proposed policy processes, reflect on proposals and options, articulate preferred options, and mandate representatives to speak on their behalf, with measures created for accountability and feedback.

It is also critical to examine who participates in the decision-making arena, and whose voice is heard. In the South African context, the relative inaccessibility of information on government decision making and the lack of resources and abilities required to engage in participatory processes, has resulted in the domination of such spaces by the elite— those who are organized and have access to resources, such as NGOs, businesses, and other similar interest groups. The groups that lack resources find it difficult to have influence. Existing public participation measures and processes are biased toward the organized and those with resources; therefore, the outcomes of these processes are of questionable legitimacy, as are their value and impact.

As alluded to earlier, while the state expects participation on its terms, through the use of "invited spaces" (Cornwall 2004), social movements have rejected this, refusing to participate on the state's terms. They have come to be seen as social *pariahs,* because they have opted to use the murky space of popular protest, which is often very confrontational, yet an important part of the participation terrain in South Africa. This form of participation is strongly discouraged and denigrated by the state, despite the fact that social movements have organically risen from within communities, as a direct response to the nondelivery of basic services by the state. Indeed, the state's often aggressive and heavy-handed response to civil protest is cause for serious concern.

Description of the Initiative

The Centre for Public Participation (CPP) is a nonprofit organization based in Durban, South Africa. Its mission is to strengthen public participation in governance. Over the years, the CPP has undertaken a diverse range of initiatives to promote meaningful public participation in local government development planning, policymaking, and program implementation, working with citizens, politicians, and government officials.

The Centre for Public Participation recently implemented an initiative on public participation policy research and advocacy, in partnership with the Rural and Economic Development unit of the Human Sciences Research Council (HSRC), and the School of Politics at the University of KwaZulu-Natal (UKZN), in Pietermaritzburg. This research initiative gathered information on the ways in which citizens can currently participate in local governance, community experiences, and aspirations; and the attitudes of local government officials and citizens, their capacity to undertake public participation, and good practices emerging in the sample province of KwaZulu-Natal (KZN). The initiative originated from the CPP's own analysis of weaknesses in local authorities' approach to public participation, based on feedback received from community groups' workshops, and research findings on community experiences of engaging with local governance processes.

The aim of this work was to formulate recommendations to inform local government public participation policy and practice, and to strengthen knowledge and capacity among local citizens. Working through local government and civil society networks, the aim was to share these findings and recommendations with partners across the country, thereby popularizing the research findings and policy interventions, by providing this information to community groups, academics, and local citizens to raise awareness around these issues. The uptake of policy recommendations was supported by advocacy, training, and planning work with individual local authorities.

This collaborative research initiative resulted in a number of recommendations. First, in light of the policy vacuum, the research revealed a clear need for the institutionalization of public participation. Particular recommendations were put forward for the creation of public participation units, and other institutional measures. Second, the sphere of local governance, in particular, requires resources to make public participation effective. There is a need for dedicated administrative staff and funding for the training of councilors, ward committee members, and community members, to meaningfully engage in public participation. Third, beyond a policy framework, there is a need to develop guidelines to strengthen existing public participation mechanisms and to introduce new mechanisms. Bureaucrats, who have been left to their own devices, require assistance to design adequate public participation mechanisms to give effect to constitutional and legislative requirements. Finally, more effort needs to be placed on strengthening and involving CSOs, which can play a crucial leadership role in community consultative processes. Municipalities can help strengthen civil society by initiating constructive partnerships to facilitate meaningful dialogue on policy questions and options. The radical proposal underlying this recommendation is the building of more diffuse forms of social power to create a more critical civil society, one that is autonomous from political parties. This is vital to addressing the current power imbalances, and to prevent capture by local elites, so that public participation mechanisms have a fighting chance at success.

During the research process, interest and response from local authorities and the KZN provincial legislature was encouraging. The CPP was constantly called upon to make presentations on public participation, and develop training and planning interventions for individual local authorities, in response to conversations arising from the research process. A very productive dialogue was convened, where representatives from local government, civil society, academia, and the national Department of Provincial and Local Government (DPLG) came together to actively deliberate on the research findings and recommendations.

In the midst of this research project, the CPP was contracted by the national DPLG to help transform the existing national policy framework on public participation into a full-fledged draft national policy document. The CPP drew on the collaborative research project's findings and partnered with the UKZN School of Politics, and the Good Governance Learning Network (GGLN), a network of South African NGOs working toward strengthening participatory local governance, to identify and respond to policy gaps in relation to public participation.

Significantly, the initiative to develop a full-fledged policy on public participation emerged out of a bilateral agreement between the South African government and donor partner Gesellschaft für Technische Zusammenarbeit (GTZ), with the GTZ country representative apparently wielding great influence in pushing this agenda. In addition, a senior bureaucrat within the DPLG, the head of the Public Participation and Empowerment Unit, shared a strong commitment to getting public participation policy in place. The South African public service experience shows that it is critical to have a *champion* within a department to drive a process; otherwise it may lose political favor and momentum. While this colleague certainly held the process together and provided a critical contact point within the DPLG, over time it became apparent that this was a political process designed primarily to ensure the DPLG met its constitutional and legislative obligations. It was also evident that this veneer of commitment lacked any underlying genuine appreciation of the value of meaningful public participation, by the bureaucrat and her colleagues within the unit.

The drafting team prepared a draft policy document and attended planning meetings with DPLG representatives. The final draft policy document was submitted to DPLG stakeholders and was received most favorably. Team members noted with amazement, however, that they were given absolute carte blanche in drafting the policy document. No significant contributions or modifications were received from departmental officials participating in policy review presentations.

The team's sense of delight in including everything it felt should be present in departmental policy was short-lived, because an internal staff reshuffle led to the *champion* within the department being moved to a new post. The draft policy has since remained within the department, and has yet to be formalized as policy. The CPP and GTZ were unable to obtain any information on when this will be taken up.

Political Will: An Analysis of its Apparent Absence, and Thoughts on How to Build it

Lack of Political Will

South Africa has a range of legislative and constitutional provisions for public participation. There are legislative provisions for consultation; ward committees, elected community representative structures chaired by the ward councilor; citizen voice in planning; and for citizen participation in assessing the performance of local authorities. This set of entitlements appears to go beyond that of most developing countries. Most government officials, however, seem to lack a genuine desire to see meaningful public participation and, instead, merely set out to satisfy some of the official requirements.

There are various reasons why officials may lack genuine political will. Many may find it hard to meet the challenges of their jobs, and lack a real understanding of the true meaning and value of public participation. They may think that facilitating participation is too tedious and time-consuming a task. The failure of the state to provide concrete guidelines, create appropriate structures, and allocate sufficient resources for public participation, as outlined earlier, serves to exacerbate this. Further, government officials may not subscribe to the notion that participation promotes just and efficient developmental outcomes, which even the World Bank (2006) now believes. Anecdotal evidence suggests that many officials have a technocratic approach to development, believing that they were elected into power and *know what people want*. Some would go to the extent of suggesting that too much participation can hamper the process of development. In addition, some local officials may even fear local knowledge, thinking that an overly open and participatory process may place their own jobs at risk.

On a somewhat positive note, interviewed municipal councilors and officials all affirmed the importance of public participation in local governance. They felt that public participation required the involvement of communities, political parties, and other stakeholders, and that it is important to ensure accountability and transparency. Local officials expressed a strong desire to avoid repeating the exclusionary practices of the previous apartheid era.

However, as noted, although public participation discourse is deemed politically correct, it does not necessarily translate into a commitment to ensuring that meaningful participation actually takes place. Although bureaucrats may affirm the importance of public participation in local governance, in reality many adopt a technocratic approach to local development. As a result, although the overwhelming impression is that municipalities realize that public participation is constitutionally and legislatively provided for, and therefore must be undertaken, this tends to happen after high-level planning has been undertaken and budgets are set.

In addition, research found no clear indication of a commitment to meaningful and penetrating participation. The pervading attitude among officials was that they know what people want and therefore participation is not necessary. As one top official commented "[w]e know what people's needs are, and what they will be for the next 100 years, only the rank order will change." As a result, public participation mechanisms do not adequately connect citizen voice with policy, planning, and budgeting processes, but rather aim to inform citizens of already formulated policy positions, and how these can be accessed.

Another indicator of lacking genuine political will is that, real access to existing mechanisms is limited to the privileged few. Opportunities for public participation are neither sufficiently publicized nor accessible, particularly to marginalized groups, such as women and refugee communities. Participants in policy discussion forums report very mixed experiences. Feelings of being sidelined, marginalized, excluded, and disempowered overwhelmingly dominate. These feelings were occasioned by not receiving feedback on input made in processes, not seeing any recommendations being taken up or impact from having participated, being co-opted into participating in a process with a predetermined outcome, being excluded from an *inner circle* that enjoys privileged access to decision makers and information, and not being recognized as worthy of participating (Hicks and Buccus 2007).

In understanding the participation of women, and other marginalized groups, in policy processes, it is critical to bear in mind that no political or civil society space is *neutral*. When participatory spaces are created, they are "infused with existing relations of power," which "reproduce rather than challenge hierarchies and inequalities" (Cornwall 2004, 81). This means that established patterns of behavior, perceptions, and stereotypes between groups and classes of people will *follow* these people into a participatory space, and subtly influence the decision-making process under way. These spaces need to be transformed by introducing new rules, techniques, and processes to avoid reproducing the status quo. This can be done, for example, through language-use choices, seating arrangements, rules for engagement, and decision making, and by building on existing spaces where people are already engaging (Cornwall 2004).

Current state practice, in South Africa, is an expression of a technocratic approach that views community participation as a politically correct *add-on,* rather than a core element of effective governance. This use-value approach runs contrary to the participatory culture that has always characterized the antiapartheid movement in South Africa.

As a result of the hegemony of this technocratic approach in postapartheid South Africa in particular, and in modern democratic society more generally (Heller 2008), the current local government crisis, characterized by corruption and poor service delivery, is attributed to a lack of technical skills and properly trained personnel at the local government level. The core problem, the lack of effective community participation, has not received the attention it deserves.

Cynically, it could also be argued that the reason there is not sufficient political will for public participation is because such processes serve as incubators of values related to citizen-centered development, which challenge technocratic approaches and behaviors and raise fears of *losing power* over decision-making processes.

Strategies for Building Political Will

For the past several years, the CPP had engaged in research and advocacy for the promotion of public participation and is broadly recognized as a leading and important player in the field. In its endeavors to ensure meaningful participation in developmental planning, it has (i) undertaken research into existing local government mechanisms to facilitate public participation; (ii) engaged with government stakeholders, including provincial legislatures, portfolio committees on local government, national and provincial departments on local government, and individual municipalities, to provide training on public participation, assist and evaluate existing public participation mechanisms, and develop public participation policy guidelines and programs; and (iii) designed and facilitated workshops on public participation and advocacy for community stakeholders and civil society networks to support their engagement with local authorities and other government stakeholders.

These initiatives have helped the CPP to establish its credibility and have served to build trust and direct relationships, as a basis for collaborative work around public participation. Information-sharing and capacity-building interventions with state officials, undertaken in a non-threatening, collegial manner, have contributed to changing attitudes and preconceptions relating to public participation. Adopting a collegial, rather than a confrontational, approach have served to reassure officials that the intention is not to decry deficiencies in public participation interventions, but rather to identify these and develop recommendations to address them. This approach also necessitated working within a fairly complex network, including policy makers, a donor agency, and a range of concerned stakeholders.

As a further leverage point, the CPP is a member of the GGLN, an initiative that brings together CSOs working in the field of local governance in South Africa to network and share information and lessons to strengthen participatory, democratic, local governance. The GGLN is well recognized in the local governance sector, and this helped to connect the CPP politically, with government actors and donor partners supporting DPLG initiatives. The value of this networking forum, in creating a space for learning and sharing good practices, research findings, and recommendations, strengthening the knowledge base of individual partner organizations, and providing a mechanism for formal interaction with the DPLG, is indisputable.

Outcomes of the Initiative

An initial sense of gloom, at seeing the draft policy on public participation stagnate, has somewhat lifted. During 2007, the DPLG initiated, of its own accord, a review of local government policy. This process has not been finalized, but one of the outcomes of the initial assessment phase and series of engagements with a range of stakeholders has been the identification of areas where policy is required. Public participation is among the areas identified. This demonstrates that currently there is political commitment within the DPLG to put policy on public participation in place.

The DPLG contracted a draft policy on public participation. It was developed by an institution belonging to the GGLN-body, which has good working relations with the DPLG, and this could be seen as contributing toward a shift in perception, at least at political and policy levels. As a result, there is high hope that the draft policy document will be revived and used as a starting point for more widely engaging with government and civil society stakeholders. However, as a check to this optimism, it must be acknowledged that South Africa is entering an election period, marked by an impending shuffle within the executive, which could disrupt pending policy processes.

However, these policy gains are merely an entry point. Building the interest, commitment, and capacity of frontline bureaucrats to put in place genuine, effective, public participation mechanisms is still a long way off. Effectively implementing the policy at the local level will require the development of practical guidelines, training, and resource allocation, but more importantly, for officials to become convinced of the value of, and need to invest in public participation as a result of firsthand experience.

It is difficult to assess the level of success of this initiative, but it is appropriate to state that there is potential for great success. There is currently a measure of political commitment to establishing public participation policy, and a working draft on the table. Significantly, there is an organized civil society structure in the form of the GGLN, a progressive and highly organized network, with an already established working relationship with DPLG, poised to engage on this policy area.

Challenges and Lessons Learned

Challenges

Engaging with this policy process has involved a number of important challenges, which are discussed below.

Securing political will for policy changes

The greatest challenge faced by this initiative has been to secure the political will to finalize this policy process. With a different set of individuals now working in the responsible department, it is uncertain how they will react to the draft document. The coming election year is bound to bring additional changes to executive structures and policy priorities, which could further delay the resumption of the policy review process.

Acting as consultants and activists

The Centre for Public Participation and its partners face the challenge of how best to put pressure on the department to take up the policy process. The approach so far has been a collaborative one, with the CPP playing the role of consultant, both in policy drafting and capacity-building work. To shift gears and take on the role of activists will require artful advocacy interventions and carefully selected pressure points. Because the contact person within the DPLG is no longer present to leverage entry points, the CPP, together with GGLN partner stakeholders, will need to restrategize around what interventions are required to revive finalizing the public participation policy. The CPP will need to push for the draft policy to be taken up, call for meaningful, broader consultation on the policy itself, and reposition itself, no longer in the role of consultant, to put forward its recommendations on institutionalization, support, and resources required for the policy to be effective.

Building popular support

For the team that researched and developed the policy proposals to take on a public advocacy role will require some careful constituency building around the issue. This will mean bringing on board mass movements and community-based organizations to take up the call for a transformation in how municipalities engage with communities. Unfortunately, the research process itself did not assist in this regard, as the envisaged popularizing of research findings, reporting back to research groups, and discussions on what further action is required to deepen and strengthen public participation, could not take place beyond the dialogue referred to earlier. However, the research process did lay some groundwork and, together with partner organizations in the GGLN, there is an expansive network of civil society stakeholders with which the CPP could engage.

Working in an unsupportive environment

In South Africa, there is an emerging sense among some political analysts that the current protests, being billed as *service delivery protests*, are actually manifestations of the lack of accountability of municipalities and elected representatives, rather than just inadequate service delivery. This acute sense of being ignored, not listened to, and not consulted appears to be driving frustrated groups to take their issues to the streets in the manner of antiapartheid activism of the 1980s. As reflected earlier, the state is reacting harshly to this criticism and these actions. Therefore, any call for improved public participation, coming from this quarter, may well result in a negative reaction from the state. The CPP would be wise to pick up on this aspect in its advocacy interventions, and put forward the notion of improving public participation mechanisms, as a means to strengthen linkages between citizens and the state processes and to deal with the forms of frustration witnessed.

Lessons Learned

Despite these challenges, key lessons have been learned from this experience. With the benefit of hindsight, the following ideas about different strategies that could have yielded greater success have emerged.

Work with a team or institution that can support the policy

This important lesson is related to working with *champions* within a state institution. There are committed individuals within government who appreciate support and input from external sources, such as CSOs and academic institutions, but their ability to keep a project in favor with political powers can be tenuous. The lesson is to work with the *champion*, but to encourage and support him or her to build a team within the department to work together on the project, so that there is a critical mass of support within the department and the project is anchored to more than a single inspired individual.

Encourage project ownership by all involved

Although it may seem ideal to be able to craft the policy without *interference,* not involving departmental stakeholders does not produce the sense of product ownership required for officials to fly the flag when required. If such a team is built around the project *champion,* and is encouraged to undertake drafting sections of the policy, or to deliberate on recommendations in a better facilitated manner than a formal presentation, it may be possible to secure a team that will work to push for the policy document to be taken up and finalized. Currently, there do not appear to be any officials remaining who particularly care about the product.

Provide support and interact with the team

Apart from strongly recommending to the *champion* that he or she develop a team of fellow bureaucrats with vested interest in public participation, CSOs can provide assistance by sharing best practices unearthed through research initiatives, providing training, offering to facilitate strategic planning processes or deliberative workshops, to create more participatory and meaningful spaces within departments, and assist with the design and facilitation of broader consultative processes with community stakeholders.

Secure political impetus for the project alongside donor support

There are also lessons to be learned about the impact donors have on a policy process. Although donors bring financial muscle, influence departmental policy prioritizing, and may assist civil society in getting public participation on the policy agenda, unlocking the resources required to finance this, there are limitations on the influence they wield. Donor interventions assist in opening up the space for policy advocacy, but do not eliminate the need to secure the political impetus required for actual implementation. This could include setting up formal presentations to political structures, such as parliament, provincial legislatures, and provincial executive authorities; identifying current gaps in policy and practice, that effectively render state institutions noncompliant with constitutional and legislative provisions; and putting forward recommendations in this regard. This could be strengthened through pressure from partner organizations and making use of the media. Also, it could extend to legally challenging policy decisions, which have not complied with public participation provisions.

Involve community groups in the entire process

The intention of the research team was to take findings back to communities and to distribute them in a manner more accessible than a professional publication. This work still needs to be done. An obvious lesson is that the solidarity and support of community groups is essential to push for policy reform. As previously referred to, this could have been nurtured from the outset by more actively involving community groups in the crafting of the draft policy.

Conclusion

Perceptions from both community and state perspectives reveal that public participation is not in a healthy state in South Africa. Officials and community members appear to share the view that public participation mechanisms are generally poorly developed, making little or no difference to local governance and development. Transforming this state of affairs will require significant investment of resources in public participation, especially money and training for staff, effective institutionalization of public participation, through public participation policy, and, most importantly, by developing the political will to make it happen.

The experiences highlighted here reveal three primary reasons for the state's current lack of political will to put the necessary policy, structures, and resources in place to champion public participation. First, there is a lack of a real understanding of the nature and value of public participation, how to design and facilitate meaningful public participation mechanisms, and the potential impact of ensuring the crafting of responsive policy in a manner that gives significant expression to community knowledge and aspiration. A second reason for political *won't* appears to be policy makers' fear that public participation will involve handing over power to civil society groups. A cynic would argue that the state does not seek to actively support the creation of autonomous, critical civil society structures and stakeholders, but would rather consolidate its power and authority and close off key decision-making processes. Third, there is an arrogance and assumption, on the part of public officials, stemming from a lack of appreciation of the nature of public participation, that they understand the complex web of societal issues, and do not need to engage with citizens in this regard. This reveals a disregard for community knowledge and expertise, and a failure to create meaningful and accessible spaces for a diverse range of community stakeholders to engage in agenda-setting, policymaking, and its implementation and review.

Finally, this chapter has identified a number of key strategies for CSOs to build the political will required to drive processes geared at strengthening public participation policy frameworks, institutionalized structures, and implementation mechanism. The first strategy is to build relationships of trust with government counterparts, positioning CSOs as a resource and collaborative partner, and developing the necessary expertise and profile to be able to undertake interventionist work aimed at strengthening public participation policy and mechanisms. The second strategy is to recognize the value of a strategic network. This can provide a vehicle to pull together key stakeholders in the sector to bring resources and expertise to bear in building a repository of research and best practice, in relation to public participation. This can then be positioned to provide support, undertake advocacy interventions where needed, and ensure necessary capacity-building, policy development, and consultative processes by the state. Third, CSOs should exert the necessary pressure to create an environment for political will to champion public participation, through awareness-raising and a variety of advocacy interventions. A fourth strategy is to ensure any public participation policy development initiative is securely located within a government department, beyond a single *champion,* and that appropriate measures are taken to ensure active engagement and ownership of the policy project by relevant bureaucrats, to anchor this process and secure momentum and support. Finally, it is crucial for CSOs to ensure that grassroots stakeholder groups are brought on board from the outset and kept informed of policy developments, implementation challenges, or failures on the part of the state, to put necessary mechanisms, structures, and resources in place. It is essential to actively create opportunities for constituency-building and to provide support for advocacy interventions in this regard.

References

Republic of South Africa. 1998. *White Paper on Local Government.* Constitution of the Republic of South Africa, Act 108 of 1996.

Cornwall, A. 2004. Spaces for transformation? Reflections on issues of power and difference in participation and development. In *Participation: From Tyranny to Transformation.* Hickey, S. and G. Mohan eds. London: Zed Books.

Habib, A. and H. Kotze. 2002. Civil society: Governance and development in an era of globalisation. Unpublished manuscript.

Heller, P. 2008. Democratising developmental local government: South Africa through Indian and Brazilian lenses. In *Consolidating Developmental Local Government: Lessons from the South Africa Experience.* Van Donk, M., E. Pieterse Swilling, and S. Parnell eds. Cape Town, South Africa: University of Cape Town Press.

Hicks, J. and I. Buccus. 2007. Crafting new democratic spaces: Public participation and policy-making. *Transformation,* no. 65: 94–119. South Africa: University of KwaZulu Natal Press.

Meth, C. 2004. Ideology and social policy. *Transformation,* no. 56: 9. South Africa: University of KwaZulu Natal Press.

Republic of South Africa, Municipal Systems Act, No 32 of 2000.

Swilling, M. and B. Russell. 2002. *The Size and Scope of the Non-profit Sector in South Africa.* Witwaterstrand, South Africa: Copublished by the Centre for Civil Society, University of KwaZulu Natal, and the Graduate School of Public and Development Management, University of the Witwaterstrand Press.

World Bank. 2006. *World Bank Development Report: Equity and Development.* Washington, D.C.: Oxford University Press.

Note

1. *Batho Pele, or People First,* was adopted in 1997 as a framework that formed the inner core of the White Paper on Transforming Public Service Delivery (Notice No 1459 of 1997). It aspires to enable citizens to hold public servants to account.

CHAPTER 13

BUILDING POLITICAL WILL FOR ENHANCED CITIZEN ACCESS TO INFORMATION: LESSONS FROM LATIN AMERICA

Anabel Cruz

Introduction and Background

Information is power, and the right to information is a unique and basic human right. Countless stories, from Latin America and around the world, give evidence to the power of the right to information as a tool in the hands of the people. This basic human right, to seek and receive government and public information, empowers people with the knowledge they need to demand political, economic, and social rights from their governments, ranging from the right to food and water to the right to be free from torture.

The right to information has been recognized under international and inter-American instruments. Article 19 of the Universal Declaration of Human Rights states that "Everyone has the right to freedom of opinion and expression; this right includes freedom to hold opinions without interference and to seek, receive and impart information and ideas through any media and regardless of frontiers." Furthermore, the International Covenant on Civil and Political Rights requires that member countries acknowledge this right in their domestic laws, and Article 13 of the American Convention on Human Rights, also known as the San Jose Pact, an international human rights instrument adopted by the Nations of the Americas, states that "Everyone has the right to freedom of thought and expression. This right includes freedom to seek, receive, and impart information and ideas of all kinds, regardless of frontiers, either orally, in writing, in print, in the form of art, or through any other medium of one's choice."

In 1766, Sweden enacted a law recognizing the right of the press to seek, obtain, and publish information held by the government, making it the first country to legally guarantee people the right to access information. Almost two hundred years elapsed, however, before another country (Finland, 1951) approved legislation on the right to access to information.

Currently, more than eighty countries, from all regions of the world, have either enacted right to information laws or put systems in place to provide people with access to government-held information. It has been a slow process, with a rather recent outburst. The 1980s and 1990s, and the first few years of the twenty-first century have auspiciously seen the approval and enactment of access to information laws in more than seventy countries.

Latin America has been part of the global trend of legal recognition of the fundamental right to access information. In 1995, Colombia approved its Law Ordering the Publicity of Official Acts and Documents, and six countries, Mexico, Panama, Peru, Argentina, the Dominican Republic, and Ecuador followed suit in 2003 and 2004. Between 2006 and 2008, five additional Latin American countries adopted access to information laws. In 2006, Honduras approved its Law on Transparency and Access to Public Information; in 2007, Nicaragua approved its Access to Public Information Act; and, in 2008, Chile enacted and promulgated its Law on Transparency of Public Functions and Access to Information of the State Administration. In 2008, Uruguay and Guatemala approved respectively Laws on Access to Public Information and Protection of Information, both of which are expected to be promulgated in 2009.

By analyzing the cases of Honduras, Nicaragua, Chile, and Uruguay, this paper explores the processes whereby citizens' groups and other stakeholders sought to build political will and positive conditions for the approval and enactment of right to information laws. There are similarities, but also important historical and cultural differences among these four countries, two of which are in South America and two of which are in Central America. All four countries suffered repression of their civic liberties in the twentieth century. The dictatorship of the Somoza dynasty ruled Nicaragua for more than forty years, and Honduras was ruled by a military dictatorship from the 1972 to 1980. Uruguay, from 1973 to 1985, and Chile, from 1973 to 1990, also endured military regimes. Indigenous civil society and citizen groups have been trying to strengthen democracy in the four countries for several decades, using a variety of methods, tactics, and alliances. Despite the unique context of each country, this chapter identifies a number of common problems, approaches, and lessons learned in their paths to enhanced access to public information and social accountability.

The Road to Enhanced Access to Information

Until late 2006, active efforts by citizens' groups in Honduras, Nicaragua, Chile, and Uruguay to lobby for the adoption of access to information laws brought little progress. In Nicaragua and Uruguay, coalition groups were officially formed, and in Chile and Honduras groupings of organizations also networked. Information campaigns using mass media, publication of specialized materials, national and international seminars, lobbying activities toward parliaments, and public awareness-raising activities took place in all four countries. Each country received technical and financial support from international agencies and donors in carrying out these activities.

Regional initiatives were also used to enhance access to information in Latin America, and communication, collaboration, and networking efforts between countries enriched the process. For example, the *Alianza Regional para la Libertad de Expresión e Información* (Regional Alliance for Freedom of Expression and Information) was created in 2005 by several organizations working on access to information in their respective countries. Today the alliance has twenty-six member organizations from most countries in Latin America. Civil society organizations (CSOs) from Nicaragua, Honduras, and Chile have been very active in the alliance since its creation, and groups from Uruguay will join soon. The alliance has the support of the Trust of the Americas, a foundation associated with the Organization of American States, and also has received support from the National Endowment for Democracy and the Open Society Institute. The alliance has become an important platform for CSOs to discuss achievements and obstacles in their work, and has been a unique space for member organizations to exchange information, conduct joint applied research, and organize capacity development activities. Members of the alliance have also worked on comparative legislation and lobbied governments through the Organization of American States (OAS).

After vehement and passionate discussions, the National Congress in Honduras approved its Law on Transparency and Access to Public Information. After months of consultations with CSOs, international experts, and donors, and after two days of debate in Congress, the thirty-eight articles of the law were approved on December 1, 2006. The press, CSOs, and many government officials expressed their satisfaction with what they considered an important step toward combating corruption and promoting social accountability in Honduras. This made Honduras the first country in Central America with an access to information law. During the whole year of 2006, a group of CSOs sustained public pressure on the National Congress to pass the law. Their strategies included mass demonstrations, publication of articles in mass media, organizing press conferences, and the ongoing targeted lobbying of legislators. The law established the creation of an *Institute for Access to Public Information*, composed of three commissioners appointed by congress.

In June 2007, Nicaragua, a neighboring country of Honduras, followed suit by approving its own Access to Public Information Act. Through very detailed regulations and a 104 article enacting code, this act established the mechanisms for Nicaraguan citizens to request information from state institutions and private companies providing public services.

The struggle in Nicaragua began many years earlier. The 2003 formation of a civic coalition, called *Grupo Promotor* (Promoter Group) for the law, was a crucial development. The group was highly diverse, composed of the *Coordinadora Civil* (the national network of CSOs), other nongovernmental organizations (NGOs), citizens' groups, the owners of mass media companies, journalists, the association of librarians, academics, university departments, and government officials. On several occasions, the group submitted comments and suggestions on the draft law to the National Congress, and their work was influential. For example, the first version of the enacting and implementation instructions was prepared by the Promoter Group itself, and submitted to the executive branch of the national government for its approval. In a highly politicized society, such as Nicaragua, the broad and diverse composition and inclusiveness of this Promoter Group was an important a factor for success. The group included representatives from across the economic, political, and social spectrums, which enabled it to gain credibility and access to media to disseminate information and exert public pressure. The law established the creation of a National Commission for Access to Information, composed of representatives from the different public agencies involved, as well as local and regional autonomous governments.

In August 2008, Dr. Michelle Bachelet, the President of Chile, signed the enactment of the Law on Transparency of Public Functions, which was approved by congress in January of 2008. In her speech at the ceremony of the law promulgation, she insisted that the new law was a benchmark in the Chilean administrative system, one that would change the relationship between citizens and the state, and would put the country in the highest ranking of public transparency. The law's principle of *active transparency*, commits the state to proactively providing citizens with up-to-date information, in easy and accessible formats. In order to monitor and control the different state agencies, the new law created a *Consejo para la Transparencia* (Council for Transparency), an independent body of four members charged with promoting access to public information and ensuring the implementation of the new norms and instructions.[1]

Two years earlier, in November 2006, following cases of state corruption that provoked a national scandal, the president appointed a group of experts to advise her on the best measures to make the state more transparent and accountable. This group of experts, composed of government officials and civil society representatives, was crucial in the design of proposals to improve transparency and accountability, including measures incorporated into the Law on Transparency of Public Functions. The group was made up of renowned individuals, respected for their expertise in different fields, particularly human rights, public accountability, and transparency. They worked together with CSOs to raise public awareness about the need for an access to information law, and closely followed and informed the discussion that took place in congress. International networking was also an important tool in this process. Among other actions, an international seminar on access to information took place in October 2007 and was attended by experts from the Federal Institute for Access to Public Information in Mexico, and other experts from Argentina, Ireland, Peru, the United Kingdom, and the United States to discuss comparative experiences with access to information, and to analyze possible lessons for Chile.

Uruguay, the smallest country in South America, has also witnessed a long fight for an access to information law. An initial bill was presented for parliamentary approval in 1996, but was never discussed. Later, in order to reach a consensus on issues related to human rights and the disclosure of information archived by the military regime, the Public University of the Republic initiated discussions on a national archive system and its relationship with access to information. A new group, known as the *Grupo de Archivos y Acceso a la Información Pública* (Archives and Access to Information Group) (GAIP), made up of members of the Public University, the Uruguayan Association of Journalists, as well as several NGOs and human rights groups, was founded in 2005. This group prepared two draft bills, one with regard to public archives and the other about access to information. The group sought the advice of experts, journalists, lawyers, and CSOs and used a variety of means to lobby and put pressure on legislators and decision makers to pass the new laws. Members of GAIP frequently met with lawmakers and congresspersons to discuss articles to be included in the law, and make concrete proposals regarding implementation mechanisms. Through its Web page, and other media, GAIP, with the participation of experts from other countries, such as Argentina and Guatemala, tried to promote public awareness about the need for new legislation, and organized seminars and talks about access to information.

In October 2008, more than three years after the GAIP was founded, the Uruguayan parliament unanimously approved the Law of Access to Information and Protection of Information. A GAIP press release on the same day declared "its satisfaction for this historical step of the democratic institutions," but cautioned that this was not "the end of the road, but just the beginning of even more arduous work." The law was not the same as the one originally submitted by the GAIP, which included the creation of a *Comisionado Parlamentario para la Información Pública* (Commission on Public Information), to advise parliament and public information officials within all concerned public agencies, both of which are independent from the executive branch of the government. The Uruguayan parliament considered GAIP's proposals, but made important modifications. Instead they created an *Unidad para el Accesso a la Información* (Access to Information Unit), within the Agency for e-Government, Information and Knowledge (AGESIC), which in turn is under the executive branch of the government (office of the president), a measure that has been criticized by experts and activists.

Enabling Forces and Challenging Tensions

The four cases summarized here reveal common lessons learned. Initially, political will for the approval of the laws was partially lacking, not only on the part of government, but also, in some cases, on the part of other social forces. Mistrust among social actors is prevalent in several Latin American societies, as a result of their history of colonization by foreign powers, colonialism, and decades of dark military dictatorship. Such societies are often ruled by secrecy, not by mutual trust. This affects relationships among social and political actors at many levels. Given this context, efforts to promote transparency have also faced resistance and hostility from some civic groups that mistrust the state, or suspect that it is merely seeking new forms of control.

Although civil society groups were active and tirelessly worked to promote the laws, these efforts required comprehensive strategies, smart alliance tactics, and a clear understanding of the obstacles. Some of these obstacles, such as resistance from different political parties and the need to acquire a majority vote in parliament, were visible and explicit, and strategies to address them were easily outlined. However, other obstacles were more difficult to deal with, because they represented hidden forces with deep cultural roots.

The following pages will provide an analysis of the following: political will and government support, or lack thereof, for the enhancement of access to information practices; strategies that were used to build political will; key obstacles and factors of success in building political will; key outcomes; and lessons learned. The chapter will also try to answer some key questions, such as the following: What were the main tensions that arose in the course of efforts to get access to information laws approved?; Was lack of political will a key obstacle in achieving access to information?; Did other factors obstruct the strategies to enhance access to information in the four countries?; What strategies were used to build political will for these initiatives?; Which strategies were successful and which ones failed?; and What has happened since the laws were approved and how are relationships among the different actors evolving? The answers to these questions are complex and multifaceted. They also require understanding some common issues and challenges, which are outlined below, that were identified across the four countries in this regional case study.

Lack of a Culture of Transparency

As different actors in the four countries were interviewed, a unanimous voice emerged regarding the lack of a *culture of transparency*. Actors in each of the four countries cited a clear lack of political will on the part of power-holders to enhance public access to information, and citizens' and civil society's limited experience in demanding information and seeking accountability. For example, one interviewee from Honduras expressed that in this country a culture of transparency and accountability does not exist, and these elements conspire against good practices.

Owing to different cultural and political factors, for many years the tendency and dominant culture in Latin America has been to transgress norms of good governance and tolerate corruption. Power relationships have not been egalitarian in Latin America, ever since foreign powers, including Spain, Portugal, and the United Kingdom, arrived in the region and exerted unilateral dominance. This dominance was based on mistrust and subjugation and, in many cases, installed systems of corruption and exploitation. Colonial forms of governance represented the antithesis of democratic values and put in place none of the checks and balances required for a real democracy (Arbulu 2006, 121–142). As a consequence of this historical legacy, in many Latin American countries a public mentality of secrecy prevails at both the community and societal levels. This culture of opaqueness and mistrust has profound roots in the history of the region such as forced colonization, domination of indigenous cultures, and military rule. The challenge has not only been to gain government support for the approval of freedom of information legislation, but also to fight against the cultural norms and habits that prevent people from sharing and requesting information. The adoption of access to information laws will have little impact, unless there is also will on the part of civil servants to implement the law, and will on the part of the people to demand information.

Corruption and Access to Information

The situation of corruption is different in the four countries analyzed here, but, in general, it is an important issue across Latin America. Transparency International's Corruption Perceptions Index (CPI) shows diverse and interesting data for the four countries.[2] Among the thirty countries from Latin America and the Caribbean included in the 2008 CPI, Nicaragua and Honduras are among the eleven countries that scored less than 3, on a scale of 10, indicating rampant corruption. Uruguay and Chile are better off, scoring between 6 and 7.5 over the past eight years; however, Chile descended slowly during the last decade.

Knowledgeable citizens and informed communities, with broad access to government information, are able to participate in public life, determine priorities for public spending, demand and receive equal access to justice, and hold their public officials accountable. Inadequate access to public information creates the opportunity for corruption, and back-room deals that serve the interests of the few rather than the many. As former U.S. President Carter has said "[a]ccess to information is a crucial element in the effort to reduce corruption, increase accountability and deepen trust among citizens and their governments" (Carter 2002). Government transparency and access to information is, therefore, an essential anticorruption tool, and it is not surprising that efforts to improve access to information can face obstacles and resistance from those that *benefit* from corrupt practices. The withholder of information has power, and that power can be exerted in illegal ways, from requesting bribes to make information available, to profiting from a cloud of secrecy that harbors corrupt practices.

Human Rights and Personal Privacy Issues

Access to information, however, must be balanced with protection of personal privacy and narrowly defined state interests. Many societies in Latin America have suffered long periods of dark dictatorships, which is an influential factor when access to information is discussed, promoted, and implemented. On the one hand, many pending and painful issues with previous military regimes have not yet been resolved. In Uruguay and Chile, for example, many families have been fighting for decades to receive information about missing people and political prisoners. Human rights groups, therefore, have been very active in some of the coalitions pushing for access to information laws. On the other hand, making information about different forms of human rights violations public can be very sensitive, and some cases require specific analysis and processing. Historians and activists sometimes have different opinions and views on this issue. As a result of the different historical reasons that have been discussed, people tend to strongly defend their own right to privacy and this can sometimes be an obstacle to social will to enhance access to public information.

When the right to information is discussed, the right and need to protect privacy and sensitive data must also be part of the discussion. In the case of Uruguay, for example, the debate on access to information was intensely linked with the right to privacy, or the so-called *Habeas Data*, which is a constitutional right granted in several countries in Latin America. It varies from country to country, but in general, this right is designed to protect an individual's image, privacy, and honor, and the right of a person to know what types of data are stored on himself or herself. Privacy concerns arise wherever uniquely identifiable data relating to a person or persons are collected and stored, in digital form or otherwise. In some cases, these concerns refer to how data is collected, stored, and associated, and in others the issue is who has access to information.

The parallel process and discussion related to right to privacy, or *Habeas Data* and right to access to information led to the 2008 passage of two different laws in Uruguay (Delpiazzo 2008). Both laws refer to confidentiality, privacy, obligations, and human rights. Law 18331, or the Law of Protection of Personal Data or *Habeas Data* (article 8), states that the right to protection of personal data applies both to persons and organizations, or juridical personalities, and that such data "cannot be used with aims that violate human rights or are illegal or against the public moral." The Law on Access to Public Information (article 12) specifies that confidentiality will not apply if "the information requested relates to violation of human rights or is relevant to investigate, prevent, or avoid human rights violations."

Recent human rights violations, in numerous countries in the region, complicate the issue of freedom of information and raise a number of important questions regarding equitable and fair access to information. In some cases, the new laws have tried to address these issues, but it will be a challenge for years to come.

Key Actors and Stakeholders

To whom do access to information laws apply, and who are the organizations and institutions that must make information accessible and become more accountable to the public? These questions were topics of debate and dispute during the process of constructing political will for the passage of the information laws, and will be, according to actors in all four countries, important issues requiring attention in the implementation of the laws.

Chile's access to information law is the most explicit in pointing out to whom the law applies, and is very state oriented. Even the name of the legislation, the Law on Transparency of the Public Service and Access to Information on the State Administration, clearly identifies who is expected to be accountable and to make information accessible. Article 10 clearly asserts that any person in Chile has the right to demand and receive information "produced by any agency belonging to the State Administration." It covers information included in events, resolutions, minutes, notes, records, proceedings, reports, agreements, and information regarding the public budget. Furthermore, the Chilean Law (Article 2) names the institutions to which the law is applicable, namely all ministries, local governments, municipalities and counties, the Army Forces, and all public services, public banks, and public enterprises created by law, and companies in which the state holds more than 50 percent of the shares, or a majority of board seats.

Uruguayan freedom of information legislation considers access to information to be the right of all persons, and there should be no discrimination as to who has the right to access information, and no person should have to justify why he or she needs certain public information. The law defines public information as all pieces of information produced by any public agency, belonging to the state or not. Although the initial proposal submitted by civil society through GAIP, made private corporations and private organizations with state funding subject to the law, the final approved version of the law did not include this. The law's reference to public agencies, whether or not they are state agencies, leaves some ambiguity as to whom the law applies and will be a question of debate in 2009.

In the case of Honduras, the law goes much further. The Law on Transparency and Access to Public Information applies to all agencies and offices of the three branches of government—the executive, legislative, and judicial—and also to all CSOs and NGOs that are granted, or in any way administer public funds, be they from government or foreign donors, such as bilateral or multilateral aid organizations, international NGOs, or foundations. A debate persists as to whether applying the laws to CSOs is positive and justifiable, or if this is a new way for the state to unduly control and regulate CSOs.

Challenges of Practical Implementation

Informants in Honduras point out that the country has "too many good laws but they are not enforced." They lament that the body of laws in the country is "scattered and saturated, confused and sometimes contradictory, completely unknown to for the vast majority of the population, and thus not implemented" (Ver a través 2008). They fear this may also be the case with the new access to information legislation. In order to address this problem, CSOs are organizing a public information campaign aimed at making the new law known to the public, so that people become the real owners and users of the legislation. Apparently, internal meetings and education campaigns for CSOs and other stakeholders are also necessary, in order to discuss the content of the new law and issues regarding its adequate enforcement.

In Nicaragua, the scope of institutions subject to the law is extensive and includes public universities, or those receiving state funds, and private companies and NGOs that administer or are granted public funds. The law applies to all forms of information, with the exception of secrets of the state. All concerned institutions must organize information as instructed by the law and the enacting procedures, and they must establish their own Offices for Access to Public Information (OAIP). Institutions named in the law must open their OAIP to the public within a set time frame.

Organizations in Nicaragua—public, private, state bodies, and CSOs—are currently discussing and coordinating efforts to enforce the law. While the law is ample in coverage, its implementation will imply, without a doubt, important challenges for all actors involved.

Building Political Will: A Never-Ending Need

The complex range of strategies, that led to the approval of access to information laws in each country, demonstrates the need for building political will at different levels, different specific moments, and with different audiences and goals specific to the situation. *Lack of awareness about how to effectively use the laws* is a key issue. Citizens, CSOs, and other actors are confronted with this problem. In all four countries, the participation of CSOs, citizen coalitions, and civic groups was crucial to the passage of access to information laws. Organizations promoting access to information in each country believe that broader and more equitable access to public information is essential to improving the quality of life of citizens in their respective countries. The majority of the population, however, is not necessarily aware of these benefits, and not all public officials who are supposed to play leading roles in providing access to public information, are aware of their responsibilities. Local governments, often geographically and politically distant from national decision-making processes, are not in the best position to make their own information accessible to the public, while local people are often unaware of their information rights, and do not know whom to ask or what to ask for.

Political will is not only necessary from the government and citizens, but also from private companies and corporations. Unless they *buy into* the benefits and advantages of the law, its implementation will be difficult or impossible. Norms and legislation without corresponding practice are dead letters. Indeed, the approval of laws by parliament is only a first step. Those norms and laws need to be promulgated, implemented, and enforced. The meaningful implementation of an access to information law requires an informed and educated citizenry that demands information. It also requires a set of public and private agencies willing and able to respond to that demand and, ideally, package information according to the needs of different users. In some countries with a longer history of access to information legislation, such as Mexico, an access to information index is regularly used to analyze how much the laws are being used, how useful they are judged to be, and to address problems or flaws. For example, the most recent index in Mexico found that in 2007 demand for information increased by more than 122 percent, compared to the previous year, and was at its highest level in recent years.[3]

In efforts to build political will, the importance of broad-based coalitions cannot be overemphasized. In all four countries, CSOs and civic groups were leading actors in pushing for the approval of the laws. They were instrumental in providing technical assistance to legislators in the drafting of access to information laws and in educating and engaging the public. The *Grupo Promotor* in Nicaragua, the GAIP in Uruguay, coalitions in Honduras, and in Chile several organizations, such as the NGOs *Fundación Pro Acceso* and *Chile Transparente,* played an important role working with parliamentarians, the media, and public opinion to build the political will necessary to get the access to information laws passed by Congress.

Civil society actors were also successful in building coalitions among groups that seldom speak to one other, and in engaging voices that are not frequently heard. The coalitions *Grupo Promotor* in Nicaragua and the

GAIP in Uruguay amalgamated different organizations working to strengthen democracy, for women's or children's rights or in public policies, regardless of the political inclinations or partisan preferences of the organizations. This strategy allowed the creation of a broad coalition, which could also access funding from international organizations for developing their work to lobby and build political will to get the law passed. As soon as the law was approved and later enacted and regulated, however, new challenges emerged. How to promote information campaigns to empower people to understand, appropriate, and use the law? How to reach out to populations at the local level, helping them to see the law as a tool to satisfy their own needs? Finally, how to educate ourselves to become wiser and more powerful in order to demand the right information in the right format?

Persuasion Versus Coercion

In trying to build legitimate political will, the coalitions and organizations that promoted the passage of information laws tried their best, in many different ways, to persuade diverse stakeholders about the important benefits of enhanced access to public information, including, more informed and empowered citizens, more transparent and fair societies where social investment can flourish, strengthened democracy, and enhanced human development. Information campaigns, lobby meetings, press releases, coalition building, workshops, and lectures at universities and colleges, were used to publicize these benefits and build public support.

It is important to mention that the civic organizations and coalitions that promoted the laws never used force, intimidation, or coercion. Public officials, members of parliament, owners of mass media, and a broad range of stakeholders from the four countries acknowledge that these organizations secured legitimacy, because of their democratic methods.

This is not to say, however, that the organizations and coalitions concerned were always courteous or polite. Discussions were vibrant, sessions in parliaments were animated, and as much public pressure as necessary was exerted. There were no violent riots, but instead well- organized civic engagement, backed up with well-thought out arguments, and characterized by a high level of patience and tolerance. Successes to date can be attributed to a combination of broad-based coalitions, open-minded participation, clear goals, and focused persistence.

The Challenges Ahead

Some future challenges have already been mentioned. Although significant political will was necessary to achieve the approval of access to information laws in Chile, Honduras, Nicaragua, and Uruguay, much remains to be done, and more political will is necessary to ensure proper implementation of the new laws.

Now that the four countries have approved their respective laws, the need for political will on the part of state and nonstate stakeholders is greater than ever. Passage of an access to information act is only the first step. Unless governments adequately implement and enforce the laws, they will not increase citizen trust or government accountability. Experience in all four countries suggests that appropriate emphasis must be placed on three distinct phases of developing an access to information culture: (i) *the adoption of legislation,* (ii) *the implementation and enforcement of that legislation,* and (iii) *active efforts to encourage the public's use of the law.*

The use of the law is a multidimensional phenomenon. Nicaragua and Honduras, the two countries where access to information laws have been in effect the longest, have experienced the practical implications of this complexity. It is clear that CSOs, working in partnership with the media and educational institutions, can play an extremely important role in raising awareness of citizen rights and promoting citizen knowledge and subsequent use of access to information laws.

In turn, the laws require official institutions, and those entrusted with public funds, to compile and organize their information and make it available to the public, in different formats and by different channels. Actors in Nicaragua and Honduras found that in discussions about the implementation of the access to information law, it was taken for granted that the concerned institutions had the knowledge and capacity to compile, organize, and disseminate information. This assumption starkly contrasts with the actual state of information disorder that characterizes Nicaragua, which lacks even a basic functioning system of libraries and archives. If the state and official institutions' budgets are not increased to organize and manage their information, the demands of well-informed citizens will not be met, and the efforts of CSOs to promote and enhance access to information will have been futile.

In Chile, where the new law only became effective as of April 2009, and in Uruguay where implementation has not yet been regulated, most stakeholders consider the new legislation as a progressive and modern milestone, but are already thinking ahead to implementation challenges. The first challenge is the *institutionalization* of the law with the formal appointment in Chile of the four members of the Council for Transparency, responsible for the execution and practical implementation of the law. In Uruguay it is the appointment of the officer in charge of the Access to Public Information Unit responsible for overseeing the implementation of the new act.[4]

These new institutions will have to play a proactive and dynamic role in order to overcome the prevailing culture of secrecy and to nurture a new organizational and societal culture that promotes transparency and facilitates access to information by ordinary citizens. International experience suggests that demand for information could be strongest during the initial phase of implementation. However, this could generate a major problem, unless *adequate resources are made available in a timely fashion.* The political will that was nurtured to get the laws approved, must now be applied to mobilizing the resources required for their effective implementation.

Another challenge, in each country context, is the issue of *the independence and democratic functioning of the oversight mechanisms.* Besides being autonomous from government, oversight mechanisms should involve elected or appointed members that represent a diversity of opinions and communities. This is equally valid for the Council for Transparency in Chile, the Access to Public Information Unit in Honduras, the National Commission for Access to Information in Nicaragua, and the Access to Public Information Unit in Uruguay, which is already criticized for being under the supervision of the Office of the President. A culture of transparency and accountability can only be achieved by genuinely independent mechanisms, equipped with adequate technical and financial resources, and working in cooperation with a range of social actors. Experience shows that institutional autonomy and continual citizen monitoring and oversight are necessary to ensure the effective functioning of these mechanisms. Social control, mutual accountability, and respect for human and citizen rights are other compulsory ingredients for this process.

Conclusions

Access to public information is an important condition for democratic governance. Thus, promoting and developing mechanisms for citizen access to information are essential elements in public policies. However, the right to access to information implies responsibilities, for the state, citizens, and CSOs. Access to information ensures transparency and accountability of all public actors and contributes to addressing power imbalances, combating corruption, and promoting citizen participation, citizen control, and peoples' empowerment.

It has been proved that the adoption of an access to information law is an important first step. However, the promulgation of legislation does not represent much if government, supported and democratically pressed by informed and active citizens and citizens' organizations, does not implement and enforce the laws. Building political will to ensure citizen access to public information appears to be a long road, and much work must be done along that road. When the laws have been passed, new stages will require renewed political will and the concerted efforts of diverse actors to make progress visible and real.

References

2007. Presentations at the international seminar entitled *Towards a new institutionality in access to public information*, Chile.

2008. *Uruguay: Se aprueba ley de acceso a la información*. Press release by the GAIP, Uruguay.

Bachelet, Michelle. 2008. Speech presented at the ceremony for the promulgation of *Ley de Transparencia de la Función Pública y de Acceso a la Información de la Administración del Estado*. Chile.

Carter, Jimmy. 2002. Forward to *Access to Information: A Key to Democracy*. Atlanta, Georgia: The Carter Center.

Centro de Estudios de Justicia de las Américas. 2005. *Access to Judicial Information Index*. Santiago, Chile: Centro de Estudios de Justicia de las Américas.

Delpiazzo, Carlos. 2008. Habeas data: A propósito del acceso a la información a la información pública. In: *Transparencia y Ciudadanía Responsable II*. Montevideo, Uruguay: Centro Latinoamricano de Economia Humana.

Instituto de Comunicación y Desarrollo. 2008. *Ver a Través. Poder, Sociedad Civil y Rendición de Cuentas*. Montevideo, Uruguay: Fundación Kellogg.

Inter-American Specialized Conference on Human Rights. 1969. *American Convention on Human Rights*. San Josi, Costa Rica: Inter-American Specialized Conference on Human Rights.

Ley de Acceso a la Información y de Amparo Informativo 2008, Law 18381 (17 October, 2008). Montevideo, Uruguay.

Ley de Acceso a la Información Pública 2007, Law 621, (16 May, 2007). La Gaceta, Managua, Nicaragua.

Ley de Transparencia y Acceso a la Información Pública, Decreto of 2006, Law 170-2006, (30 December, 2006). La Gaceta, Honduras.

Ley de de Transparencia de la Función Pública y de Acceso a la Información de la Administración del Estado 2008, Law 20285, (20 August, 2008). Chile.

Tantaleán Arbulu, Javier. 2006. La corrupción en la Colonia. Pizarro, el primer corrupto en la historia del Perú. In *Socialismo y Participación*, no. 100: 121–142.

United Nations High Commission on Human Rights. 1948. *Universal Declaration of Human Rights*. New York: United Nations.

Notes

1. The council, and other institutions created by the law, will be established by April 2009.

2. The annual Corruption Perceptions Index, first released in 1995, is produced by Transparency International. The CPI ranks 180 countries according to their perceived levels of corruption, as determined by expert assessment and opinion surveys.

3. Other efforts to measure access to judicial information include studies conducted by the Center of Studies of Justice in the Americas. See, for example, CEJA, 2005. Access to Judicial Information Index.

4. While in Chile the four members of the council were appointed and formally took office in April 2009, the appointment of the Access to Public Information Unit officer was still pending at the time of publication.

CHAPTER 14

TRANSPARENCY INTERNATIONAL'S ADVOCACY AND LEGAL ADVICE CENTRES: EXPERIENCES IN FOSTERING CITIZEN PARTICIPATION AND GOVERNMENT RESPONSIVENESS

Angela Keller-Herzog

Overview and Summary

The core domain of Transparency International's (TI's) activism is anti-corruption. Integrally linked to fighting corruption is a preoccupation with issues of integrity, accountability, and transparency. Since its inception in 1993, TI has invested significant effort to generate so-called political will, initially under the organization's avowed approach of constructive engagement and multistakeholder dialogue. Transparency International has taken part in literally thousands of dialogues and consultations, has made countless visits with heads of state, politicians, and high-level officials, and has been instrumental in getting anticorruption issues onto the World Bank and G8 agendas. While TI's overall agenda and activities would make a useful case study to explore *how to generate political will,* this chapter focuses specifically on the experiences and lessons learned of TI's Advocacy and Legal Advice Centres (ALACs).

The ALACs, which currently operate in more than twenty countries around the world, provide legal advice and assistance to victims and witnesses of corruption. It helps citizens pursue corruption-related complaints, encouraging them to come forward. By using information gained from individual cases or common themes running through a variety of cases, the ALACs are able to advocate for very specific reforms, based on concrete evidence. The ALACs translate citizens' concerns about corruption into systemic changes for better local and national governance. Included in systemic changes are practical reforms in procedures or loopholes; improvements in administrative practice, which put an end to

245

localized or high-level abuses of power or neglect of the responsibilities of office; institutional reforms that implement and enforce laws; and in some cases legislative reforms. All of these require political will.

This chapter is written in the tradition of the participant observer. It describes the unfolding ALAC experience as I am learning to understand it, and being part of it. This description is followed by an analysis of what the ALAC experience can potentially teach us about how civil society can generate political will for functioning participatory governance and participatory democracy. My conclusions are that the ALACs' success, in getting governments to respond, is first due to a methodology of *connectedness* that generates credibility and legitimacy for the TI ALACs, by tying together evidence-based advocacy with directly empowering citizens to act on their own concerns and individual interests. Second, success generating political will for reforms is due to an approach that works mostly *with,* rather than against, existing public corruption complaint mechanisms and institutions, using an advocacy approach that is legally professionalized, consistent, and, above all, very *persistent* in its demands for political and public sector responsibility for follow-up to instances of alleged corruption.

Starting out Perspectives on Political Will

How can civil society encourage governance toward greater participation and responsiveness? The unique political and institutional life and times of different countries is extremely important. A central characteristic of this context, in which national or local civil society organizations (CSOs) are operating, is *political will.* Often reflection on past activities, and especially on the failure of civil society efforts to achieve hoped for changes, is blamed on *lack of political will.* Similarly, donors reflecting on failed reform agendas will speak of lack of government buy-in and ownership, and then again come back to *lack of political will.*

These can be *shorthand* and sometimes *coded* statements, implying that there were other dominant interests, other power agendas being played out, and other changes underfoot during a particular period. These types of *cloaked* statements, using the term *political will,* are also common when it is not safe to speak to the actual issues at play. For example, in the anticorruption context, it may not be safe to overtly accuse the ruling regime or president of grand corruption.

Setting aside this use of *cloaked* language, there is the danger that the language of *lack of political will,* when employed by civil society seeking greater participation, simply becomes a fatalistic, shrug-of-the-shoulders statement of disempowerment. At worst, *political will* becomes something akin to a light switch that has been turned on or off by fate. Clearly when it is *off* we are *in the dark* and are bound to fail. Our construct of the primary determinant that shapes progress toward better governance is an abstract, intangible, untouchable, and unpredictable *political will* at the highest level. This also shows the *disconnectedness* of the CSO from the political and governmental agencies of change. This sense of disconnectedness is then typically bolstered by pairing it with observations about a larger surrounding international context of idiosyncratic geopolitical processes and circumstances, factors which the agency of local civil society is *powerless* to change.

As a result of this backdrop of discourses on *political will,* which are about disconnection and disempowerment, I think that conversations in civil society that are seeking to discuss, analyze, and describe success in generating political will for more participatory governance, need to take some care in at least two regards. First, the points of *connectedness* and engagement with agencies of power, as well as with the public, need to be identified and described more carefully. Second, within this sociopolitical space, it is important for CSOs to build an understanding of how and where we see ourselves and how we construct ourselves, as active agents shaping the context in which political will is exercised. These two critical lenses will be examined further in the chapter.

Perspectives and Background

Having bought into the intersubjective version of understanding reality[1], I must tell the reader that I am not an external observer of the ALACs, but a participant observer working at TI's Secretariat in Berlin.[2] I am committed to, and tasked with, globally supporting and promoting the ALACs in the TI network. Therefore, I have my own agency and very active interest in this. I am also a part of a close community of colleagues, some of whom I name further on, each of whom casts his or her own interpretation of the significance and success of the ALAC approach. Of course, we plan to do a great deal of measuring and tracking of results in the future, and some of this work has begun. However, the primary purpose of this chapter is to provide a case study of the ALAC so far, and its interpretation in the context of understanding fruitful civil society activism and *political will* as a constraining factor.

Furthermore, I cannot *represent* the ALACs directly, given the identity and nature of the TI movement. Transparency International, the leading global coalition against corruption, consists of a network structure connecting autonomous local CSOs. Transparency International is not a unitary or hierarchical organization. Transparency International's Secretariat

(TIS) accredits local organizations as *TI national chapters*. The secretariat, then, only oversees that commonly agreed upon principles and standards are observed by all chapters, and provides some support in common services, for example in the areas of corruption measurement methodologies, anticorruption conventions advocacy, and global communications.

Advocacy and Legal Advice Centres: The Contextual History

The ALACs started in 2003, when the TIS, along with three TI national chapters in Bosnia-Herzegovina, FYR Macedonia, and Romania, approached the German Ministry of Foreign Affairs and the European Commission about funding an initiative that was a significant evolution of previously existing Anticorruption Resource Centres.

In terms of citizen engagement and service, the proposed ALACs would create national anticorruption hotlines and walk-in centers, listen to citizens, or victims and witnesses of corruption, and provide legal advice to help citizens file their corruption complaints with the responsible authority. On the advocacy side, the ALACs would analyze the corruption complaint statistics, identify clusters of complaints, find the *soft spots* of corruption in the system, and then lobby and advocate for corresponding administrative, institutional, or legislative changes to make the system less prone to corruption. By linking citizen complaints with advocacy, the advocacy becomes grounded in real cases of abuse of authority and power.

The preparation of the proposal provoked quite lively debate at TIS, and the yea sayers won—meaning, organizationally, TI's traditional domain of research and *systemic* anticorruption advocacy was expanded to include service provision and proactive citizen engagement. The Transparency International experience now shows that it is a very significant step for an advocacy and research organization to open their doors to direct public and citizen contact.

Naturally, TI holds no patent for the invention of a legal aid centre, for thinking of a hotline, or for organizing a resource centre on corruption. However, what we believe to be unique is pulling these elements together into building a centre of highly contextual expertise on corruption, which then explicitly sets out to advocate for changes based on citizens' corruption complaints. Interestingly, there is affirmation from TI people who worked as anticorruption activists for years, such as Adriana Krnacova in the Czech Republic and Srdjan Blagovcanin in Bosnia and Herzegovina, that the ALACs are bringing forth new cases and deeper understandings of the workings and complexity of corruption in their societies. The experiential information that citizens are bringing to TI's ALACs offers an alternate knowledge dimension of corruption to the country Corruption Perception Index scores and rankings that Transparency International is famous, and both loved and reviled, for.

In 2005, TI commissioned an external evaluation of ALACs (McCarthy 2005). The study found that ALACs had dramatically exceeded all expectations. Thousands of people called the anticorruption hotlines, and hundreds of anticorruption complaints were formally submitted. Arguably, relatively few cases received full formal investigation or successful public prosecution. However, the responsiveness of public institutions to citizen corruption complaints demonstrably increased and, to the satisfaction of the ALACs clients, corruption complaints were informally remediated many times. ALACs were also shown to be highly cost-effective on a per-case basis.

Transparency International then consciously set out to develop the ALAC model and practice. This push was enabled by several factors, including support from Europe and Central Asia Department of the TIS, support at the International Board Level, where Boris Divjak, from Bosnia and Herzegovina, had firsthand insight into the success and potential of the ALAC approach, and consistent donor support,[3] particularly from the German Ministry of Foreign Affairs, which was looking to find concrete ways to manifest its support for the Stability Pact principles.[4]

Cross-training workshops between TI national chapters, on the methodology of the ALACs, hosted by TI Romania in 2005, and in Transparency Azerbaijan in Baku in 2007, further got the ball rolling, and the second generation of ALACs began to spring up in countries like Azerbaijan, Bulgaria, the Czech Republic, Moldova, Montenegro, and Serbia. Production of systematic documentation, including production of an ALAC manual and case management database, further underpinned efforts to develop a *quality* ALAC model and practice.

Currently, inside the TI movement, the ALACs are considered to be a leading new-generation approach to increasing the effectiveness and broadening the base of the TI movement. They are seen to strengthen public demand for transparency, integrity, and accountability; raise the credibility and visibility of TI national chapters, as effective and relevant advocacy organizations; and provide a methodology that allows TI national chapters to formulate advocacy interventions on a citizen-demand-led basis.

In 2008, there were more than twenty ALACs operating in over a dozen countries; by 2009 there were more than thirty. The ALACs have received tens of thousands of citizen contacts and are helping people resist and prevent corruption. Expanding beyond Eastern Europe and central Asia, in 2007 and 2008 ALACs were launched in Guatemala, Haiti, Kenya, and Zambia. A third wave of expansion in 2009 is set to include over a dozen new ALACs across Africa, the Americas, Asia-Pacific, and the Middle East.

Operationally, ALACs enjoy a great deal of flexibility, and making national and subnational adaptations to achieve greater local effectiveness is encouraged. For example, in Azerbaijan the Baku-base ALAC is being decentralized into five local ALACs in different regions of the country, and work is being done in local mobile outreach, where lawyers visit remote villages and give legal anticorruption clinics to more marginalized, and in some cases ethnic and internally displaced, communities. Transparency International Russia is working on developing a virtual ALAC on the Internet that can contribute to corruption prevention, citizen awareness of rights, and provide responses to police abuse by human rights defenders. The ALAC in Zambia is using a theatre and drum group to raise legal awareness, bring forward complaints, seek recourse, and engage with communities in the participatory identification of local corruption issues. Usually, in trainings I speak about the *ALAC approach* rather than ALACs as a fixed methodology. This reflects two central facets of TI's practice. First, a culture of cross-learning in the TI movement exists, a component of which is respect for diversity. Second, there is intent within the movement, expressed in the secretariat's mandate, to translate knowledge, learning, and innovation into effective anticorruption practice.

The ALAC practice still needs to fully identify and grapple with several layers of gender issues around access to and benefits by women of ALAC services. Not only do cultural factors, traditional roles, and family responsibilities act as barriers to women approaching the advice centers, but in many countries the political economy of corruption is seen as a more male domain, and anticorruption organizations project a *male persona* that is less welcoming to women. It is clear that ALACs, like other demand-side participatory approaches, are not automatically inclusive.

In some TI national chapters running ALAC operations, there has been some stress because the ALAC has become all-consuming and displaced other streams of activity. In most cases though, national chapter staff and boards are inspired that they are engaged in work and actions that are concrete and directly helpful to citizens who are victims and witnesses to corruption. Working at the systemic advocacy level, the first generation of TI work is no doubt where the most strategic entry points are. However, matching this work with citizen engagement and service, or better yet, directly informing strategic advocacy by the evidence of case-based knowledge and information, has provided an additional infusion of purpose, self-worth, and public legitimacy. Commercial advertising and publicity for the anticorruption hotlines has also served to generate significant visibility for many of the ALACs and TI chapters.

Tactics

In analyzing the ALAC case study, as an example of citizen participation and civil society advocacy for change, it is important to note that the starting point of citizen engagement is more often than not a case of self-interest. In complaining about corruption, individual self-interest is often paired with some measure of individual risk. For example, the risk to the citizen complaining about bribe-taking by petty officials can be minor, whereas the risks for complaining about paying mafia protection money can be high. Individual interest often coincides with wider public interest. For example, if one taxi driver complains about having to pay a bribe to get a license, it is in the interest of the majority of taxi drivers and taxi passengers to reduce this illegal cost in the industry. In more rare cases the ALACs are approached by whistle-blowers who are acting entirely in the public interest and at personal risk. For example, complaints that unreasonable or excessive fees, side payments, and kickbacks are being demanded, that scheduled social support payments or services are not being delivered, and that public procurement projects and contracts are not being fairly awarded and implemented, are all instances of localized and specific social and economic injustice, or corruption. The first type of citizen participation that ALACs support then is to help, or *empower*, citizens to more effectively act in their *own* interest. In the first instance, this is done by making citizens aware of their rights, entitlements, and obligations, as well as applicable laws, regulations, and procedures. Second, ALACs support and encourage citizens to submit official complaints using available channels in responsible agencies. Some countries have specific anticorruption agencies; others have institutions of public accountability such as ombudsman offices and supreme audit institutions. In most cases some kind of public complaints channel exists, though it may be within the same institution, for example, where parents with a complaint about a teacher complain to the principal of the school, where complaints about the school management are directed to the oversight education board or ministry of education. Typically, this involves helping citizens draft a formal letter. In some countries, like Montenegro, ALACs also help citizens use channels, provided for under access to information laws, to obtain supporting information and evidence of possible corruption and malfeasance.

It is fairly typical for government offices to simply ignore a complaint from an individual, but to pay attention when the complaint is accompanied by an ALAC cover letter and formulated with reference to the relevant legal code. The ALAC accompaniment can also protect complainants from threats and intimidation from minor officials. Typically, cases of administrative corruption can then be *resolved* through some type of administrative remedy, where the corrupt act is then administratively reversed. Examples include the issuance of a license or service without illegal fee payment, the return of a bribe, the reappearance of pension or social payments, and the reversal of hiring, promotion, and dismissal decisions. Although the resolution of individual cases and private interests is not public interest advocacy, the ALACs' persistent push of public offices toward responsiveness to citizens' complaints, through hundreds of *legalistic* letters, is real and useful civic pressure.

In cases where there is no administrative response, where a reasonably free press exists, and where citizens are willing *to go public* with their evidence, the citizen can go to the media. Transparency International is cautious not to speak for the citizen, not to take sides in cases of alleged corruption, and not to become, or be perceived as, embroiled in partisan politics. However, it is clear that a citizen who has full awareness of his or her rights, from consultation with the ALAC lawyer and can comment on existing abuse of power in legal terms, will have a better chance attracting media attention and mobilizing pressure. The relationship between ALACs, advocates based on mostly legal means and knowledge, and the media, who in the case of investigative journalism can be powerful advocates making information public, can be mutually supportive. There are even cases where ALAC lawyers have advised media under threat of defamation suits. While corruption abounds, solid evidence of corruption is difficult to come by, given its secret and conspiratorial nature.

The third avenue of individual recourse for victims of corruption is through the judicial system. Clearly, where a citizen corruption complaint with sufficient evidence of criminal malfeasance is submitted to a public agency, it is then the duty of the public prosecutor's office to launch an investigation. In reality, this seldom happens. Sometimes internal audits are launched, and there are some instances of ALAC lawyers fully taking on individual cases in court, but usually this representational work is referred to legal aid clinics or left to commercial lawyers. Risks are high. Arguably, in national environments characterized by a strong rule of law, political will for change can be gained through legal means. Public interest litigation, as an advocacy method, deserves a separate chapter, and with regard to building political will, the debate on judicial activism and judicial restraint is germane. On the opposite end of the spectrum, in national environments that are not characterized by rule of law, but by impunity, there may be a role for high-profile example litigation cases to break the pervasive culture of impunity. The TI chapter in Papua, New Guinea, is putting forward this argument and is about to launch an ALAC.

Interestingly, ALAC lawyers are pulled into cases of corruption, where there is need for legal advice, letters, and follow-ups. However, ALAC volunteers, often third- or fourth-year law students, trained hotline operators, and legal assistants often cover a much wider spectrum of caller or visitor inquiries. Citizens need to know what kind of services their governments have promised to provide and at what cost. These can be simple questions. For example, how do I get a passport and how much should it cost, and should I have to pay for a tuberculosis diagnostic chest X-ray at the district hospital, or is this supposed to be free. Or the questions can be more involved, such as why is there no equipment or material support for nurses in a particular Moldovan subdistrict, where did this budget go, and why are nurses being threatened with censure when they ask these questions.

There are strong connections between the availability of public information and the right to access information. In many countries in Europe and Latin America freedom of information laws, or access to information laws, have been passed over the past two decades. Although not always well implemented, the existence of these laws can be a critical tool for civil society. Accountability of the public service and the state administration is strengthened when civil society is able to access information on budgets, expenditure, and public procurement processes. The forced transparency, which arises from these public claims to information, is a hook for generating political will.[5]

Information and statistics provide the bridge between individual cases and individual interest to ALAC public interest advocacy for systemic change. Occasionally, one case will reveal a depth of information on how corruption is being practiced in a particular sector or area. Once the particular nature of the corrupt practice is understood and the ins and outs, or the network of individuals more or less identified, action can be taken. However, typically it is not a depth of information, but many dots of individual alleged corruption cases clustering around one area or institution that provides the evidentiary base. This is even more critical in environments that are characterized by high levels of insecurity, such as Guatemala, where corruption complainants want to stay anonymous because they fear for their safety.

Based on statistical evidence of where abuse and corruption hot spots are, ALAC advocacy takes many different forms. There are some instances where ALACs and their TI chapters have mobilized people into public street protests, for example, in Tirana, Albania, on urban waste management issues, but this tends to be the exception. More often, the dry material of pie charts and statistical breakdowns of alleged corruption incidence are the initial fodder for press conferences and meetings, and then serve as launch pads for follow-up meetings, discussion, and lobbying public bodies and politicians.

A basic approach of most ALACs early on is to enter into Memoranda of Understanding (MoU) with key government ministries, establishing contacts at multiple levels. We have learned to interpret the willingness of ministers to sign MoUs cautiously. A quick willingness to sign an MoU should not necessarily be interpreted as evidence of political will to combat corruption. A willingness to sign can be based on short-term political opportunism, such as the photo opportunity. A hesitation to sign can signal that there is serious intent and that the ministry first wants to rethink its own internal processes and procedures for dealing with corruption revelations.

It is also clear that no government acts monolithically. All governments have branches and departments cooperating or chafing against each other, which are placed in a variety of hierarchical, supervisory, and oversight roles vis-à-vis one other. There are always champions of reform and greater justice, and usually there are some doors open for dialogue and constructive engagement with civil society. This includes CSOs that are sure to be critical of government behavior sooner or later. It is important to find these entry points. Some examples are the ALAC in Bulgaria, which maintains a regular dialogue with the prosecutor's office, the ALAC in the Czech Republic works with the Ministry of the Interior, the ALAC in Kazakhstan is working with universities, and the ALAC in Guatemala is working with the vice president's office.

We have also found that it is extremely useful to have entry points at different levels in the same structure. Working-level officials who are supportive of the ALAC mission will be freer to work in greater collaboration and depth with the ALAC, if a minister or deputy minister has blessed the work that the ALAC is doing. Similarly, ministers and high-level officials will be much more likely to attend scheduled meetings and dialogues, if their staff has provided them with reassuring briefings. This lesson also translates to regional, local, and national structures and institutions, where cases of corruption are acted on and resolved locally by those vested with executive or judicial power. At the local level this works well, but sometimes it is also useful to be able to call on someone in the power structure, who is not complicit in local corruption to *generate political will*.

Effective advocacy must propose solutions and specific proposals for change that politicians can adopt and administrators can implement. At this point, ALACs act as intermediaries and produce priorities and proposals for change based on problems identified by citizens. In a host of countries, ALACs have scored consistent successes in advocating systemic and structural changes, many of which have required political buy-in or political will at various levels. For example, in 2004, TI Romania, informed by a number of cases of public sector whistle-blowers, successfully advocated for a whistle-blower law and its implementation in Romania. In Albania, the advocacy of the ALAC has focused on judicial reforms, and environmental issues, where public trust has been betrayed. Access to information laws and their implementation, land restitution and real estate registration, public procurement and the administrative practices of inspectorates, are other systemic corruption-prone areas that have seen strong and successful advocacy from ALACs. Advocacy interventions have included legalistic approaches based on administrative law, informal dialogues and consultations, and public campaigns and citizen mobilization.

Privatization and reallocation of public assets to private-public-partnership (PPP) structures are often corruption prone. The ALACs have received appeals for help from groups of workers, for example in Croatia, and in some cases have received documents that attest to corruption at very high levels, for example in Bosnia and Herzegovina. The questions then become: are there *checks and balances* institutions with sufficient power and political will that can be mobilized; will the police launch a criminal investigation against the current prime minister; and will the prosecutor's office give consideration to documents incriminating a powerful minister. Often the answer to the question on whether there is *political will to fight corruption* depends on what side of the line in the sand the corruption is on. Trying to move that line, and testing the waters, is not without risk. The ALAC in Bosnia and Herzegovina had to be evacuated in the summer of 2008, due to death threats and a state-sponsored smear campaign against the ALAC.

In trying to assess the ALACs' success in increasing the political will to fight corruption, it is clear that there are mutually reinforcing agendas at play, especially in Eastern and Southeastern Europe. Because the European enlargement process criteria include justice sector and anticorruption reforms, there have been other powerful drivers alongside TI's advocacy. However, many specific administrative, institutional, and legislation changes, that ALACs and the TI chapters have lobbied for, clearly would not have happened without the ALACs. In the cases of specific administrative practices, attribution is especially clear.

Some Lessons

How can we understand and interpret these successes in a participatory governance framework? It is time to return to the two lenses or lines of analysis proposed earlier: engagement or *connectedness*, and how we construct our own agency. A third thread, that is traceable through the work and successes of the ALACs, concerns the political power of information.

Engagement of Citizens and Institutions:
A Practice of Connecting at Both Ends

The Advocacy and Legal Advice Centres can be understood as a tool or mechanism that enables better-informed and more effective *direct* citizen participation in the fight against corruption. The ALACs facilitate wider engagement of a given population in the fight against corruption, and provide for enhanced transparency and accountability of governing institutions. They can be seen as deriving their effectiveness from direct engagement with citizens and aligning private incentives with TI's anti-corruption public interest objectives. In these senses, ALACs are a mechanism for democratic citizen participation. The fact that tens of thousands of citizens have come forward and contacted the ALACs , which have helped these citizens engage with their state authorities, is a remarkable achievement in an era of declining voter participation in the new Eastern European democracies. Voter turnouts, especially in the new member states for the last European parliamentary elections, were at strikingly low levels, for example at 16.7 percent in Slovakia, 20.4 percent in Poland, 38.7 percent in Hungary, and 27.9 percent in the Czech Republic. The fundamental assumption of the ALAC mechanism is that citizens are not apathetic by nature, and will act if given simple, understandable, realistic ways of stepping forward. Most grandly perhaps, ALACs have been described by Dr. Miklos Marschall, director of the Europe and Central Asia Department at the TIS, as the *democratization* of the fight against corruption (Fig. 14.1).

As legitimate intermediary institutions (legitimate in the sense of being legitimated by a statistical and evidence-based set of complaints and corruption cases, and legitimated by success in greatly increasing the responsiveness of public agencies to citizen corruption complaints), ALACs are able to play a *representative* interest role. ALAC advocacy, which translates corruption complaints into calls for change, is pursued and practiced on principles of multistakeholder engagement.[6] Before a new ALAC is launched, a crucial aspect of preparation is to understand, and, if necessary, create channels of communication and cooperation with official

Figure 14.1. ALAC Client Interviewing on Behalf of his Daughter's Rights—Lenkaran, Azerbaijan

institutions theoretically or practically responsible for responding to citizen corruption complaints.

Often, ministries and agencies have effectively *stonewalled* ALAC demands for follow-up to individual corruption complaints for the first few months, or longer. Thus, the ALAC case study tends to show that positioning engagement with citizens and creating working interfaces with offices and persons in power is not sufficient. The second requirement is what one might call *persistence and consistency in agency*.

Self-Aware Agents of Change: Constructing Our Own Agency to be Consistent and Persistent

As a consequence of TI's network structure, the nature of the individual national chapters is quite diverse, and capacity tends to be uneven. In many cases, national chapters are founded by the proverbial *small group* of committed people, who are willing to work together for the common cause of fighting corruption. There is a common interest, a direction, and purpose; there is a sense of wanting to become and build an *agency* of change. In this sense, TI chapters are akin to the diverse world of civil society in general. Often, we are characterized by short bursts of volunteer-driven advocacy energy, responding to crisis, or taking advantage of opportune timing to advocate for change, and also the structural short-termism created by donor project cycles. Against this familiar backdrop, we can look at the ALACs through a managerial lens.

Although the concept of an ALAC is extremely simple, the practical requirements of running an ALAC are reasonably complex. They include, an office with regular hours of operation, a phone that *must* be answered professionally, a legal capacity, an administrative capacity capable of managing a large number of case files, a mentoring and organizing capacity for the legal volunteers, a coordination capacity for managing these human resources, and a political and professional capacity to manage the relational aspects of advocacy with government institutions. Therefore, it is not surprising that an initially unexpected side effect of starting and operating an ALAC has been a professionalization and maturing of the functional capacity of the local CSOs, or TI national chapters.

By design, construct, and arrived at through practice, ALACs have addressed the corruption complaints of their individual clients and advocacy demands to the authorities in a *persistent* and *consistent* manner. This is reinforced by the legal underpinning of ALACs. Chosen strategies are less on the creative and surprising side, and more in conformity with the legal framework, such as calling on institutions, as frequently as needed, to perform their duties, responsibilities, and mandates as required by law. This persistence is further reinforced by the ALACs' accountability to their clients, who return for news and progress on their case. We believe that it is this persistence and consistency of work, achieved through professionalization of capacity, which accounts for the success of the ALAC approach.

Ben Elers, an important and dedicated craftsmith of the ALAC approach at TI, would also point to the flipside of this coin, noting that the potential lack of quality in too rapid and unsupported expansion of the ALAC model can result in failures, disappointments, and a lack of credibility, in the eyes of the public and government agencies. Elers is an untiring proponent of total quality control of TI's tools and products. He encourages everyone to take responsibility for the quality and full completion of each part of the whole effort. He is right—nothing undermines civil society advocacy more than the revelation that the facts cited are not solid, and the key messages are nothing but thinly grounded hyperbole.

Public institutions are easily able to ignore single calls for change from civil society. Politicians are more likely to respond to calls for change that are accompanied by savvy media work. However, it still tends to fall to bureaucrats and technocrats to implement changes at administrative and institutional levels. Legislative reform work tends to be drawn out over time, and can easily lose momentum. Even if legislative reforms are passed, working out the regulations necessary to implement the prescriptions of various acts and legislations is the domain of public officials. With public officials, consistency and persistence are often a winning strategy.

There is a philosophical and sometimes passionate debate and self-awareness among the founders, senior advisors, and key people in TI on how TI's capacity for effectiveness is constructed, or how to shape the *agency*. One approach would be to construct ourselves as building a flexible but strong *capacity to respond* to the exigencies and unpredictable opportunities for anticorruption advocacy. According to this view, we will never be able to foresee the next plot twist, corruption scandal on which TI will be asked to substantively comment, or the next entry point for advocacy and anticorruption reforms, so we should stay nimble and not seek to technocratize and professionalize. Alternatively, TI could strengthen its staff complement of specialists and professionals, *who really know what they are talking about* in order to build TI's capacity and effectiveness. Ever since the time of the German sociologist Max Weber, organizational theory has assumed that social institutions begin as charismatic organizations and must be transformed into formalized structures, if they are to grow and be sustainable.

Examining the ALAC operations, it is evident that clear procedures and processes are required, so that legal volunteers and assistants can effectively staff the front lines of the ALACs. Clear case management is required for the legal capacity of the ALAC to be brought to bear. Therefore, the work and methodology of ALACs contain an inherent driving force toward increasingly formalized structured capacities in the host chapters, as well as toward becoming a civil society *mediating* institution, connecting citizen participation with responsible public institutions.

The Political Power of Information

Probably one of the most important insights in the tactics of advancing change in the area of anticorruption, accountability, and integrity is the power of information. As Ana Castro, ALAC coordinator in Guatemala, told her peers at a workshop, "ALACs *are* information." It is useful to deconstruct the ways in which this is true. First, having primary, original-source information is the legitimate basis for evidence-based advocacy. Second, where the evidence is based on statistically significant numbers of citizens' contacts and cases, this *can* become the beginning of an interesting story of civil society advocating for a specific change.

I say *can,* because we live in a time of information overload, what might be called *information devaluation.* The quantity of information that technology has made accessible to an ever-increasingly *connected* population is growing every day. However, people's willingness to take information at face value seems to be declining. There is a sense of distrust in facts and statistics that are put forward to motivate political action and participation. People wonder if this is another spin doctor having a go. There is the postmodern sense of no truth to be had, and there is the cynicism and political apathy that devalues what could be called the direct motivational impact of information regarding social and economic injustices. It is difficult to generalize globally, but these trends insulate politicians and powerholders from evidence- and information-based demands for action.

The anecdotal evidence of many informally shared stories by ALAC staff also points to another aspect of information. The case and statistical information that citizens bring to ALACs has a great deal of political content, political in the sense that information can give one person more or less power over someone else. A middle-level bureaucrat or back-bench politician is probably not as worried by the public reaction to a potential disclosure, via the media, that she or he is guilty of a corrupt act. Tomorrow's page three will have other news. More worrisome is the reaction of those left out of the deal, political competitors who will have a long memory of this allegation or proven malfeasance and use this information later.

Thus, the correctly or incorrectly perceived threat of disclosure of information can become the key motivator of action by public figures. Persons of power may not know exactly what information the ALAC has received, but they may think ahead about what information the ALAC could receive in the future. The lesson might be that as citizens act in self-interest in approaching the ALAC, public figures' level of *political will* in taking appropriate action may depend more on their own personal perceived interests than anything else.

The mostly implicit threat of media disclosure has often been a significant lever of influence for ALACs—the information tools of transparency, and shining the light, and speaking truth to power. It can be used in very different ways, and there are enormous choices in timing and choices of stakeholder spaces. The same set of information may have very different legal, ethical, personal, financial, or political power aspects. Client confidentiality, the unproven nature of criminal allegations, potential misinformation, and potentially unfair damages to reputations and livelihoods are ethical considerations that loom large in the responsible handling, protection, and use of information. Thus, evidence-based advocacy for a specific public interest objective may be put forward by an ALAC on legal grounds, but the political will to make the change may be rooted in the personal or political calculations of various decision makers. Where the individual interest of the decision maker is *aligned* with the desired public policy change, it is more likely that the political will for change will materialize. Where the direct personal interest of the public officeholder is directly entangled with the outcome of a public policy decision, whether the alignment is positive or at odds, is called a *conflict of interest*. Most countries have legislation where conflict of interest, in terms of direct financial interests and personal financial gain, must be declared and avoided. Other boundaries are placed on lobbyists trying to wield undue influence, political party financing laws, and transparency and reporting requirements. However, these safeguards have clear limitations of scope and are often not easily or well implemented. More broadly, when it comes to personal and political interests, we look to the overall structure and incentives of a political system to provide guidance and boundaries.

Some Conclusions

The evidence of the ALACs shows success in strengthening the citizen-responsiveness of public institutions and their ability to receive and act upon corruption-related complaints. This is achieved through constructive engagement with public institutions, focusing on helping them understand the need to effectively process complaints and develop the capacity to do so. The ALACs have proved successful in promoting systematic administrative, institutional, and legislative changes in over a dozen countries in Eastern Europe and the Caucuses. It is too early to know how the approach is faring in Central America or in Africa, but success in advocating for systemic change and in supporting citizens' cases have been achieved in a variety of political climates.

The key ingredients of success seem to be an *apolitical* politics of engagement, which is rooted in the strong base of legitimacy and credibility that ALACs have developed through direct citizen engagement. Advocacy is *evidence-based*, meaning that it is connected to real cases, and a *mediating* approach that seeks to formally connect with the complaint-taking mechanisms or *windows* of responsible authorities, officials, and institutions is practiced. Perhaps it could be said that, just as in the case of individual clients where ALACs can empower them to act on their own behalf by explaining the legal framework, the terminology, and the recourse options, ALACs can help institutions and politicians find ways forward in the anticorruption agenda, by mapping out practical steps to help them deal with citizens' direct demands, and making governing, adjudicating, and administering institutions less prone to corruption. One antidote that the ALAC case study presents, to the pessimism of the untouchable and intangible *lack of political will* is for CSOs and public interest organizations to structurally organize work approaches to *become better connected* with ordinary citizens, politicians, and administrators.

A second key factor of success is the consistency and persistence of the ALACs' advocacy efforts, which requires significant managerial and professional capacity. In this sense, seeking governance that is responsive to legally empowered citizens is not a spontaneous communitarian or libertarian direct expression of popular will. Transparency Internationals' ALAC experience demonstrates that civil society can be effective in its agency, getting from political *won't* to *will*, when it has constructed its own institutional capacity to productively engage governing institutions. In a way, CSOs need to become responsible institutions, if they are to effectively engage with responsible institutions and authorities, and, in turn, arouse the civic courage and political will of ordinary citizens, inside reformers, and whistle-blowers for better governance.

It is clear that the promotion of transparency and access to information is a first key step toward participatory and responsive governance, and in holding those in power accountable. Exactly how all forms of information can be legally and ethically used to lever the political will for action is far from a straightforward process, as is apparent in the discussion about influence and the *undue* influence of lobbyists. It is important to realize that a given set, or *packet* of information can be seen as a set of evidence with a particular public interest advocacy objective. The *same* packet of information can also have personal, financial interest and political power dimensions for different stakeholders and power-holders. Therefore, the political will to act can be motivated by information *qua* evidence, and equally by personal or political interest to have or not have certain information in the public domain.

References

Eigen, Peter. 2003. *Das Netz der Korruption: Wie eine weltweite Bewegung gegen Bestechung kämpft.* Frankfurt, Germany: Campus Verlag.

Geertz, Clifford. 1984. From the native's point of view: On the nature of anthropological understanding. In *Culture Theory: Essays on Mind, Self, and Emotion,* ed. R. A. Shweder and R. LeVine, 123–136. New York: Cambridge University Press.

Inter-American Development Bank. 2008. *Anticorruption Activities Trust Fund: Report on Preparatory Activities.* Available at the Inter-American Development Bank Web site.

Keller-Herzog, Angela. 2008. *Participatory Mid-term Evaluation: TI Advocacy and Legal Advice Centres in Baku, Ganja and Lenkoran*

Azerbaijan. Report available from Transparency International Secretariat.

Li, Tania. 2007. *The Will to Improve: Governmentality, Development, and the Practice of Politics*. Durham, NC: Duke University Press.

McCarthy, Paul. 2005. *Drivers of Change: An Evaluation of Advocacy and Legal Advice Centres*. Report available from Transparency International Secretariat.

Pope, Jeremy. 2000. Confronting corruption: The elements of a national integrity system. In *TI Source Book 2000*. Berlin, Germany: Transparency International.

Notes

1. Reality is subjective in both a postmodern and ethnographic sense; see, for example, the work of anthropologist Tania Li (2007). Communication, on the other hand, requires intersubjectivity–shared meanings to be constructed and agreement on meanings and definitions.

2. Participant observation has a well-established place as a methodology in social anthropology, but limitations are also evident (Geertz 1984).

3. Other supportive donors were the Finnish and French Foreign Ministries and USAID. The current (2009) third wave of ALAC global expansion receives significant support from the UK Department for International Development.

4. The Stability Pact is the international community's attempt to replace the previous reactive crisis intervention policy in the Balkans/Southeastern Europe, with a comprehensive, long-term conflict prevention strategy. Under it, more than forty partner countries and organizations seek to strengthen the countries of Southeastern Europe in their efforts to foster peace, democracy, respect for human rights and economic prosperity in order to achieve stability in the whole region.

5. For a report bringing together a series of country studies on the theme of corruption, transparency, and access to information, see Inter-American Development Bank (2008).

6. In general, Transparency International seeks to engage all parties in dialogue, on the basis of an understanding that change is much more likely to be achieved through working with people and institutions. TI[0] also sees corruption as a systemic issue, where a less corruption-prone system of governance can only be achieved and maintained through a strengthening of the many different institutions composing a national integrity system–including public sector institutions and political parties, civil society, the private sector, and media.

PART 5

CONCLUSION

CHAPTER 15

PARTICIPATORY GOVERNANCE: WHERE THERE IS LACK OF WILL, IS THERE A WAY?

Carmen Malena

Introduction

Around the world, growing numbers of committed practitioners and activists are working to promote citizen participation in public decision making. The preceding chapters of this book have presented more than a dozen examples of such efforts, from as many countries. The case studies represent a diverse mix of experiences and contexts, ranging from the village to the national level and including efforts to strengthen dialogue between citizens and local government authorities (Chapters 4, 5, and 6), promote participatory monitoring and evaluation of public services (Chapters 7 and 8), give citizens a say in the allocation of public funds (Chapters 9, 10, and 11), empower citizens to hold elected representatives accountable (Chapters 7, 8, and 11), and create a more enabling environment for participatory governance (Chapters 12, 13, and 14).

What the cases share is a common concern for how to build political will for participatory governance. In every case, lack of political will was identified as a key obstacle, and the authors have described the challenges they faced, the strategies they employed, and the successes they achieved in overcoming *political won't*. This chapter seeks to distill key findings and lessons from the cases examined. It includes an analysis of the principal reasons for *political won't*, successful strategies for building political will, key factors of success, and essential lessons learned.

Understanding Political Won't

The case studies reveal a wide spectrum of reasons for lack of political will for participatory governance. From these, a core group of fundamental and frequently encountered obstacles emerge. As hypothesized in the introductory chapter, some of these relate to lack of *political want,* while others are related to a weak sense of *political can* or *must* (Fig. 15.1).

Lack of Political Want
Fear of losing power

The case studies suggest that one of the most important factors blocking government authorities from *wanting* to support participatory governance is *fear of losing power*. This is particularly true in so-called *hybrid* states where the political mantra is *retain power at all costs,* but, even in a much broader set of political contexts, government authorities appear to hold a zero-sum perception of power and fear that participatory processes will erode their own personal power base, along with its related privileges. In Guelph, Canada, for example, Pinnington notes that government authorities are accustomed to having power *over citizens,* versus sharing power *with* citizens. Mumvuma states that as a result of this logic, government authorities see "no benefits in sharing political power." The notion that, by empowering citizens and tapping into the incredible potential of the people, public authorities can actually enhance their own performance, popularity, and power is not widely understood or embraced.

Unaware/unconvinced of benefits

A second important reason for lack of *political want* is that power-holders do not believe in participatory governance, or are not convinced of its potential benefits. Unless they have witnessed or experienced the benefits of a successful participatory governance initiative firsthand, most public authorities have little desire or incentive to experiment with an unfamiliar approach, especially one that can appear potentially complicated, messy, risky, or time-consuming. If a politician or bureaucrat does not perceive participatory governance as serving their self-interests, or if the costs of participatory governance appear to outweigh the benefits, then they are likely to lack *political want*.

Poor civil society–state relations

Weak or hostile relations between civil society and state actors is another major obstacle to participatory governance. In many case studies, initial

Figure 15.1. Key Reasons for Political Won't

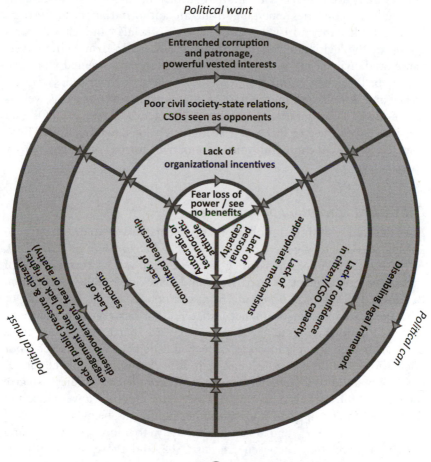

relations between government officials and citizens/civil society organizations (CSOs) were marked by mutual suspicion, distrust, or disrespect. Especially in countries emerging from an authoritarian past, such as Bolivia, Tajikistan, and Uganda, government officials can lack an appreciation of the legitimate role of CSOs and citizens in democratic governance, and civil society actors involved in governance-oriented work can quickly be labeled as *political opponents* or *rebels*. Such attitudes of intolerance and domination on the part of government authorities, as well as the resulting confrontational or aggressive tactics of some CSOs and activists, have served to fuel and perpetuate tensions, making it very difficult to pursue meaningful and productive forms of participatory governance.

Entrenched corruption or patronage

A serious and widespread problem that prevents power-holders from supporting participatory governance is *entrenched corruption or patronage*. As has been shown, participatory governance can be a powerful means of enhancing government transparency and checking public corruption. Power-holders who are *benefiting* from corruption are likely to resist or sabotage participatory governance initiatives that risk revealing their misdeeds. Situations of entrenched patronage are particularly pernicious because they create relationships of fear and dependency between poor populations and their patrons, making it difficult and risky for the former to speak out and seek systemic change. However, the case studies also give some cause for optimism. In several cases, participatory governance initiatives led to corrupt and nonperforming politicians being voted out of office (Chapters 4, 7, and 8) and, ultimately, to more productive and strengthened relations between citizens/CSOs and those public officials who took a stand in favor of transparency and accountability.

Lack of Political Can

Lack of capacity of government actors

The hypothesized link between *political can* and political will is validated by several case studies in this book. A number of chapters attribute lack of political will, at least in part, to a *lack of capacity,* on the part of government actors, to put participatory governance principles into practice. Public officials rarely have specialized knowledge about participatory approaches and frequently lack awareness of even basic dialogue or collective decision-making techniques. Elected representatives or bureaucrats, who feel incompetent or insecure about their capacity to fulfill even their core governance functions, due to limited knowledge, skills, or experience, can be reluctant to openly engage with citizens, for fear of revealing these weaknesses. In Zimbabwe, for example, Mumvuma describes how local authorities were initially afraid that participatory budgeting would expose their own limited capacity to stakeholders who regarded them with *esteem and admiration.*

Lack of appropriate mechanisms

Lack of appropriate systems and mechanisms for participatory governance is also an important cause of *political can't.* As Cruz points out, in many developing countries, "colonial forms of governance represented the antithesis of democratic values and put in place none of the checks and balances required in a real democracy." Even in stable democracies, systems of representative democracy rarely provide an enabling context, or adequate mechanisms, for participatory governance. Even committed champions of participatory governance can be paralyzed by an absence of institutional mechanisms for implementing participatory governance or organizational systems that purposefully or inadvertently block or discourage such practices. Except in those rare cases where there is an established tradition of citizen participation, promoting participatory governance usually requires challenging accepted practices, inventing new platforms and mechanisms, and experimenting with new approaches, most often without organizational support or additional resources. This is a daunting task, even for a staunch supporter of participatory governance.

Lack of citizen/civil society capacity

An important reason for a sense of *political can't,* on the part of government officials, is a *lack of confidence in the capacity of citizens or CSOs.* Participatory governance, by definition, requires the active involvement of multiple stakeholders. Political will for participatory governance is jeopardized when citizens/CSOs lack the requisite knowledge, skills, or interest, or where power-holders, rightly or wrongly, lack confidence in their capacities. As outlined by Clark, elected representatives may be understandably cautious about sharing the responsibility and trust bestowed upon them, and, before doing so, need to feel sure that adequate capacity, experience, credibility, and representativity exists. In many of the case studies, significant efforts were required to address a lack of information, skills, and engagement on the part of citizens. Zipfel, for example, describes how participatory governance advocates in the United Kingdom had to struggle with "political disengagement" on the part of ordinary citizens and "a cultural tendency to rely on government and the welfare state to resolve problems and meet needs." In numerous cases (Chapters 4, 7, and 8), significant efforts were also required to address lack of capacity on the part of local CSOs.

Lack of Political Must

Autocratic or technocratic tendencies

A final set of reasons for lack of political will, emerging from the cases in this book, relates to political leaders and bureaucrats feeling no sense of real pressure or compulsion to support participatory governance, in other words, a lack of *political must*. One factor cited as contributing to this is the lack of any *sense of obligation or duty*, on the part of many power-holders, to listen to, respond to, or account to ordinary citizens. Whether due to arrogance, an elitist mind-set, or an autocratic or technocratic political paradigm, the result is the same—little sense of personal or professional compulsion to reach out to and involve ordinary citizens. Namisi reports that in Uganda "many local leaders had no respect for the illiterate community representatives that made demands on them." Hicks and Buccus found "the pervading attitude among officials was that they know what people want and therefore participation is not necessary." The type of education and training that public officials and administrators receive and the norms and expectations of the institutions in which they function can lead power-holders to believe that they alone know *what is best*, that nonstate actors are unable to truly understand complex political issues and trade-offs, and that there is, therefore, no need to engage with ordinary citizens.

Lack of committed political leadership

Just as high-level support for participatory governance can serve to generate political will throughout an entire political system or bureaucracy, a *lack of committed political leadership* is a serious lacuna that can result in disinterest and inaction at all levels. If there is no, or even only a nominal, commitment to participatory governance on the part of political leaders and top-level bureaucrats, and no signals or directives coming from the top in support of participatory governance, then government actors throughout the system are unlikely to feel compelled to take action or invest personal time and energy to promote participatory governance. Zipfel presents a rare case where local government authorities are strongly encouraged, by top-level political leadership, to become champions of participatory governance. A more typical scenario, however, is that government officials are expected to follow directives from above, rather than to respond and account to citizens. In the Canadian context, for example, Pinnington found that current New Public Management approaches led government officials to place very little value on civic engagement and the role of citizens.

Lack of sanctions

The *legal, regulatory, and policy frameworks* in which state actors function, serve to guide their behavior and control their actions. When it comes to participatory governance, legal provisions guaranteeing citizen rights, calling for popular participation, or requiring public information-sharing or consultation are frequently weak or absent. In the case of Washington, D.C., Jacksteit laments the lack of established norms and legal provisions to support citizen participation or downward accountability. Even if certain constitutional requirements or policy directives are in place, experience shows that such provisions can have little impact, unless they are actively enforced. Unfortunately, several cases (Chapters 7, 8, and 12) show us that constitutional and legal provisions regarding citizen rights and popular participation are often no more than lip service, frequently lacking any clear implementation mechanisms or enforcement measures.

Lack of public pressure/citizen engagement

Finally, as discussed in the introductory chapter, and illustrated in Chapters 7 and 8, creating and maintaining public pressure can be a powerful method for creating a sense of *political must*. Where there is a lack of citizen mobilization and engagement, there is a corresponding lack of pressure on power-holders to act. Whether it is due to a history of political repression, a culture of fear or secrecy, lack of organized civil society, or citizen disillusionment and apathy, the lack of active public demand for participatory governance is a final important reason for lack of political will. As pointed out by several chapter authors, the challenge is often not only to gain government support for participatory governance, but also to fight against cultural norms and habits that prevent people from actively engaging.

Strategies for Building Political Will

Chapter authors describe a broad spectrum of strategies for building political will for participatory governance. In some cases, efforts have focused exclusively on nurturing a particular element of political will, *political want, political can,* or *political must.* In other cases, practitioners have developed strategies aimed at addressing all elements simultaneously. One thing this group of experiences shows, is that there is no simple blueprint for addressing the complex and multifaceted challenge of building political will for participatory governance. In each individual case, strategies for building political will must take into account the specific context and nature of the situation at hand, and adapt to ever-changing political circumstances and stakeholder dynamics.

The cases, however, do reveal a number of core strategies that have proved successful in building political will in multiple contexts. These include: *(i) strengthening familiarity and trust between civil society and state actors; (ii) seeking critical collaboration; (iii) demonstrating concrete benefits; (iv) empowering and mobilizing citizens; and (v) lobbying for and making use of legal/policy reforms.*

Strengthen Familiarity and Trust Between Civil Society and State Actors

In essence, participatory governance is about establishing more productive relations between the *governors,* such as elected representatives and bureaucrats, and the *governed* (citizens and nonstate actors). Again and again, the case studies identified *a lack of familiarity and trust* between state actors and citizens/CSOs as an obstacle to building political will and implementing participatory governance. Too often, both government and CSO actors adopt a *them and us* mentality, based on assumptions, suspicions, and stereotypes rather than firsthand knowledge and understanding.

Oftentimes, government officials are woefully unaware of civil society and how it operates. Likewise, civil society actors are frequently ill informed about, or sometimes disrespectful of, government systems, laws, regulations, and programs. In many country contexts, government and civil society representatives inhabit different worlds and rarely have the opportunity to meet one another in a *neutral* space to productively and honestly share views and discuss issues.

Given this reality, a key strategy for building political will for participatory governance is to strengthen relationships between civil society and state actors. This is obviously easier in some contexts than others but experience suggests that, even in situations of political repression or crisis, it is almost always possible to establish links and build relations *at some level,* even if these are limited to the very local level or between technical staff. Where civil society–state relations are tense or hostile, it is all the more important to try to maintain direct communication and avoid polarization into isolated camps.

As shown by several of the experiences recounted in this book, uneasy relations between civil society and state actors are sometimes the result of a mutual lack of understanding, rather than genuine disagreement. In such cases, the simple act of creating formal or informal opportunities for direct dialogue can often go a long way toward defusing tension and improving relations. In Aga Khan Foundation (AKF) countries, significant time and energy were invested in helping local CSOs and local government authorities learn more about one another and to understand each other's respective ways of working, for example, by preparing a directory of local CSOs for local government authorities and convening workshops to explain government systems/programs to CSOs and vice versa. These approaches require a willingness to learn about one another and capacity, on the part of stakeholders themselves or a third-party facilitator, to seek out relevant information. Methods used in other case studies to strengthen civil society–government relations included the following: one-on-one meetings and the development of personal relationships (Chapter 10); organizing joint government–CSO meetings on common concerns (Chapters 5 and 9); introducing platforms for regular communication (Chapters 4, 8, and 11); and conducting joint research projects or training events (Chapters 4 and 13).

Seek *Critical Collaboration*

Participatory governance requires that multiple stakeholders agree to work together. This does not mean that civil society and state actors necessarily have to *agree* with one another, but it does necessitate a basic willingness to interact and treat one another with respect. Unfortunately, in many country contexts, government officials are unwilling to accept criticism or dissenting opinion, and, lacking meaningful opportunities for dialogue, civil society activists resort to unilateral and confrontational advocacy tactics. In such circumstances, it is common to hear government officials refer to *good CSOs,* meaning collaborative, service delivery-oriented CSOs, on the one hand, and bad *CSOs,* meaning critical, advocacy-oriented CSOs, on the other.

Participatory governance challenges all stakeholders to explore and create a new middle ground between these two extremes, calling on CSOs to ensure that criticisms are *constructive* and encouraging government counterparts to be more *tolerant* and *open* to alternative viewpoints. These case studies offer a number of valuable recommendations for replacing confrontation with more productive forms of *critical collaboration,* which result not only in concrete outcomes but also serve to enhance relations and build mutual confidence between civil society and state actors. This is not to suggest that civil society should never use confrontation as a strategy for achieving social change; it can in fact be an important tactic for building public pressure and creating *political must*. However, the danger is when confrontation and *punishment-based approaches* become a habit, and opportunities for more collaborative forms of interaction are overlooked.

Proposing Versus Opposing

A recurring theme in several of the chapters is the importance of *proposing versus opposing*. In order to nurture productive working relationships and build political will for participatory governance, it is essential for civil society actors to not just flag problems, but also to propose solutions. Hicks and Buccus (Chapter 12) describe how by "adopting a collegial rather than a confrontational approach" civil society actors were able "to reassure officials of an intention not to decry deficiencies in public participation interventions, but rather to identify these and develop recommendations to address them." In Washington, D.C., community activists were able to gain the respect and trust of the local advisory council by offering *new ideas and solutions*, breaking the usual dynamic of conflict and complaint. In Tanzania, civil society intermediaries helped community groups to "repackage demands in a way that enabled them to re-establish productive discussions with the authorities." As Holloway et al. (Chapter 4) described it, such constructive and proactive approaches allow practitioners "to light a candle, not simply to complain against the darkness."

Evidence-based Approaches

Another lesson in building political will is the importance of backing up arguments and proposals with *reliable evidence*. To overcome and manage differences of opinion, it is crucial to adopt a balanced and open-minded approach, and to seek to justify one's position, not with ideological slogans or moralistic proclamations, but with objective and verifiable facts. Adopting an evidence-based approach not only demonstrates professionalism, but it also provides a solid information base from which to accurately analyze problems and identify solutions. It also helps avoid politically motivated fudging or wishful ideological thinking. Keller-Herzog warns that "nothing undermines civil society advocacy more than the revelation that the facts cited are not solid" (Chapter 14). Namisi concludes that "research findings and hard data are key to advocacy activities and give credibility to efforts to exact accountability from government actors" (Chapter 7). Collecting reliable evidence and proposing potential solutions is much more demanding than simply pointing out problems and requires that CSOs develop, or partner with organizations that possess, solid research skills, analytical competencies, and technical expertise.

Demonstrate Benefits and Address Priority Interests

Individual actors, be they government officials or citizens, are unlikely to devote time and effort to participatory governance if they see no personal benefits. In order to build political will, it is therefore essential to ensure that participatory governance initiatives serve the self-interests of both citizens and fair-minded government actors.

Mumvuma confirms that "for political will to be enduring, participatory governance initiatives must quickly generate positive tangible results" for citizens. This means not just abstract talk about *citizen rights* and *good governance,* but significant and visible improvements in people's everyday lives, such as improved roads and market spaces in Zimbabwe; better water, health, and education services in Tajikistan, Kenya, and Tanzania; enhanced public security and conflict resolution in Uganda; reduced crime in Canada; and the resolution of individual citizen complaints by Transparency International's Advocacy and Legal Advice Centers (ALACs). These achievements again necessitate considerable capacity on the part of CSOs, requiring a mix of participatory governance expertise, social mobilization skills, and technical knowledge.

MacLean-Abaroa attributes the success of Popular Participation in Bolivia to the fact that it "made participatory governance attractive to those holding political power" and adds that "political support began to grow once . . . elected authorities, realized that . . . popular participation was of advantage to them." MacLean-Abaroa recounts how Popular Participation made the lives of mayors, like himself, much easier, by helping citizens better understand resource constraints and by challenging citizens to prioritize needs themselves, thus defusing the pressure on mayors to respond to an impossible-to-satisfy list of demands. This also boosted the popularity of local government officials, leading to unprecedented rates of reelection. Other case studies similarly describe how participatory governance gained support by serving the self-interests of government actors, for example, by increasing tax revenues and attracting donor funds in the Philippines, boosting the legitimacy and status of neighborhood commissioners in Washington, D.C., and ending a history of citizen protest against local government authorities in Mutoko, Zimbabwe. Zipfel relates the story of a ward councilor in the United Kingdom who, after four years in politics, described a participatory budgeting decision-day as "the best day ever." While discovering the satisfaction and joy of working together meaningfully may be a more intangible benefit of participatory governance, it can also be a powerful one, and a surefire source of political will.

Building political will can also require investing time and energy in documenting and publicizing the concrete benefits of participatory governance approaches. Pinnington describes, for example, how quantifying the monetary value of volunteer hours devoted by community members, which totaled over CAD$2,000,000, helped raise awareness of and respect for both the process and benefits of participatory budgeting. Zipfel notes that, in the United Kingdom, independent academic research has provided an important evidence base for participatory governance reforms. In other cases, such as the Philippines, peer-to-peer campaigning as well as media coverage, demonstration projects, study tours, and cross-country exchanges have all proved effective mechanisms for documenting and publicizing the benefits of participatory governance.

Empower and Mobilize Citizens

Active and engaged citizens are the lifeblood of participatory governance. It is, therefore, no surprise that almost every case in this book relied on *citizen empowerment and mobilization* as a core strategy for building political will and for successfully implementing participatory governance practices. The power of "reawakening the sleeping giant," as Namisi puts it, through a wide range of public education, citizen training, and community mobilization techniques, is that it simultaneously addresses the three key elements of *political want, political can,* and *political must.*

Mobilizing large numbers of citizen-voters in support of participatory governance initiatives creates a very strong incentive for vote-seeking, popularity-hungry politicians to get on board. Credible elected representatives want what their constituencies want, so strong demonstrations of public support for participatory governance, particularly during strategic preelection periods (as in Chapters 7 and 8), can be very effective in stimulating *political want* and political will.

An informed and active citizenry is also essential to nurturing a sense of *political can.* Public officials who see citizens as uninformed, uninterested, or unengaged are unlikely to support participatory governance. On the other hand, working to educate and empower citizens, not just instructing citizens on what to think or say, but providing them with the information and support they need to deliberate on public issues and voice their own opinions and ideas, can serve to greatly enhance power-holders' confidence in the ability of citizens to participate in governance processes. Forums that mobilize large numbers of citizens and directly demonstrate their capacity for collective, ideally nonpartisan, deliberation and decision making can be especially effective in convincing public officials of the feasibility and enormous potential of participatory approaches.

Finally, large numbers of empowered citizens can create enormous public pressure and communicate a clear message of *political must.* Namisi reports that "once large numbers of citizens became aware and simultaneously began to demand change . . . local leaders had no choice but to collaborate and share information with communities." Abad argues that when government fails to listen, the objective must be to make it politically costly to resist citizen demands. The popular revolution that swept her country in the mid-1980s, and deposed a dictator, is an impressive example of the incredible power of the people and a warning to those power-holders who fail to honor it. According to Abad, especially in contexts where systems of political corruption and patronage are entrenched, "nothing can change until the power balance shifts . . . in the favor of the powerless—not just in favor of CSOs."

Legal/Policy Reforms

Enabling legal and policy frameworks have the capacity to contribute to *political want,* by creating *incentives* for participatory governance, to *political can,* by creating appropriate *spaces* and *mechanisms* for citizen participation, and to *political must,* by placing *legal requirements* on government officials to incorporate participation in their administrative processes. Several of the case studies focus on creating a more enabling environment for participatory governance, by lobbying for freedom of information legislation (Chapter 13), developing a national policy on public participation (Chapter 12), or introducing procedural/regulatory reforms to control corruption and enhance public oversight (Chapter 14). In other case studies, decentralization legislation and other specific reforms proved crucial in building political will for participatory governance and creating new democratic spaces and channels for citizen engagement. For example, Bolivia's 1994 Popular Participation Law, the Philippines' Local Government Code of 1991, and recent policy reform in the United Kingdom, have proved *revolutionary* in creating space and building political will for participatory governance. Passing laws that directly *empower citizens,* for example, by giving citizen *vigilance committees,* the power to freeze municipal funds as in Bolivia, and laws that *create incentives,* for example, by basing local government assessment on the quality of community participation as in the United Kingdom, have proved particularly effective.

However, legal provisions are of limited use if they are not effectively implemented and enforced. According to Cruz, "the adoption of access to information laws will have little impact unless there is also will on the part of civil servants to implement the law and will on the part of the people to demand information." Hicks and Buccus similarly found that "policy gains could be meaningless without sufficient pressure *from below* for their subsequent uptake and effective implementation." Therefore, it is important not only to lobby for legal/policy reforms, but, ideally, to actively involve citizens in these efforts and to subsequently promote and support citizen/CSO awareness of, and use of, legal frameworks.

Factors of Success

In addition to outlining strategies for nurturing political will for participatory governance, the cases presented in this book reveal a number of factors that were critical to the success of these initiatives. Among others, these include: (i) *a high level of professionalism;* (ii) *emphasis on inclusion;* (iii) *investing in capacity development;* (iv) *drawing strength from networks and coalitions; and* (v) *timing.*

Professionalism

An important strategy for building political will for participatory governance is to prove it works and can result in real benefits outweighing potential costs and risks for key stakeholders. Experience shows that this requires a high level of *professionalism and commitment* on the part of participatory governance practitioners. Strong capacity with regard to participatory process, including facilitation, mediation, and conflict resolution skills, is important. Depending on the nature of the participatory governance initiative, a considerable level of technical, financial, and/or legal expertise may also be required to make participatory governance work.

As discussed, one of the key precepts of participatory governance is to promote approaches that go beyond making complaints to seeking collective solutions. This challenges CSOs to not only remain constructive and diplomatic under sometimes trying and emotionally charged circumstances, but also to demonstrate a high level of professionalism with regard to collecting and presenting accurate evidence, preparing well thought through arguments, and proposing realistic solutions.

As the case studies show, building political will for participatory governance also requires a high level of patience, persistence, and long-term commitment. Advocates of participatory governance must, therefore, be willing and able to sustain efforts and support over the long term, well beyond typical *development project* timelines.

Finally, in order to successfully advocate for more transparent, responsive, and participatory government, CSOs must themselves strive to become models of the values and practices that they preach. A common reason given by government actors for refusing to listen to or collaborate with CSOs is the charge that they are not truly representative or accountable or are themselves controlled by elite or foreign interests. To build political will for participatory governance, CSOs must have their own house in order and hold themselves to high standards of internal governance and good operational practice, in particular, ensuring that they empower and account to the constituencies they aim to serve. This is essential both to achieve goals of social justice and to earn credibility and respect in the eyes of government and the public at large.

Inclusion

One of participatory governance's most important benefits is ensuring that democratic processes not only respect the majority view, but also recognize and respond to minority interests, especially, marginalized minorities. Around the world, economic and social inequities result in the political exclusion of women, poor people, and disadvantaged minorities. In the South Africa example, Hicks and Buccus report that the inaccessibility of information and lack of resources and abilities have resulted in the domination of participatory spaces by the elite, by those who are organized and have access to resources. In the case of marginalized groups, "feelings of being sidelined, excluded, and disempowered overwhelmingly dominate."

In order for vulnerable and marginalized groups to participate in and benefit from democracy, their specific needs must be prioritized. Civil society organizations need to maintain a strong focus on *social justice* and develop the capacities and skills required to promote *social inclusion* and guard against agenda-setting and decision-making processes being *captured* by more powerful or influential stakeholders. Many CSOs claim to speak on behalf of the poor, marginalized, and *voiceless,* but only rarely are opportunities created for affected groups to obtain information, deliberate on options, and directly negotiate social change themselves, articulate preferred options and mandate representatives to speak on their behalf, with measures created for accountability and feedback.

Constant and specific efforts are required so that marginalized stakeholders remain at the forefront. Many of the participatory governance methodologies described in this paper are specifically designed to promote the equitable participation of marginalized groups. In Washington, D.C., specific efforts were made to recruit leaders from disadvantaged sectors. In the Philippines, Peoples' Manifestos were designed to articulate the specific needs of women, youth, fisherfolk, and other traditionally excluded groups. In Uganda, the *Pressure From Below* initiative specifically highlighted the plight of internally displaced persons, one of the country's most vulnerable groups.

Numerous case studies attribute their success to the fact that they were able to reach out to and strengthen the voice and power of traditionally marginalized groups of citizens. However, Namisi points out that much more work is required to achieve genuine social inclusion. She underlines, for example, the long-standing and urgent need to address gender issues, not just by promoting the inclusion of women in participatory governance initiatives, but by seriously analyzing and addressing the underlying reasons for persistent gender subordination and unequal access to resources, services, and benefits in every public sphere.

Invest in Capacity Development

As previously discussed, lack of political will for participatory governance is often directly linked to a *lack of capacity* to deliver participatory governance, on the part of both government and CSO actors. Therefore, investing in capacity- and confidence-building is a key strategy for building political will for participatory governance. Training, knowledge-sharing, and skills-building activities were important elements of almost every case presented in this book. For example, Areño recounts how Iloilo Caucus of Development NGOs (ICODE) identified the limited competencies of community leaders to take advantage of opportunities for meaningful participation in local governance processes as a fundamental gap, and, as a result, organized an extensive training program, even going so far as establishing a School of Local Governance in partnership with a local university. Large-scale capacity-building activities were also a core component of all three AKF country experiences. In each case, learning and training events were carried out jointly with government and civil society participants, resulting in not only increased knowledge and skills, but also in greater shared understanding and stronger relationships.

Networking and Coalition Building

Strategic networking and coalition building was critical to the success of nearly all initiatives described in this book. As previously discussed, building broad-based support for participatory governance, especially at the grassroots level, but also at higher levels, is essential to building strength and credibility. Cruz points out that "in efforts to build political will, the importance of broad-based coalitions cannot be overemphasized." For example, AKF found that supporting the clustering of village organizations was key to achieving greater coherence and negotiating power. The organization of candidates' forums in the Philippines required the coordination of CSOs, churches, peasant and labor organizations, media, sector professionals, and academics.

The most effective alliances sometimes involve unusual partnerships. Bringing together diverse stakeholders, not only demonstrates unity and broad support, but also helps ensure a balanced and holistic vision of societal needs, experiences, and preferences. Coalitions for access to information in Latin America, for example, were coordinated by national CSO networks, but also comprised citizens' groups, the owners of mass media companies, journalists, library association members, academics, university departments, and government officials. As noted by Cruz, in a highly politicized society, such as Nicaragua, the broad and diverse composition and inclusiveness of the Promoter Group for the Law was an important factor of success.

Establishing such broad-based coalitions is not always easy. In South Africa, for example, where Hicks and Buccus describe civil society as "distinctly compartmentalized," it is difficult to establish partnerships between NGOs, who accept collaborating with government in *invited spaces,* and social movements that refuse to participate on the state's terms and opt for protest. In Uganda, Namisi identifies the need for concerted action among diverse civil society actors, such as community groups, the media, trade unions, academics, professional associations, and political party representatives, as an ongoing challenge and an important gap. New information and communication technologies can be critical in building broad networks and supporting effective public mobilization and information sharing. Building the capacity of, especially grassroots level, CSOs to effectively access and utilize such technologies remains a challenge.

A common theme running through the case studies is the importance of strengthening links with media actors and including them in these coalitions. Using the media in strategic and creative ways is identified as a factor of success in a number of case studies. For example, broad media coverage was key to the success of Candidates' Forums in the Philippines and People's Manifestos in Uganda. Media strategies also served to build public support for participatory budgeting in Guelph, Canada, to raise public awareness of popular participation reforms in Bolivia, to create public pressure for the adoption of access to information legislation in Latin America, and to prompt government action on corruption complaints in ALAC countries.

Timing

Experience suggests that timing can be key to building political will. Several of the cases (Chapters 4, 7, and 8) took strategic advantage of election periods or seized particular policy moments to push certain *hot* agendas. Several cases also suggest that periods of crisis, chaos, or transition can actually be important opportunities for building political will for radical change. In Bolivia, for example, MacLean-Abaroa describes how a combination of economic and social upheaval served to put great pressure on the state to collaborate with local communities. In Washington, D.C., Jacksteit remarks that the "urgent situation helped spur change in attitude and willingness to try something new," and Areño describes how widespread discontent over political injustices and social inequities has been the trigger for change in the Philippines. The ability to identify and take advantage of opportunities, even sometimes less obvious opportunities, for social change and to be strategic in the timing of public demands and initiatives is a final success factor in building political will for participatory governance.

Lessons

In addition to factors of success, the case studies reveal a broader set of lessons learned with regard to building political will for participatory governance. Important lessons relate to: (i) *the need for political and power analysis;* (ii) *strengthening and complementing formal democratic institutions;* (iii) *supporting participatory governance champions;* (iv) *institutionalizing or codifying participatory governance practices;* and (v) *appropriate forms of external support.*

Political/Power Analysis

As discussed in the introduction to this book, the concept of power lies at the heart of participatory governance. The goal of participatory governance is to achieve greater social justice and collective well-being, by trying to level the playing field, enhancing the power of those who lack it, such as ordinary citizens, and, in particular, the poor, vulnerable, and marginalized, and building the will of those who hold power to *share* and use it to the benefit of the needy many rather than the privileged few. Therefore, building political will for participatory governance requires understanding, in any given setting, where different types of power lies, how it is exercised, and the nature and dynamics of relationships among power-holders and between the powerful and powerless.

It is essential to start by understanding the political context and power dynamics of the country, municipality, or locality in question (Cammack 2007). Tools, like the Swedish International Development Agency's *power analysis* approach (Swedish International Development Agency 2005), or Department for International Development's *Drivers of Change* methodologies (Department for International Development 2004) can help to do this. A key question is how public decisions are made? What logic and whose vested interests are driving decision making? Because decisions are frequently made behind closed doors and outside formal channels, it is important to identify and map power *networks*.

Selective support for participatory governance can be used by political players to score political points, such as branding one's self as the *transparent* or *clean* candidate, to punish opponents, for example by encouraging public scrutiny of an opposition party or member, or to check the power of another level of government, for example, by mandating citizen groups to oversee local government expenditures. Therefore, it is important for participatory governance advocates to understand who supports, owes, opposes, or competes with whom, and how these relationships and dynamics might potentially be leveraged to gain support for citizen participation and social accountability. Who are the actors that potentially have something to gain from supporting participatory governance? What are their relationships with other power-holders?

Most of the case study experiences were led by practitioners with high levels of political intelligence and relied on a very careful analysis of constantly changing political realities and power dynamics. A lesson of this volume is the importance of participatory governance practitioners honing their political and power analysis skills. While an increasing number of tools and methods have been developed to assist with mapping and analyzing power relationships, this is an area where many civil society practitioners need further capacity development and support.

It is also crucially important for practitioners to honestly assess and understand power dynamics within civil society, within their own organizations and among the populations they serve. Do participatory governance initiatives serve the interests of the weakest and most vulnerable? Do CSOs truly represent and empower the poor? Are CSOs themselves genuinely participatory? Are they susceptible to co-optation or elite capture?

Strengthening and Complementing Existing Democratic Institutions

Public officials are likely to resist participatory governance initiatives if they see them as undermining or bypassing mainstream democratic institutions. According to Zipfel, even though *participatory democracy* and *representative democracy* are complementary, power-holders tend to see them in opposition to one another. As Clark stresses in his chapter, it is essential to ensure that participatory governance *strengthens and improves,* rather than *erodes* or *supplants,* representative democracy.

In Mumvuma's chapter, practitioners worked to reassure local authorities that the objective of participatory budgeting was to strengthen, not challenge, the local council. Pinnington and Jacksteit both emphasize the need to avoid competing or overlapping with the mandate of local government. In both cases, civil society efforts were strong and persistent, but always *supportive* and *complementary* to the role of local government.

Participatory governance is based upon the fundamental truth that neither government nor civil society can fully achieve their respective goals on their own. Recognizing this *interdependence* can be an important step toward building political will for participatory governance. In Zanzibar, for example, CSOs became committed to seeking collaboration with the government when they "realized the futility of equipping communities to participate in local development without the support of local government authorities."

Aiming to reinforce, and also simultaneously to reform and improve existing institutions, requires a judicious equilibrium of determination and compromise. For example, Jacksteit and her colleagues in Washington, D.C., refused to abandon their ultimate goals of community development, but made the strategic decision to support the existing Neighborhood Advisory Group in pursuing identified priorities, rather than taking on that mandate themselves. Knowing when to push or ease off, when to give in or hold one's ground, or even when to utilize a *good cop/bad cop* strategy in partnership with other civil society actors, requires good judgment and strong political instincts.

In supporting and collaborating with state institutions, CSOs must also be alert to the risk of being co-opted or subsumed. Zipfel, for example, points out that as a result of recent reforms in the United Kingdom, many CSOs now work alongside the statutory sector and are increasingly dependent for their survival on income from service-related contracts, a situation which "can compromise their independence and reduce their capacity for community development . . . [and] advocacy work." In a context like the Philippines, Abad warns that participatory governance efforts can serve to legitimize structures of dominance and inequity and even transform CSOs into conduits of political patronage.

Supporting Participatory Governance Champions

The cases illustrate both the importance of supporting government *champions,* and the challenges and limitations of doing so. Numerous cases mention the important role played by an enlightened leader in advancing the participatory governance agenda, and how civil society actors were able to support them by sharing best practices, rallying public backing, and helping to design and facilitate participatory processes. Several cases, however, also highlight the fragility of individual champions. Pinnington, for example, describes how the principal promoter of participatory budgeting in the Guelph Community Development Department was suddenly dismissed without justification. In South Africa, efforts to prepare a national popular participation policy ground to a halt when the main government point person was moved to a different unit, leaving no one to carry the initiative forward.

Institutional champions are incredibly important, but also limited by organizational constraints and top-down controls. It's therefore necessary to not just collaborate with inspired individuals, but to encourage and assist champions to build up a critical mass of support, both within and outside their institution. As Hicks and Buccus conclude, "movement and power dynamics in government departments means that *champions* can easily be sidelined or transferred. Without a sufficient body of internal stakeholders with a vested interest . . . initiatives that rely on a single *champion* are extremely vulnerable." Similarly, Keller-Herzog reports that ALACs have found it "extremely useful to have entry points at different levels in the same structure."

Institutionalization/Codification

Another lesson from the case studies is the importance of codifying and/or institutionalizing participatory governance practices. In many contexts, there is no clear shared understanding about the respective rights and responsibilities of citizens/CSOs and state actors, or their obligations to one another. Reaching consensus on such issues, even with regard to one very specific question or concern, and putting it in writing, in the form of a social contract, local charter, or terms of reference, can go a long way toward avoiding misunderstandings and promoting collective political will. Keller-Herzog, for example, explains how Transparency International supported ALACs' systematic attempts to enter into Memoranda of Understanding with key government ministries early on. Mumvuma and Areño both describe how the use of social contracts served to clarify roles, responsibilities, and relationships, and helped manage expectations, allay fears, avoid conflict, and promote mutual understanding and good working relations.

Areño also explains the added advantage of *institutionalizing* the social contract process in the form of a municipal ordinance, thus integrating it into the public administration cycle and increasing the chances of regular and sustained implementation. Experience shows that political will is most enduring when it is institutionalized and not dependent on particular persons (Kpundeh and Dininio 2006). An essential aspect of institutionalization is to establish appropriate and lasting mechanisms for enhanced citizen–state interactions. A key feature of the AKF approach, for example, was to create new platforms for government and CSO actors to dialogue and deliberate on a regular basis.

Appropriate Forms of External Support

A number of cases highlighted the value of *certain forms* of external support in building political will for participatory governance. A common theme running through several cases (Chapters 4, 5, and 9) was the important role of a third-party facilitator, especially in helping to broker new relationships and facilitate productive dialogue and working relationships between citizens and state actors. This mediator and intermediary role for CSOs, focused on strengthening and facilitating relations between citizens and the state, is key to participatory governance, and there is a need to further develop this function and related set of skills. This role is often best played by a local CSO or individual, but one that is trusted by both sides as an honest broker. Abad reminds us that it is dangerous for CSOs to play anything but such a mediating and support role.

Several chapters underline the important impact of international support, in pushing for policy reforms (Chapter 9), offering technical assistance (Chapter 11), sharing best practice (Chapter 13), and providing financial support (Chapter 8). At the same time, Mumvuma cites suspicions about donor motives, on the part of government, as an obstacle and Hicks and Buccus relate how the efforts of an external donor ultimately failed to achieve policy reform, leading them to conclude that "donor interventions assist in opening up the space for policy advocacy, but this does not eliminate the need to secure the political impetus required for actual implementation." The lesson would seem to be that external assistance is important, but only if leadership and ownership remain in the hands of local stakeholders.

Conclusions

The cases examined in this book show that building political will for participatory governance is a complex and multifaceted challenge. It necessitates a combination of political savvy, technical know-how, patience, and persistence. It requires paying attention to the interrelated elements of *political want, political can,* and *political must.*

Experience shows better results when power-holders come to genuinely appreciate and *want* to support participatory governance goals, but that does not mean creating and exerting external pressure is not necessary. Meaningful change usually results from a combination of pressure from within, for example, the commitment of an internal champion or an enlightened leader, and from without, such as an active citizenry willing to engage for change, as well as from demonstrations of how participatory governance can lead to better results.

Efforts that focus on only one dimension of political will often achieve only limited success, for example, initiatives that focus exclusively on capacity-building, without regard for other elements of political will, or confrontational advocacy activities that force or shame the government into short-term concessions, but jeopardize relationships and the achievement of longer-term goals. In South Africa collaboration with a government department led to the preparation of a progressive policy on popular participation, but a lack of active citizen engagement meant that there was little leverage to keep things moving when the internal champion was transferred and the process ground to a halt. In Uganda, citizens achieved certain short-term gains through *Pressure From Below,* but lost opportunities for more sustained participation in decision making because of their *reactionary approach* and the fact that "they were not always diplomatic or tactful in their interactions."

To make participatory governance work, civil society and state actors must be willing to interact in a constructive, if critical, and solution-oriented manner. In practice, it can be extremely challenging to establish and maintain a balanced relationship of *critical collaboration,* especially in contexts where CSOs' relationships with government tend to be either unquestioning and apolitical on the one hand, or confrontational and hostile on the other. More work is needed to study and learn from the growing number of current CSO efforts to *simultaneously support and challenge* government institutions and to establish new forms of relationships with state actors, based on principles of *critical collaboration.*

Too often, lack of political will has been used as a catchall excuse for development and governance failures. As noted by Keller-Herzog, there is a risk that the term can become "a fatalistic shrug-of-the-shoulders statement of disempowerment." A fundamental conclusion of this book is that, although it is neither easy nor straightforward, it is in our power to build political will and to influence its determining factors. Political regimes and cultural norms can be changed; systems of repression, patronage, and corruption can be overcome; economic and social inequities can be challenged; apathy can be unlearned; and active citizenship can be nurtured. We all have a potential role to play in building will for participatory governance. As citizens, we can get informed and get engaged. As civil society activists, we can work to empower citizens, strengthen *critically collaborative* citizen–state relationships, and create more enabling spaces and conditions for participatory governance. Political will does not just happen; we collectively make it happen.

References

Cammack, D. 2007. The logic of African neopatrimonialism: What role for donors? *ODI Development Policy Review,* 25(5): 599–614.

Department for International Development. 2004. *Public Information Note: Drivers of Change.* London: Department for International Development.

Kpundeh, S. and P. Dininio. 2006. Political will. In *The Role of Parliament in Curbing Corruption.* R. Stapenhurst, N. Johnston and R. Pelizzo eds. Washington, D.C.: World Bank Institute.

Swedish International Development Agency. 2005. *Methods of Analysing Power: A Workshop Report.* Stockholm, Sweden: Swedish International Development Agency, Division for Democratic Governance.

INDEX

A

Access to Public Information Act
(Nicaragua), 230

Accountability, 6, 79, 87, 124, 130,
138, 253

Accountability, Not Lip Service, 145

Active citizenship, 7

Advisory Neighborhood Commission
(Washington, D.C.)
background, 73–74
Collaboration DC assessment, 74
Community Benefits Coordinating
Committee, 76–77
Community Benefits Task Force,
75–76
political will, building of, 79–83
political will, evolution of, 83–87
political will, issues of, 77–78
structural issues, 79–80

Advocacy and Legal Advice Centres
(ALACs)
advocacy, effective, 255
evaluation, external, 249
formation of, 248–249
gender equity in, 250
growth of, 249–250
legal resources at, 253, 258
management of, 258
Memoranda of Understanding,
252
operational stress, 250–251
overview, 245–246

role of, 256–257
success of, 277

Aga Khan Foundation, 13
capacity building, 282
civil society and state relationship,
275
integrated approach to
development, 68
Kenya, Coastal Rural Support Programme, 57–62
Local Good Governance Capacity
Assessment Tool, 52
overview, 51
Tajikistan, Mountain Societies
Development Support
Programme, 52–57
Tanzania, NGO Resource Center,
62–67

Agenda-setting, in participatory governance approaches, 4, 10

Alarcon, Elvira, 143

Albania, ALAC advocacy, 255

*Alianza Regional para la liberad de
Expresión e Información*, 229

American Convention on Human
Rights, 227

Anticorruption Resource Centres, 248.
See also Advocacy and Legal
Advice Centres

Apathy. *See* Citizen apathy

Archives and Access to Information
Group (Uruguay), 231

Assessment tools
    Local Good Governance Capacity
        Assessment Tool, 52
    needs assessment survey
        (CIVICUS), 6
    as social contract strategy, 142
Author-bias, 247
Autocracy
    curse of the autocrat, 197
    political must, lack of, 272
Azerbaijan, Baku-base ALAC, 250

B
Bachelet, President Michelle, 230
Baku-base ALAC (Azerbaijan), 250
Bangladesh, female political agency,
    44–45
Banzer, Hugo, 192
Blagovcanin, Srdjan, 248
Blears, Hazel, 98, 99, 110–111
    continued stay in office, need for,
        110–111
    support of, 98, 99
Bolivia
    citizen-state relationships, 199–204
    decentralization, 198–199
    dictatorship, effect of, 196
    Fondo Social de Emergencia (Social
        Emergency Fund), 192
    governance, history of, 191–192, 196
    government, support for, 14–15
    La Paz, reform of, 200–201
    Law of Popular Participation, 189,
        192–195, 277
    Minister of Finance, role of,
        202–203
    National Dialogue, 202, 204
    overview, 190–191
    participatory budgeting in, 10,
        204–205
    participatory governance
        practices, 4
    Plan de Todos (Plan for All), 193
    political will, building of, 197–199
    political will, lack of, 195–197

Brazil, participatory budgeting in, 175
Britain. *See* United Kingdom
British Labour Party, 37–38
Budgets. *See* Public budgets

C
Canada, participatory budgeting pro-
        grams, 176 (*see also* Guelph
        Neighborhood Support
        Coalition)
Capacity building
    in ICODE (the Philippines),
        140–141
    lack of, 270–272
    and political will, lack of, 282
Carter, President Jimmy, 234
Castro, Ana, 259
Center for the Analysis of Social
        Exclusion, 96
Centre for Public Participation (South
        Africa)
    challenges, 230–231
    lessons from, 221–223
    outcomes, 219–220
    overview, 213–216
    political will, building of, 218–219
Chama Cha Mapinduzi, 63
Champions, institutional
    types, 20
    importance of, 286–287
    political will, building of, 149, 151
Champions Participation workshops
        (Sussex University), 105–106,
        107–108
Chile
    Law on Transparency of Public
        Functions, 230–231
    Law on Transparency of the Public
        Service and Access to Informa-
        tion on the State Administration,
        236
    political prisoners, information on,
        235
    right to information, legislature,
        228, 240–241

Citizen apathy, 40–42. *See also* Voter
  turnout
Citizen empowerment, 7
  definition, 14
  as objective, 32–33, 97
  political will, strategy for, 278
Citizen engagement, need for, 273
Citizen report cards, 11
Citizen-state relations development
  Bolivia, 199–204
  Kenya, 60–62
  the Philippines, 147–149
  poor relationships, 268, 270
  Tajikistan, 55–56
  Tanzania, 66–67
  Zimbabwe, 168–169
CIVICUS Participatory Governance
  Programme, needs assessment
  survey, 6
Civil society
  capacity, lack of, 271–272
  government, relationship with,
  274–275
Civil society actors, co-optation of,
  16–17
Civil society organizations, role of,
  32–33
Climate change, cooperation for policy
  change, 43
Coalition building, 282–283
Coastal Rural Support Programme
  (Kenya), 57–62
Coded statements, on political will,
  246
Codification, of participatory
  governance practices, 287–288
Collaboration,   in ICODE
  programmes, 147
Collaboration DC, 74
  capacity of, 75
  community roundtable event, 84
Collegiality, importance of, 276
Colombia, right to information, legis-
  lature, 228
Communication tools, 124–125

Community monitoring, 11
Conflict resolution, 118–119
Constructive engagement, 31, 245,
  254, 261
Converted champions, 20
Co-optation, of civil society actors,
  16–17
Corruption
  and access to information, 234
  administrative remedies, 252
  entrenched, 270
  and privatization, 255
  and risk in complaining, 251
Corruptions Perception Index, 234
Covenant for Transparency and
  Accountability (the Philippines),
  138–143
Critical collaboration, 147, 274–275,
  289
Critics, exclusion of, 16
Cultural transparency, lack of, 233–234
Curse of the autocrat, 197

D
Decentralized development
  in Bolivia, 198–199
  limitations of, 69–70
Demand for good governance, 9
Democracy
  in ancient Greece, 38–39
  obstacles to, 40–44
  paradox of, 39
  representative democracy (*see* Rep-
  resentative democracy)
Demos kratein, 38–39
Department for International Develop-
  ment, Drivers of Change
  methodologies, 285
Development Network of Indigenous
  Voluntary Associations
  (Uganda), 114, 119
Diakonia-Sweden, 140
Divjak, Boris, 249
Donor support, impact of, 222–223
Drivers of Change methodologies, 285

E

Education. *See also* Training
   regressive distribution of, 44
   Uganda, programmes in, 119
Elections, 35, 40, 44, 96, 124, 131,
      256
   in Bolivia, 198, 205
   in Philippines, 135–138
   in Zimbabwe, 166
Elers, Ben, 258
Elite capture, 16
Empowered participatory governance,
      175. *See also* Participatory
      budgeting
Empowerment. *See* Citizen empower-
      ment
England. *See* United Kingdom
Entrenched corruption, 270. *See also*
      Corruption
Entrenched patronage, 270. *See also*
      Patronage systems
Estenssoro, Victor Paz, 192
Evidence-based advocacy, 142, 246,
      259–260
Evidence-based approaches, 122,
      176

F

Fear, as obstacle to democracy, 41–42

G

Gender equity promotion
   in ALACs, 250
   in the Philippines, 143
   in Uganda, 121–122
Glorious Revolution (Britain), 39
Good governance
   Philippine conference, 152
   Uganda National Development
      Plan, 116, 120
Good Governance Learning Network
   Center for Public Participation,
      membership in, 219
   University of KwaZulu-Natal, part-
      nership with, 215

Governments
   capacity, lack of, 270–271
   civil society, relationship with,
      274–275
   direct benefits to, 14–15
   entry points, 254
   press right legislation, 228
   stakeholders, 12, 20
   supporters (*see* Institutional cham-
      pions)
   support of, 6–7
Great Britain. *See* United Kingdom
Greece, ancient democracy, 38–39
Greenpeace, 38
Grupo Promotor (Promoter Group, in
      Nicaragua), 230
Guatemala, right to information, legis-
      lature, 228
Guelph Neighborhood Support Coali-
      tion (Canada)
   basic information, 176–177
   Family and Children's Services, role
      of, 179, 184
   outcomes, 184–186
   participatory budgeting, 177–180
   political will, building of, 182–184
   political will, lack of, 180–181
   Terms of Reference, 178, 185

H

Habeas Data, 235
Hardy, Keir, 37
Health services, in Uganda, 120
Heavily Indebted Poor Countries,
      203–204
Honduras
   Law on Transparency and Access
      to Public Information, 229–230,
      236–237
   participatory governance
      practices, 4
   right to information, legislature,
      228, 240–241
Housing, tenant management
      movement (U.K.), 103

Human rights
    international covenants, 227
    and personal privacy issues,
        234–236

I
Iloilo Caucus of Development NGOs
        (the Philippines)
    capacity building, 282
    model of, 138
Inclusive policies, 281–282. *See also*
        Gender equity promotion
India, Champions of Participation
        workshops, 107–108
Individual advocacy, 23
Information
    political power of, 259–261
    right to. *See* Right to access infor-
        mation
Institutional champions
    converted, 20
    importance of, 286–287
    political will, building of, 149, 151
Institutionalization, of participatory
        governance practices, 287–288
Internally displaced persons, in
        Uganda, 118–119, 125
International Covenant on Human
        Rights, 227
Internet-based ALAC, 250
Investigative journalism, 252

J
Jameson, Neil, 105
Joseph Rowntree Foundation, poverty
        research, 96
Judicial system, in resolution of
        corruption, 252–253

K
Katakwi Urafiki Foundation (Uganda),
        118–119
Kenya
    Coastal Rural Support Programme,
        57–62

participatory governance practices, 4
Krnacova, Adriana, 248

L
La Paz (Bolivia), reform of, 200–201
Latin America. *See also* individual
        countries
    corruption in, 234
    cultural transparency, lack of,
        233–234
    regional initiatives, right to
        information,
    right to information, legislature, 228
    social actors, mistrust among, 232
Law of Access to Information and Pro-
        tection of Information
        (Uruguay), 232
Law of Access to Public Information
        (Uruguay), 235
Law of Popular Participation (Bolivia),
        189, 192–195, 277
Law of Protection of Personal Data
        (Uruguay), 235
Law on Transparency and Access to
        Public Information (Honduras),
        229–230, 236–237
Law on Transparency of Public Func-
        tions (Chile), 230–231
Law on Transparency of the Public
        Service and Access to Informa-
        tion on the State Administration
        (Chile), 236
Leadership
    political, commitment of, 272–273
    recruiting for, 82
Legal reform, 279–280
Lobbying
    boundaries of, 261
    in Pressure from Below initiative
        (Uganda), 125–126
Local Good Governance Capacity
        Assessment Tool (LOGOCAT)
    application of, 52
    good governance, elements of, 68–69
London Citizens, 105

London School of Economics, research
    on poverty, 96
Loveys-Smith, Janette, 180

M
Marginalized groups, inclusion of,
    281–282
Marschall, Miklos, 256, 257
Media
    corruption charges, investigation
        of, 252
    Guelph (Canada), use by, 183–184
    information disclosure, threat of, 260
    public support, building of,
        283Meetings
    good process at, 82–83
    in Uganda, 123
Memoranda of Understanding, 252
Mexico, access to information legisla-
    tion, 238
Millenium Development Goals
    (MDGs), 5, 296
Montenegro, ALAC support in, 251
Morales, Evo
    ascendency, to presidency, 205
    Popular Participation, opposition
        to, 200
Multistakeholder partnerships, 16
Museveni, President (Uganda), 113
Mutoko participatory budget initiative
    (Zimbabwe)
    budget action committee, 160–161
    budgeting cycle, 161, 162–163
    cause of, 158–159
    objectives, 159
    outcomes, 165
    social contract, 161, 164
    strategic plan, 159–160
    success, factors for, 169–170
    training in, 164–165

N
National Dialogue, 202, 204–205
National Endowment for Democracy,
    229

Natural champions, 20
Needs assessment survey
    (CIVICUS), 6
Neighborhood council systems
    governing principles, 87
    Los Angeles, California, 78–79
    Portland, Oregon, 78
    Washington, D. C. (*see* Advisory
        Neighborhood Commission)
Neighborhood renewal, in U.K.,
    103–104
Newcastle City Council (U.K.), 106
New Public Management, 176
NGO Resource Center (Tanzania),
    governance structure, 62–63
Nicaragua
    Access to Public Information Act,
        230
    participatory governance
        practices, 4
    right to information, legislature,
        228, 237, 240–241
Nongovernmental organizations
    (NGOs)
    distrust of, 42
    NGO Resource Center (Tanzania),
        62–67

O
Open Society Institute, 229
Organizational behavior theory, 23–24
Organization of American States, 229
Outreach methods, in Washington,
    D.C., 86

P
Palabrica, Matt, 147
Participatory budgeting
    in Canada (*see* Guelph
        Neighborhood Support
        Coalition)
    overview, 175
    in U.K., 100, 106
    in Zimbabwe (*see* Mutoko partici-
        patory budget initiative)

Participatory governance
  benefits of, 12–14
  collegiality, importance of, 276
  deficiencies of, 44–45
  definition, 7, 9
  evidence-based approaches,
    276–277
  at international level, 10 (see also
    individual countries)
  at local level, 4, 7
  mechanisms, lack of, 271
  obstacles to, 45–46, 69
  patronage system, 144
  political will, overcoming lack of,
    143–147
  power analysis, need for, 284–285
  risks of, 15–17
  stakeholders, 12
  strategies, 141–142
  supporter types, 20
Participatory governance practices
  examples, 4, 6 (see also individual
    practices)
  importance of, 5
  institutionalization, 287–288
Patronage systems, in the Philippines,
  144
Patron-client relationship, 35–36
People's agenda, in the Philippines,
  137–138
People's rule, 38–39
The Philippines
  citizen-state relations, 147–149
  Covenant for Transparency and
    Accountability, 138–143
  electoral forums, 142
  Good Governance for Change;
    Change for Good Governance
    conference, 152
  Iloilo Caucus of Development
    NGOs (ICODE), 138
  Local Government Code, 137–138
  participatory budgeting, 15
  participatory governance
    practices, 4

political history, 135
political patron-client relationship,
  35–36
social contract process, 137–138,
  139
social contracts, 136–137,
  149–152
Planning, participatory governance
  approaches to, 10
Policymaking, participatory
  governance approaches to, 10
Political agency, of females, 44–45
Political behavior
  political systems theory, 24
  rational actor models, 23
Political can (ability)
  citizenry, role of, 278–279
  gaining of, 21
  lack of, 269, 270–272
Political donors, income distribution
  of, 40
Political leadership, commitment of,
  272–273
Political must
  citizenry, role of, 279
  lack of, 269, 272–273
  overview, 21–22
Political parties
  British Labour Party (*see* British
    Labour Party)
  Chama Cha Mapinduzi party (Tan-
    zania), 63
  CONDEPA (Bolivia), 200
  definition, 39
  ZANU-PF party (Zimbabwe), 166
Political prisoners, information on,
  235
Political process, 34–35
Political stability, 15
Political systems theory, influence on
  political will, 24
Political want
  lack of, 268–272
  overview, 19–21
  self-interest, as source of, 20–21

Political will
    building of, 33–34, 60, 66, 79–83,
        122–126, 273–280
    coded statements on, 246
    definition, 18
    elements of, 8, 19–22
    external support for, 288 (*see also*
        Institutional champions)
    factors influencing, 22–25
    importance of, 157
    indictors of, 18–19, 212
    lack of, 6–7, 180–181, 216–218
    professionalism, as strategy to
        enhance, 280
    for right to access information
        laws, 237–239
    timing, 284
Port Alegre (Brazil)
    versus Guelph (Canada) model, 179
    participatory budgeting model, 175
Poverty
    research on, 95–96
    in Uganda, 116
    in U.K., 93–94
Poverty gap, in U. K., 93–94
Power
    participation and, 34–35
    of public authorities, 268
Pressure from Below initiative
        (Uganda)
    challenges, 129–130
    impact of, 126–127
    lessons learned, 127–129
    lobbying and advocacy, 125–126
    media use, 126
    outcomes, 118–120
    overview, 115–118
Priority Boards (Dayton, Ohio), 79
Privatization, and corruption, 255
Professionalism, 280
Promoter Group (Nicaragua), 230
Public budgets
    examples, 15 (*see also individual
        countries*)
    overview, 10

Public expenditure tracking, in partici-
        patory governance practices, 11
Public hearings, 10, 105, 160, 171
Public oversight, in participatory gov-
        ernance practices, 11–12

R
Rational actor models, of political
        behavior, 23
Representative democracy. *See also*
        Democracy
    deficits in, 42–44
    strengthening of, 285–286
Research, on participatory governance
    in South Africa, 213–215
    in Uganda, 122
    in U.K., 95–96
Responsiveness, 148, 246, 249, 252, 256
Right to information
    Access to Public Information Act
        (Nicaragua), 230
    and availability of public informa-
        tion, 253
    enforcement issues, 240–241
    instruments, 228–229
    Law of Access to Information and
        Protection of Information
        (Uruguay), 232
    Law of Access to Public
        Information (Uruguay), 235
    Law of Protection of Personal Data
        (Uruguay), 235
    Law on Access to Public Informa-
        tion, 235
    Law on Transparency and Access
        to Public Information
        (Honduras), 229–230
    Law on Transparency of Public
        Functions (Chile), 230–231
    Law on Transparency of the Public
        Service and Access to Informa-
        tion on the State Administration
        (Chile), 236
    and right to privacy, 235
    social contract process strategy, 141

Romania, ALAC advocacy, 255
Rule of law, 252–253

S

Sanchez de Lozada, Gonzalo
  Partipacion Popular, drafting of,
    198
  support for economic reform, 192,
    193, 194
Sanctions, 273
San Jose Pact, 227
Self-interest
  and corruption complaints, 251
  political want, source of, 20–21
Service delivery protests (South
    Africa), 221
Shorthand statements, on political
    will, 246
Social accountability, 9
Social actors
  mistrust among, 232
  and right to access information leg-
    islation, 238–239
Social capital, 80
Social contract process
  stages, 137–138, 139
  strategies, 141–142
  success, factors for, 149–152
  in Zambia, 161, 164
Social Emergency Fund (Bolivia), 192
Social inclusion, 281
Societal factors, influence on political
    will, 25
South Africa
  Centre for Public Participation
    (*see* Centre for Public
    Participation)
  coalition building, difficulties in,
    283
  legal framework, for participatory
    governance, 212
  participatory governance
    practices, 4
  political will, lack of, 216–218
  service delivery protests, 221

Stakeholders, 12
  and access to information laws, 236
  collaboration among, 275–276
  in government, 20
  multistakeholder partnerships, 16
Statistical evidence, in anti-corruption
    advocacy, 253–254
Strategic networking, 282–283
Sussex University, Champions Partici-
    pation workshops, 105–106,
    107–108
Sweden, press rights legislation, 228
Swedish International Development
    Agency
  power analysis tools, 285
  Tajikistan Governance and
    Livelihood Programme, 52–53

T

Tajikistan
  Mountain Societies Development
    Support Programme, 52–57
  participatory governance
    practices, 4
Tajikistan Governance and Livelihood
    Programme
  objectives, 55
  overview, 52–53
Tanzania
  NGO Resource Center, 62–67
  participatory governance
    practices, 4
Technocracy, 42
  political must, lack of, 272
  in South Africa, 216, 218
Tenant management movement (U.K.),
    103
Training. *See also* Education
  access to information seminar, 231
  ALAC workshops, 249
  for participation and public engage-
    ment skills, 88
  for participatory budgeting,
    164–165
  voter education, 146

Transparency, 138, 140–143
Transparency International
  agenda, 245
  ALACs (*see* Advocacy and Legal
    Advice Centres)
  capacity, for effectiveness, 259
  Corruption Perception Index, 234
  network structure, 247–248
  participatory governance
    practices, 4
  virtual ALAC, 250
Trust of the Americas, 229

U
Uganda
  Access to Public Information Act,
    115
  coalition building, 283
  community meetings, 123
  conflict resolution, 118–119
  Development Network of
    Indigenous Voluntary
    Associations, 114, 119
  Domestic Relations Bill, 122
  gender equity promotion, 121–122
  internally displaced persons,
    118–119, 125
  legal framework, for participatory
    governance, 114, 128
  Local Government Act and Decen-
    tralization Policy, 115
  National Objectives and Directives
    Principles of State Policy, 114,
    128
  participatory governance practices,
    4 (*see also* Pressure from Below
    initiative)
  people's manifesto days, 124
  political history, 113–114
  political reform, need for, 131
  political will, building of, 122–126
  poverty, 116
United Kingdom
  Blair, Tony, 93
  Blears, Hazel, 98, 99, 110–111

community empowerment, implant-
  ing of, 99–101
community response capacity,
  102–105
Comprehensive Area Assessment,
  101
current policy development, 98–99
democracy, evolution of, 39
government agenda, 95–98
Labour Party (*see* British Labour
  Party)
local government response capacity,
  105–107
London Citizens, 105
National Empowerment
  Partnership, 100
National Strategy for
  Neighborhood Renewal, 94
neighborhood renewal, 94,
  103–104
participatory budgeting, 100
participatory governance practices, 4
political will, creation of, 108–110
poverty gap, 93–94
poverty research, 95–96
tenant management movement, 103
United States Agency for International
  Development (USAID)
  Bolivian decentralization
    programme, aid to, 193
  Zimbabwe agreement, 158
United States of America
  Dayton, Ohio, Priority Boards, 79
  Los Angeles, California, neighbor-
    hood councils, 78–79
  participatory governance
    practices, 4
  political donors, 40
  Portland, Oregon, neighborhood
    councils, 78
  voter turnout, 41
  Washington, D. C. (*see* Advisory
    Neighborhood Commission)
Universal Declaration of Human
  Rights, 227

University of KwaZulu-Natal (South
    Africa), 214
Urban Institute
    capacity of, 170
    Zimbabwe participatory budgeting
        initiative, implementation, 158
Urban renewal, in Washington, D.C.,
    73–74
Uruguay
    Archives and Access to Information
        Group, 231
    Law of Access to Information and
        Protection of Information, 232
    participatory governance
        practices, 4
    political prisoners, information on,
        235
    right to information, legislature,
        228, 235, 236, 240–241

V
Vigilance committees (Bolivia), 200
Virtual ALAC, 250
Voter turnout
    Eastern European democracies, 256
    United States of America, 41

Vulnerable groups, inclusion of,
    281–282

W
Washington, D. C. *See* Advisory
        Neighborhood Commission
World Bank, Bolivian decentralization
        programme, 193, 194

Z
Zambia, ALAC in, 250
ZANU-PF party, 166
Zanzibar, government collaboration
        with, 286
Zimbabwe
    Mutoko participatory budget initia-
        tive (*see* Mutoko participatory
        budget initiative)
    participatory budgeting, 15
    participatory governance
        practices, 4
    political stability, opportunity
        for, 15
    political will, building of,
        166–169
    Urban institute, role of, 158, 170

ABOUT CIVICUS

CIVICUS: World Alliance for Citizen Participation is an international alliance dedicated to protecting the rights, strengthening best practices, and increasing the influence of civil society around the globe. CIVICUS has members and partners in more than one hundred countries worldwide. Established in 1993, CIVICUS nurtures the foundation, growth, and protection of citizen action throughout the world, especially in areas where participatory democracy and citizens' freedom of association are threatened.

For effective and sustainable civic participation to occur, citizens must enjoy rights of free association and be able to engage all sectors of society. CIVICUS is dedicated to strengthening citizen action and civil society throughout the world so as to best amplify the voices and opinions of ordinary people and give expression to the enormous creative energy of civil society. CIVICUS' vision is of a worldwide community of informed, inspired, committed citizens engaged in confronting the challenges facing humanity.

CIVICUS provides a focal point for knowledge-sharing, common interest representation, global institution-building, and engagement among these groups. It acts as an advocate for citizen participation as an essential component of governance and democracy worldwide.

For more information about CIVICUS, please visit www.civicus.org.

About the Contributors

Henedina Abad has a career spanning thirty-one years of development work, focused on building and strengthening human and institutional capacities in civil society and the public sector. She served in the Thirteenth Congress of the Philippines, as the representative of the lone district of Batanes. Prior to her time in elective politics, she was founding dean of the Ateneo School of Government in Manila. She has cofounded and steered numerous multistakeholder partnerships, such as the Philippine Governance Forum, Budget Watch, G-Watch, and the Transparency and Accountability Network. She currently lectures in political science at the Ateneo de Manila University.

Emmanuel C. Areño holds a master's in rural development management from the University of Philippines in Iloilo City. He is currently the executive director of the Iloilo Caucus of Development Nongovernmental organizations (NGOs), serves as the regional coordinator of the Western Visayas Network of Social Development NGOs, and is the academic coordinator for the local governance certificate and diploma programs at the Central Philippine University, in Iloilo City. He sits on the board of the Peace and Equity Foundation, a national civil society organization (CSO) dedicated to financing grassroots poverty reduction initiatives.

Imraan Buccus is a research fellow at the Centre for Public Participation (CPP) and the School of Politics, University of KwaZulu Natal in Durban, South Africa. He is also a PhD candidate in development studies at Radboud University in the Netherlands. He holds a master's in social policy from the former Institute for Social and Economic Research at the University of KwaZulu Natal. He also writes a regular column for the *Mercury*, Durban's popular morning newspaper.

Achim Chiaji is the programme director of the NGO Resource Centre, an Aga Khan Foundation initiative based in Zanzibar, which has been a training and capacity-building center for CSOs in Tanzania since 1994. The training center has played an important role in strengthening the capacity of local CSOs and has had numerous experiences in partnering with the government. Achim was a pioneer coordinator of the civil society campaign on Millennium Development Goals, using a human rights approach. Achim previously managed local governance support programs with various international organizations in Kenya and Uganda, with particular focus on public expenditure monitoring and advocacy dimensions.

John Clark is the former lead social development specialist for East Asia in the World Bank, working primarily on governance, poverty, and civil society issues in East Asia, before which he led the Bank's engagement with civil society. During a four-year absence from the Bank, starting in 2000, he worked in the UN Secretary-General's office, advising on UN-civil society relations, was a visiting fellow at the London School of Economics, and served on a task force advising the British Prime Minister about Africa. Before working at the World Bank, he had a long career with NGOs, particularly Oxfam Great Britain, where he was head of campaigns and started the policy work. He is the author of various books, including *Worlds Apart: Civil Society and the Battle for Ethical Globalization* (2003) and *Democratizing Development: the Role of Voluntary Organizations* (1991).

Anabel Cruz is the founder director of the Communication and Development Institute, a research center and NGO support organization in Uruguay. Anabel has a long history of working to strengthen citizen participation in Uruguay and all over the world. She has conducted extensive research on the role of civil society in building democracy and citizenship and their participation in development processes in the Latin American post-dictatorship era. She has led action-research projects to map CSOs and their impact on development and good governance in the Americas and elsewhere. She is currently the vice-chair of the Partnership for Transparency Fund and the chair of the board of CIVICUS: World Alliance for Citizen Participation.

Janine Hicks holds a master's in participation, development, and social change, from the Institute of Development Studies, University of Sussex, and an LLB from the former University of Natal in Durban, South Africa. She is currently a commissioner at the South African Commission on Gender Equality, an independent statutory body established by the South

African Constitution to promote and protect gender equality and advance the status of women. Janine was the founding executive director of the Centre for Public Participation, a South African NGO dedicated to strengthening citizen participation in governance.

Richard Holloway has spent all his working life in the global south with CSOs, apart from two years working for DFID in the Caribbean. He has worked as a volunteer, frontline development worker, project and program director, aid administrator, trainer, writer, and capacity-builder in Africa, Asia, the Caribbean, and the Pacific. He is particularly interested in building competence in CSOs and improving their relations with the government and public in the countries in which they are situated, at both national and local levels. He currently heads the Civil Society program of the Aga Khan Development Network.

Mary Jacksteit designs and facilitates dispute resolution, dialogue, consensus-building, and civic engagement processes and programs. She has run two projects for Search for Common Ground, Collaboration DC, on participatory local governance in Washington, D.C., and the Network for Life and Choice, on reproductive health issues, and served as a labor arbitrator and mediator. She is currently an independent consultant and practitioner and an associate and program manager for the Public Conversations Project. She has a law degree from Georgetown University and a master's in conflict analysis and resolution from George Mason University.

Angela Keller-Herzog joined Transparency International (TI) in August 2006 as manager of global programmes. She has since taken on the challenge of globalizing TI's Advocacy and Legal Advice Centers approach, and currently leads the Judiciary Advocacy Working Group. Prior to TI, she spent three years in Indonesia working with the Canadian International Development Agency (CIDA), in poverty reduction and development. Angela first joined CIDA in 1996. She has over twenty years development experience in Asia and Africa and extensive sectoral experience, including private sector development, economics of development, gender analysis, and environmental governance issues. She holds a master's in economics from Carleton University, Ottawa.

Carmen Malena works as an independent consultant and part-time director of the CIVICUS Participatory Governance Programme from her base in Quebec City, Canada. She is a political sociologist, with special interest in the areas of civil society, participatory governance, social

accountability, and gender. She holds a master's in international development from University of Sussex. Carmen has more than twenty years
experience as a development practitioner, researcher, writer, facilitator
and trainer. She has authored a wide range of academic and operational
publications. She has held positions as a civil society and participation
specialist at the World Bank and the African Development Bank and has
worked for a range of multilateral and bilateral donors and NGOs.

Ronald MacLean-Abaroa is a leading governance expert and practitioner, with experience from the world of politics and public service. He
was the first democratically elected mayor of La Paz, Bolivia, and was
reelected four times. Appointed the youngest minister at age twenty-nine,
he has held five national cabinet positions, under three presidents, and
became the presidential candidate of the governing party in the general
election of 2002. He then joined the World Bank, as lead public sector
management specialist on governance, decentralization, and poverty
reduction. He received his master's in public administration from Harvard
University, where he taught, and became a senior research fellow. He is the
author of several articles, professional papers, case studies, and books. He
coauthored, with Robert Klitgaard and Linsey Parris, *Corrupt Cities: A
Practical Guide to Cure and Prevention* (2000), which has been translated
into fifteen languages.

Takawira Mumvuma is the coordinator of the Municipal Development
Partnership for Eastern and Southern Africa's Policy Research and Participatory Budgeting Programme and a development economics lecturer at
the University of Zimbabwe. He is currently a visiting lecturer at the
Africa University, where he teaches a course on decentralization and local
governance offered in their Public Sector Management Master's Programme. He has authored and coauthored many books, chapters, articles,
and manuals on issues of enterprise development, local economic development, trade, policy reforms, participatory budgeting, and social accountability in Africa. He holds a master's in economics from the University of
Zimbabwe and a PhD in development studies from the Institute of Social
Studies, The Hague, Netherlands.

Harriet Namisi is programme coordinator of policy analysis and governance at the Development Network of Indigenous Voluntary Associations
(DENIVA), in Uganda. She has broad experience at the international,
national, and local levels in enhancing the contribution of civil society to
Ugandan life, and interaction with a wide variety of stakeholders, including government, development partners, and leading civil society networks.

Harriet is the national coordinator of the CIVICUS Civil Society Index in Uganda. She serves on a number of eminent bodies, including the advisory board of the International Council for Non Profit Law. She holds a master's in rural sociology and community development from the University of Nairobi and a BA in social sciences (sociology and social administration) from Makerere University, Kampala. Before DENIVA, she worked with the National Association for Women Organisations in Uganda and Community Based Trainers and Development Consultants in Nairobi.

Margaret Ngari is currently working on the Coastal Rural Support Programme in Kenya (CSRP-K), a program started by the Aga Khan Foundation. The CSRP-K has been working with community-based organizations (CBOs) for more than a decade, and is currently working on strengthening networks of CBOs to actively engage in dialogue and partnership with structures of local government.

Elizabeth Pinnington is a doctoral fellow in adult education and community development at the Ontario Institute for Studies in Education, University of Toronto. Her research interests combine adult learning, participatory governance, and civic engagement. Elizabeth's doctoral research builds on her master's work at the University of British Columbia, where she studied the links between participatory governance and political power for marginalized residents in Canada. Elizabeth has been actively involved in the participatory budgeting process in Guelph, Canada, including acting as a facilitator for the 2008 and 2009 processes. Her recent publications include *Participatory Budgeting in North America* (with J. Lerner and D. Schugurensky) and *From Civic Learning to Political Engagement: Participatory Budgeting in Guelph, Canada* (with D. Schugurensky).

Shahribonu Shonasimova used to work with the Community Development Unit of the Mountain Societies Development Support Programme (MSDSP), an initiative of the Aga Khan Foundation, Tajikistan. As local governance officer, she worked closely with government authorities at all levels, to strengthen partnerships between MSDSP and government institutions. She also worked directly with rural communities and local governments in community mobilization.

Tricia Zipfel has more than thirty years experience in social policy and antipoverty work in the United Kingdom. She has worked in some of the most disadvantaged neighborhoods of the country, establishing innovative models of community participation and empowerment. In 2001, she was seconded to work for the UK government's Department for Communities and Local Government (DCLG). As senior community advisor, she made sure that the grassroots experience informed the development of national policy. Since leaving DCLG in 2006, she has advised local governments, and other public sector and CSOs, on strategies to increase community democracy and empowerment, helped promote participatory budgeting, and facilitated international learning on participation, with the Institute of Development Studies, University of Sussex.

Also From Kumarian Press . . .

Civil Society:

Transnational Civil Society: An Introduction
Edited by Srilatha Batliwala and L. David Brown

CIVICUS Global Survey of the State of Civil Society,
Vol. 2: Comparative Perspectives
Edited by V. Finn Heinrich and Lorenzo Fioramonti

A Civil Republic: Beyond Capitalism and Nationalism
Severyn T. Bruyn

Advocacy for Social Justice: A Global Action and Reflection Guide
David Cohen, Rosa de la Vega, Gabrielle Watson

New and Forthcoming:

Civil Society Under Strain: Anti-Terrorism Policy,
Civil Society and Aid Post 9/11
Edited by Jude Howell and Jeremy Lind

Building Peace: Practical Reflections from the Field
Edited by Craig Zelizer and Robert Rubinstein

Rights-Based Approaches to Development:
Exploring the Potential and Pitfalls
Edited by Diana Mitlin and Sam Hickey

Leadership for Development: What Globalization Demands of
Leaders Fighting for Change
Edited by Dennis A. Rondinelli and John M. Heffron

Visit Kumarian Press at **www.kpbooks.com** or
call **toll-free 800.232.0223** for a complete catalog

Kumarian Press, located in Sterling, Virginia, is a forward-looking, scholarly press that promotes active international engagement and an awareness of global connectedness.